CITY FATHERS

CITY FATHERS

The Early History of Town Planning in Britain

Colin & Rose Bell

BARRIE & ROCKLIFF: The Cresset Press

Produced by Design Yearbook Limited, 21 Ivor Place, London, N.W.1.
Published by Barrie & Rockliff, The Cresset Press, 2 Clements Inn, Strand, London, W.C.2.
Text set by Yendall & Company Limited, Riscatype House, 22–25 Red Lion Court, London, E.C.4.
Printed by Compton Printing Limited, Pembroke Road, Stocklake, Aylesbury, Buckinghamshire.
Jackets printed by Berkshire Printing Company Limited, Oxford Road, Reading, Berkshire.
Bound by Nevett, Key & Whiting Limited, The Hyde, Colindale, London, N.W.9.

Copyright © Design Yearbook Limited 1969.
Art Director: Ian Cameron.
Designer: Tom Carter.

First published 1969.

Printed in Great Britain.

SBN 214.65030.8

Acknowledgements
The authors are indebted to the under-mentioned for permission to reproduce illustrations as listed: those marked * are Crown Copyright. All other illustrations in the book, not listed here, are by the authors, and are the copyright of Design Yearbook Limited.

Aerofilms (p. 99 top); Public Library, Barrow-in-Furness (p. 158); Professor Maurice Beresford (pp. 17 & 39 left); Central Library, Bournemouth (p. 105); Central Library, Bradford (p. 190); Trustees of the British Museum (pp. 9, 15, 20 top right & top left, 23, 24 top left, 26, 29, 30 bottom, 51, 52, 57, 62, 63 top & bottom right, 66, 67, 68, 69 bottom, 70, 83, 86, 88, 96, 119 bottom, 120, 122 & 186); Cadbury Brothers Ltd. (pp. 200, 201, 202 & 205); Terence Davis (p. 63 left); Worshipful Company of Drapers (p. 49); The Illustrated London News (pp. 150 & 160 top); Lever Brothers & Associates Ltd. (p. 211); City Museum, Liverpool (p. 107); Ministry of Public Buildings and Works (p. 14)*; Moyses Hall Museum, Bury St Edmunds (p. 18); National Maritime Museum (p. 43); National Monuments Record of Scotland (pp. 170 & 171)*; National Monuments Record (pp. 41, 44, 64, 65, 87, 99 bottom, 165 & 173)*; National Portrait Gallery (p. 85); Oxford University Press (pp. 11, 39 bottom right, 48 left, & 49); Atkinson Central Library, Southport (p. 106); Dr J. K. St Joseph, Committee for Aerial Photography, Cambridge (pp. 21, 24 bottom left, 30 top, 31, 39 top, 82, 146, 166 & 169); Science Museum (pp. 129, 130 & 132); Tom Scott (p. 183 top & bottom left); Central Library, Shipley (p. 189); Ordnance Survey (pp. 11, 17 & 39 bottom right)*; Central Library, County Borough of Tees-side (pp. 133, 136, 138, 140, 141, 142, 144 & 145); Transport Museum, British Railways Board (p. 149); Public Library, Tunbridge Wells (p. 91); UML Ltd. (p. 208); Valentine & Sons Ltd. (p. 168 right); Victoria and Albert Museum (pp. 94 & 95)*; The Dean and Chapter, Westminster Abbey (p. 24 right); Reece Winstone (p. 168 left); Public Library, Whitehaven (pp. 112 & 113); City Library, York (p. 127 top).

Contents

Introduction

Any reader already fully aware of the long history, and immense variety, of planned towns in Britain will recognise from its size alone that this book does not pretend to give either an exhaustive historical account, or a definitive technical analysis, of its subject. Indeed, it is doubtful if any single book ought to try: the gradual accumulation of specialised studies in urban history will in the long run serve the same purpose with greater accuracy and detail than one might expect from a necessarily gigantic compilation.

What we have tried to do, both for those who do know something of our subject and for those who may perhaps be surprised to discover just how much town-planning there was before the birth of the Garden Cities movement, is to provide an introductory survey of the history, with a minimum of technical detail. The problem has always been what to leave out, and in every case our ruthlessness has been reluctant.

For example, with the passing exception of Londonderry, we have regretfully omitted Ulster (and Eire). In part because there are so many plantations – admittedly photogenic – and in part because we could find no overwhelming case for any single one. We apologise therefore to Crossmaglen, Hillsborough, Tanderagee and Cookstown – and their fellows.

We have also tried to apportion space on the principle of existing work: that is, to minimise what appeared to us to be superfluous in the context of the study as a whole; since it is quite obvious that anyone wishing to study Mediæval planning would turn to Maurice Beresford and that Edinburgh is splendidly covered by A. J. Youngson, we felt able to compress both these important sections to a minimum.

Inevitably there will be many readers who disagree with the choices we have made (and with our judgments), and we recognise that there are inconsistencies – our affection for Stourport and for the smaller Scottish foundations is all too apparent. Nevertheless, we hope that we have gone some way to filling the gap we believed to exist, and that some of those who have not already done so will be encouraged by our book to read further into the absorbing history of British towns.

We should like to record our gratitude to all those who helped us in our researches: most particularly, we are indebted to D. C. D. Pocock, of the University of Dundee, for allowing us to read his unpublished work on the development of Middlesbrough, Dr J. K. St Joseph of the Cambridge Committee for Aerial Photography for combing his files on our behalf, Miss Sue Groocock of Cadbury's for supplying us with material from the Bournville Village Trust, M. C. Moore of UML Ltd. for material on Port Sunlight, and to a number of Librarians and Curators for generous assistance, among them Colin Amery of the Town and Country Planning Association, Neil Beacham of the National Monuments Record, E. G. Twigg of Southport, Miles Shepherd of Tees-side, F. Barnes of Barrow, H. Bilton of Bradford, A. G. McKee of Shipley, Daniel Hay of Whitehaven, and Miss Catherine Cruft of the National Monuments Record of Scotland.

Before the Conquest

There is in Egypt a small town-site, Kahun, built nearly five thousand years ago. It was designed to house the workers on a nearby Pyramid, and, since it was presumably therefore planned in a commonplace style, we may assume from its regular pattern of blocks intersected by a grid of streets that the Egyptians of the third millennium B.C. saw nothing novel in wholly artificial urban planning. Since then, all manner of towns have been built on a grid, from Manhattan to Winchelsea, Richelieu to Saltaire. It is far and away the most common response to the challenge of planning a new settlement of any size.

According to Herodotus, and authenticated to some extent by modern excavation, Babylon was primarily a grid city. According to Aristotle, Hippodamus of Miletus (*f*.450 B.C.) 'introduced the principle of wide, straight streets, and, first of all architects, made provision for the proper grouping of dwelling-houses and also paid special heed to the combination of the different parts of a town in a harmonious whole.' We have already seen there is reason to doubt Hippodamus's primacy to that extreme extent, but he laid out Piræus, Thurii, Rhodes (probably), and all evinced his known predilection for the right-angled intersection, and indeed, for the fan-shaped zone. Selinus and Cyrene, whether or not Hippodamus had anything to do with their planning, are other 5th century sites based on grids.

Alexander's strategic and logistic needs – a common element in the birth of towns – produced Alexandria, Miletus, Priene, Nicæa, Pergamum and Ephesus. Piecing together contemporary evidence, and aided by the modern excavations, it seems fairly certain that all these were originally planned on the chequer-board grid. To Hippodamus's name we can, incidentally, add that of Dinocrates, employed by Alexander to build Alexandria: arguably the first two practitioners of the art of town-planning to get any historical credit.

The Greeks in general, apart from their realisation of the military advantages of the predictable street-plan, devoted endless conscientious rules and regulations to urban planning. Builders and occupiers were both subject to strict by-laws safeguarding light, air, water, structure, and against fire. The community accepted responsibility to a marked extent for the wholesomeness of its own environment, rather than leaving it to the free play of the market.

All this proves that long before we get to the Romans, and thus to ourselves, towns were built and governed on principles which still survive, relatively unquestioned, under the happy umbrella of the Town & Country Planning Acts. Britain is reached via the Romans for the very good reason that we know something of the Roman techniques of town-planning, and we know very little indeed of what went before them; what we do know is that there is yet to be discovered any sign of a British town, rather than a village or encampment, and that in any case, a town is only practicable where productive and distributive specialisation have reached the point at which townsfolk can make a living. The itinerant merchant is no more urban than the nomadic shepherd is a farmer.

Roman power, like Roman culture, was on the other hand immensely urban. Where the Romans went, their decision to stay can invariably be dated from their first town-plantation. Roman generals carried army-issue town planning schemes in their knapsacks.

When the Roman generals first arrived in Britain, they found in residence three broad groups of people – and three types of culture. The most sophisticated were the Belgic tribes, and it is Cunobelin, the great Belgic leader, who alone of British chieftains seems to have impressed the Romans as in any sense their peer. The Catuvellauni had settlements, at Camulodunum and Verulamium, which one might almost dignify as towns (they were probably much larger than Wheathampstead's 100 acres) were it not for Caesar's laconic comment that 'the Britons call it a town when they have fortified dense woodland with a rampart and a ditch'.

Next in level of civilisation (by Roman standards) came the tribes under Belgic influence: and these too had tribal centres – evidence of one has been found at Leicester – which were of some size, but little sophistication. Again, the impression that we can borrow from the Romans is of a fortified area containing both huts and open ground, the accommodation of the chief, and of his mint, being distinctly more civilised than the housing of his followers.

Finally there were the tribes untouched by Belgic influence – indeed, fighting continually to remain untouched. Some were, like the invaders, of the Iron Age, but there were also some who appear to have been still restricted to Bronze Age levels of civilisation (that is to say, not that they were unaware of the technology of Iron, but that in the organisation of their affairs and their dwellings they remained backward) and in general the settlements of this third group cannot be considered as much more than hill-forts, at best, or crude earthworks round a camp, at worst. Maiden Castle is the summit of this culture's capacities, and remarkable as it is, it can hardly be called a town.

The Romans had of course very different ideas about what constituted a town from those of even the most civilised Briton. They had a long tradition of town-planning behind them before they ever reached the remote extremity of north-western Europe, and that tradition itself, with its firm commitment to regular schemes assembled in their turn from regular plots – the *insulæ* which we shall meet again in mediæval Winchelsea – owed something to the primitive Terramare of northern Italy, built up of trapezoidal plots, and to the rectangular blocks of Etruscan planning. Even had they not already shown this predilection for square towns with cruciform main streets (the Decumanus and the Cardo), as with Aosta and Turin, the Romans would, like any soldiers, presumably have favoured right-angled grids for their military coloniæ: it is the simplest pattern to lay out with crude instruments and unskilled surveyors.

During the course of their long occupation the Romans founded many towns in Britain; a large proportion were on sites already inhabited, but in the main the Roman plan was imposed without much consideration for the older settlement. There are exceptions, which seemed to show the influence of the native form with its lower building density, and of these Silchester is the best known, and the most obvious. Calleva Atrebatum, the capital of the Atrebates, a Belgic tribe, was founded at some time between 15 B.C. and A.D. 5, and it almost certainly fitted Cæsar's quoted description of a British *oppidum* – enclosed, but hardly built-up. It fell to the Romans by about A.D. 45, and, as the principal centre of one of the most important tribal kingdoms (the Atrebates controlled

'A plan of Silchester . . . together with a scheme of the ancient streets as he conjectures them to have been, from several years observation of the Corn when Green there. Likewise the situation of a large Building whose foundations remain towards the Middle of the City.' Wright's plan testifies to the accuracy of crop-marks as a basis for mapping. The regular insulæ are obvious.

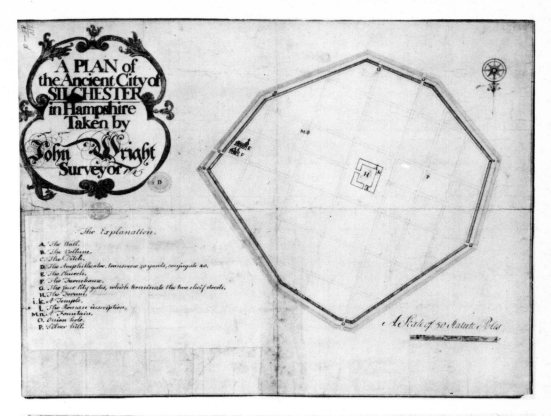

John Wright also produced these drawings of the surviving Roman walls at Silchester, sensibly incorporated for his own purposes by the 18th century farmer.

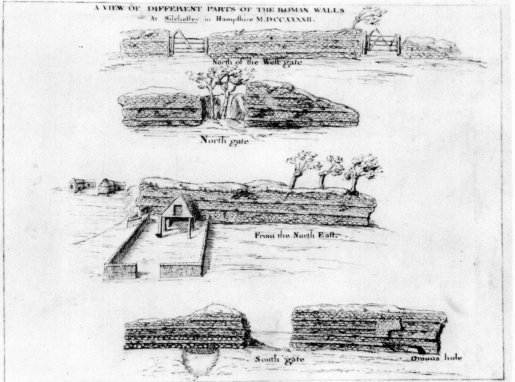

at one time Berkshire, Hampshire and large parts of Wiltshire, West Surrey and West Sussex), was developed by them into a cantonal capital – the centre of that form of native local government which co-existed with the Roman provincial government.

The Roman contribution to the planning of Silchester is easily assessed: the Forum, public baths, regular *insulæ*, wide streets (20 to 25 ft.) with cambered sides. The British contribution can be inferred. The Forum occupies an almost central position, instead of being positioned near the junction of the cruciform main streets; the shape of the town as a whole is that of an irregular octagon, rather than a rectangle or square (Winchester, Leicester, Aldborough, Cærwent, Brough on Humber, Caister St Edmund's, Alchester, Irchester, Mildenhall, Leintwardine, Dorchester on Thames, Ancaster, Mancetter, Horncastle, Hardham, Alfoldean and Iping among other Romano-British towns were rectangular); and, above all, the *insulæ* were not packed with urban housing, but occupied by small country villas, with substantial gardens. Sir Patrick Abercrombie called it a 'garden city'; and according to G. C. Boon 'if we could see Calleva in its prime we should see nothing more than a loose-built village with farms, big houses, cottages, shops, hall and places of worship and amusement, set amid gardens and paddocks'.

It may seem capricious to discuss Silchester at length, and not to mention much more typical Roman plans, like those we suspect to lie beneath Gloucester, Colchester, Lincoln or York – the four coloniæ, settled by veteran legionaries and modelled on Rome's own principles of government – but there is a point. Silchester is not only recognised to be more truly British (that is, pre-Roman) in its plan, it happens to demonstrate one of the strongest themes in all British town-planning, from the dispersed *oppida* of the Iron Age to the King's Green of Winchelsea, the allotments of Port Sunlight – and, of course, the suburbs and garden cities of the 20th century: the great passion of the British for gardens and parks.

The Roman occupation founded, over four hundred years of steady re-investment of trading profits, dozens of towns. They nearly all bore the signs of Roman civilisation – baths, temples, *fora*, stone and brick instead of wood and mud – and of Roman planning – walls, regular *insulæ*, right-angled streets – from the start, because the orderly Roman mind regarded these things as primary requirements. A town was far more the ordered juxtaposition of buildings than a concentration of people – a very different view from that of the tribes who went before them, and from that of those who came after. When the Romans left, we are accustomed to think that civilisation departed with them; but although the next five hundred years can hardly be regarded as a great innovating period in the history of British towns, we should remember that a large number of the towns the Romans founded managed to survive the Dark Ages, and that town life, the essential basis for civilisation, continued despite the apparently incessant waves of invasion. Some towns certainly died, among them Silchester itself; but others merely shrank within their walls.

The Anglo-Saxons have customarily been allowed some credit for the villages of England, but not for any towns. Were this fair, it would be para-doxical, since the impulse which made the Anglo-Saxons villagers, where the

Chichester: the modern street-plan, based as it is on the typical East-West and North-South cross of the main streets within the line of the Roman Walls, is a direct survival of the Roman Noviomagus Regnensium lay-out. The lesser streets have been substantially pushed out of their original grid by the territorial ambitions of the various religious institutions which squeezed within the walls in the Middle Ages.

British were happier in hamlets or isolated farmsteads, is presumably a similar impulse to that which makes men townsfolk. At the moment when a group of Saxon colonists chose to settle in a valley bottom, leaving the sparse ridge-top to the retreating Celts, they could hardly guarantee that what they founded would remain a village, not a town. And in fact there is some evidence of explicit town-foundation at the height of Anglo-Saxon England. Early in the 10th century, when the changing course of the River Rother ruined Romney, the community was quite capable of building their port all over again at New Romney. At about the same time, it seems probable that the Abbey of St Alban laid out a new town near the ruins of Roman Verulamium; and, not long after, the selection of a rocky outcrop by the River Wear as a safe resting place for the bones of St Cuthbert led to the birth of Durham.

About several other towns, untraced in Roman Britain and yet unequivocally thriving by the Norman Conquest, there is less certainty. Although it may well be that Lydford, Burpham, and Maldon grew from villages to their undoubted town status by the Conquest, rather than being planted *de novo*, it is equally clear that they did become towns during the time when the allegedly unurban Anglo-Saxons lived there. There is a dispute about a town of greater importance than any of these: batteries of historians can be found to prove or criticise the claim of Oxford to have been planted as an investment on the Royal lands. There are doubts and arguments about Lydford and Cricklade, Wallingford, Ipswich and Southampton; and the chances of any definite resolution of such arguments are of course remote, in the absence of documents, and given the difficulties of excavation. At any rate, it should be clear that the Anglo-Saxons not only lived in the towns they found, but were quite capable of building new ones for themselves. What kind of towns they built must unfortunately remain a little vague: although there are marked signs of rectangularity – the ubiquitous grid – in New Romney, Oxford, Southampton, Lydford and Cricklade. And although there are many kinds of plan, of which the grid is merely the simplest and most common, it is the form least likely to arise spontaneously in the growth of an organic town.

About the Romans and the Saxons we cannot really do more than make informed conjectures; but, having established that there were towns, town-plans, and town-planners before 1066, we can enter upon the history of new towns in Britain from the moment when evidence becomes more than fragmentary archæology, or reasoned inference, and becomes instead a matter of moderate certainty, documents, and surviving streets.

The Conquest

The Normans, like the Romans, arrived fully conscious of the uses of urban settlement in conquest and control. And, a factor of great importance in the ensuing centuries, of the superior profitability of the self-governing town over the captive agricultural demesne. Before they came to England, Dukes of Normandy and their greater vassals had chartered a number of new, or notably expanded, *bourgs* in the preceding generation. Caen had had two new plantations added to it by the Conqueror: Breteuil sur Iton, probably founded by William fitz Osbern around 1050, left its mark after the conquest on Hereford, Cardiff, New Carmarthen, Haverford West, New Montgomery, Brecon, Denbigh, Rhuddlan, Llanfyllin, Welshpool, Dryslwyn, Kenfig, Aberavon, Llantrissant, Neath, Laugharne, Cardigan, Deganwy, Aberystwyth, Ruthin, Flint, Overton, Hope, Caerwys, Caernarvon, Conway, Criccieth, Bere, Harlech, Beaumaris, Bala, Newborough, Nevin and Pwllheli. Every one, either directly or through one or more of the others, enjoyed the 'liberties of Breteuil'.

Maurice Beresford, on whose exhaustive and definitive *New Towns of the Middle Ages* much of this and the next chapter have gratefully leaned, cites several other indigenous Norman plantations: Cormeilles, Laval, Auffay, Dieppe, Pontaudemer, Ponts and 'at least twelve other *bourgs*'.

The incentives for the Normans were not substantially different from what we might regard as the traditional grounds for town-planning. Indeed, the most striking paradox of Norman policy is that a nation usually credited with the introduction of high feudalism to England and Wales should have created so many enclaves of free tenure and borough liberties: since it is plain the conquerors had no commitment to the principle of economic freedom, every time they conceded it they bore witness to the potency of those traditional grounds – defence, transport, industry, and landlord's profit.

A town was more profitable than bare manorial fields because: it could be built on land that might have little or no agricultural value, or at least include such land within it; far higher rents, and straight cash rents, could be charged for burgage plots than for open fields; the strangers their town attracted – normally, of course, because of its market status – could be subjected to various tolls and fees; and town dwellers, where the founder was the King, made splendid taxpayers. Furthermore, it took a great deal less effort to draw rents and taxes from a free town than to manage, at every level, a farming manor.

Nevertheless, since the Normans arrived unbidden, the first class of foundation we might examine is that designed to control the English. Eighteen of their first twenty-five plantations were in the shadow of a castle: and the first generation after the Conquest saw the erection of nearly ninety castles. Three-quarters of all new towns begun between 1000 and 1140 were castle towns – thirty out of forty. Before the Normans came, there was the threat of the Normans, sundry Scandinavians, and native robbers and rebels to be guarded against, and after they came, and the English were satisfactorily pacified, the Scots and the Welsh continued to require military foundations.

William I's first castle-town was, as one might expect, at Hastings. Like its exact contemporaries Skipsea (Yorks) and Richard'sCastle (Hereford), neither of which has survived as much more than an historical monument, Hastings was castle first, town second: indeed, it is arguable that both Skipsea and Hastings existed at or near the Norman sites before the castles came, and moved into their protective shadow afterwards. This was certainly the case with Launceston, where an existing market moved half-a-mile to be at the castle foot, and at Windsor, where the Norman castle became the centre of a town removed more than a mile from its Saxon site.

The attractions of the castle were obvious: it offered protection against external dangers, authority over internal crime, and was a major consumer of the town's goods. On occasions the town existed right inside the castle's own walls, as at Trematon (Cornwall), and all self-respecting towns in this early period were surrounded by their own fortifications, even if they had a guardian castle nearby. Sometimes, perhaps, because they had the castle and its unpredictable owner nearby.

The primacy of fear in town-planning naturally affected urban morphology. The immense cost in labour and materials of building a solid town wall, let alone a castle, makes it most unlikely that they were put up for mere show, and if the need was so strongly felt, then all other considerations must have come second to that of security. By and large, towns put up by soldiers have

straight streets; if the inhabitants grow fractious, they can be put down more easily, and if an enemy takes the town, he finds it more difficult to defend. There are examples – Montreuil is one – of a slightly more devious approach: irregularly contrived streets which can be defended yard by yard. However, from Alexander to Napoleon, soldiers have plumped for the tidy grid, and the Normans employed it as one might expect wherever it was appropriate.

It would, however, be mistaken to think that grids, or rectilinear arrangements on any scale, imply military origins, or that the grid alone distinguishes the new foundations. As we have seen in earlier periods, right-angles and straight lines are cheap and easy to survey, require little creative thought – whatever they demand of the builder on the ground – and often spring from haste as much as forethought. Kahun was put up as a temporary shanty-town for navvies, and used a grid, one must assume, because that was the quickest and simplest plan. For those who have devoted great time and attention to their plans, the grid often loses its authoritarian charm, whether to give way to a higher geometry, as in Scamozzi's ideal, or Wren's London, or to a simulation of organic development, as in Bournville. The shapes, sizes and densities of Norman plantations commonly reflect their function; and their function, economic or strategic, was to satisfy their founder's needs rather than to build utopia.

Founders, whether they were enterprising local landlords, prelates, the King, or the King in partnership with a lesser landlord, had to attract inhabitants for their foundations. They were not concerned with the ordinary sort,

Launceston Castle: immediately after the Conquest, the Earl of Mortian built a castle on the hill of Dunheved, and moved the market from the Saxon Launceston St Stephen to the new town at the foot of his hilltop stronghold. Its typical 'clustering round the skirts' form remains apparent today.

14

A Mediæval City: from the Luttrell Psalter, 1310.

those who would become porters, labourers, beggars, and would arrive in any case seeking a breath of that town air that made men free, but with the more substantial sort – merchants and craftsmen. In order to seduce these desirable citizens away from their old allegiances, new towns had to be promoted in much the same way we now promote under-developed areas: capital grants, tax holidays and investment allowances all existed in Norman times. A prospective burgess, an intending vintner perhaps, would be offered a building lot, on which he was expected to build quickly, but on which he could squeeze as many buildings as he might, without further rent, with favourable terms from the proprietor's woods and quarries, and remission or reduction of rent during building and even for some years thereafter. Edward I, whose urgency in populating his Welsh plantations was more than commercial, offered ten years rent free to those building houses in Beaumaris, Caernarvon, Harlech and Criccieth.

As a general rule, the founder offered only such physical and political inducements as encouraged trade: the amenity of the town was defined as its defensibility, the size of its market and of the plots on offer; the liberty as the frequency and scale of its markets and fairs and the relative burden of its tolls and taxes. Founders who made little or no objection to maximum-density development, encroachment on the highway, differential building-lines, grossly varying heights and styles of building, and thoroughly intermingled building use, can hardly be treated in anything but pragmatic, and mercenary, terms. Such zoning as was usual was dictated by commercial considerations: big merchants had not just to be allowed, but encouraged to build round the market-place, and poorer housing kept away from the high-rent areas.

Virtually nothing but an occasional street-line survives in England of mediæval buildings. The total failures among the plantations (and Beresford cites 41 such failures out of 256 attempts in England and Wales) have often rotted into the ground, the great successes have been rebuilt time and again, and even the static successes – those that survive unexpanded – can seldom show more than one or two rather doubtful mediæval survivals. It would in any case be surprising for a domestic building to survive for so many centuries. Fashions and accepted standards change (and before anything can become a valued antique it has to survive an apprenticeship as merely old-fashioned and out-dated), the greatest pressure for redevelopment is always at the centre, the original core, and the normal wear-and-tear of weather, traffic, wars and riot has taken steady toll. Furthermore, neither the materials nor the arrangement of mediæval houses offered any resistance to fire. Far worse than worm and rot in any wooden city, fire swept through most mediæval towns as often as the plagues.

Inevitably, therefore, we know much more about Norman castles and their owners than we do about the homes and households that squatted round their skirts. Since the Norman foundations include Newcastle upon Tyne (a self explanatory name), King's Lynn, Pontefract and Watford, among the forty, it is a great pity.

Nevertheless, to revert once more to Hastings, the Conqueror's own castle was a temporary structure, designed to guard against the English, as yet unconquered. It was close by an existing port of Hastings, already in the process of inundation. Victorious, William granted the area to the Comte d'Eu, who proceeded to build a permanent stone castle on the clifftop. The Norman town lay in the valley of the Bourne below (the Saxon, drowned, had been in the Priory valley to the west) and consisted of two parallel streets running north from the sea. The market place and All Saints' Church were at the northern end, St Clement's Church by the town wall at the sea-front; the latter also fell to the sea in 1286. It sounds very small, and very simple, but it was of considerable importance at the time; the compensation paid to its original owners, the Abbey of Fécamp, was an entire, and valuable, manor.

Despite the obvious early importance of fortified sites, it is worth remarking that, while the Normans erected castles at Hastings, Skipsea, Arundel, Richard's Castle, they simultaneously (1070) founded their first unfortified town, and an important one, at Battle. William founded the Abbey of St Martin there as a thank-offering for victory, and granted the Abbey not only six manors, but a regular Sunday market. The residents of the township at the Abbey gates ('brought hither out of the neighbouring counties, and some even from foreign countries') were answerable only to the Abbot. The town was effectively a funnel-like street running from the Abbey gatehouse down to the market place, lined with houses, and boasting two guild-halls. Its principal occupation was receiving pilgrims and, although it never officially received a borough charter, the Abbey Chronicle remarks rather smugly that 'on account of the very great dignity of the place, the men of this town are called burgesses'. Shrines were of prime economic importance: Abbot Baldwin of Bury St Edmunds, the great Saxon example, greeted the Conquest by expanding his town over five new streets running parallel to the West front of the precinct. A strict grid or chequer-board pattern, Baldwin's development according to Domesday Book produced '342 houses on . . . land

The Abbot of Bury St Edmunds' new streets after the Conquest can still be seen making a regular pattern of chequers West of the Abbey Gate. The Market has been gradually built over.

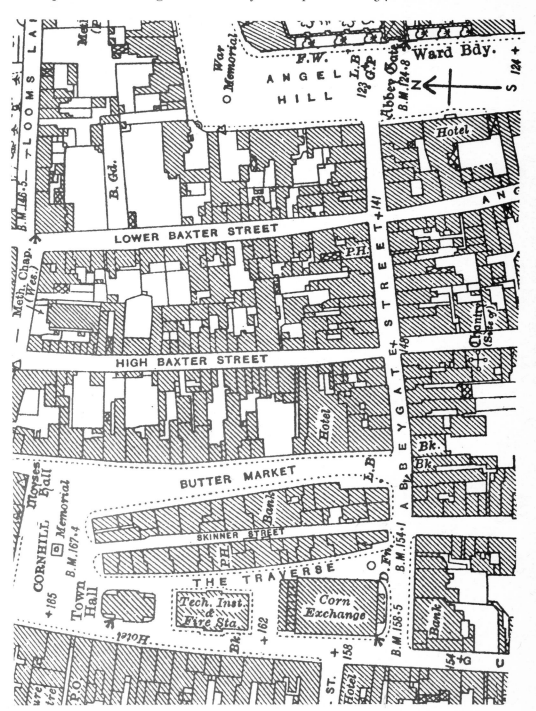

. . . which was under the plough in the time of King Edward'. It also included a splendid new market place.

The first two generations after the Conquest were naturally more acutely conscious of the need to pacify the country than their successors. We have already noted the high proportion of castle-towns in the period, and it is also a time when the King himself took a leading role in founding new towns to facilitate defence, administration, transport and trade (which means both taxes and the amelioration of discontent). William I, William Rufus and Henry I not only encouraged their greater tenants, seigneurs or abbots, to found towns, they did it themselves. A third of the foundations in the first generation after the Conquest were royal, a proportion not reached even by Edward I.

Gradually the emphasis changed from castles, from royal initiatives and strategic sites – notably in the West – to commerce, all manner of private enterprise and private interest. Battle and King's Lynn were followed by St Ives and St Neots, Newborough, Boston and Dunstable, Watford and Boroughbridge: plantations designed to exploit, and facilitate, particular commercial demands rather than to defend the realm. The differences were slight; no castle, a site chosen without defence in mind. Otherwise, these Norman foundations, like their successors for centuries thereafter, were simple ventures, with blunt and unashamed aspirations. The only civic amenities provided by the proprietor were the market-place, with, perhaps, attendant guild-hall, and the Church. Founders did not sketch in the hospital, the school, library or public baths because they did not exist in the competing organic towns, nor was there any body of planning literature to suggest it. The nearest that most mediæval foundations – even those of the latest date – got to the broader social amenities was the provision of almshouses.

Commercial foundations, however, did differ in place and shape from the stark, military eminences and peninsulæ. St Ives and St Neots are, of course, riparian foundations, but not to control the waterway and its crossing, nor to exploit the natural barricade. They were founded as rather marginal shrines at happy confluences of river and road where markets and fairs would flourish. Boroughbridge grew steadily from insignificance to great substance, because its site embraced not only the bridge over the Ure crossed by all traffic between Scotland and the South, but because that Great North Road was neatly diverted to run into the market place, at the cost of an additional bridge over a small stream.

This mercenary seduction of main roads into the arms of the town's stall-holders was very common: there is effectively a whole class of town-shapes which are based on the irresistible market place. Many towns were indeed planned to be no more than a market, surrounded with burgage plots, and safely wrapped in an outside wall, but even more ambitious grids could and did include provision to channel the carriage trade (not that it was carriage-borne until the late 17th century) past their goods. Some had no real problem; Dunstable and Stony Stratford sit firmly on the line of the old Roman road, and had their markets strung along it. Others, like Chipping Sodbury, bent the road to go through their markets, before allowing it to swing back on its former course. Not only planned towns did, and do, this. Aylesbury and Witney, just as much as planned Baldock, force the traveller to negotiate their market, and in fact there are still hundreds of towns and villages which we now condemn as bottlenecks simply because the last thing a mediæval borough wanted was to be by-passed. This view is responsible for the corner-access market: one in which no road enters and leaves in a straight line, or even in the middle of a façade, but in which all traffic is conducted through obliquely, with the maximum hesitation imposed on the stranger.

The great surge in plantation, of both classes, came to an end with the civil wars of Stephen and Matilda: between 1110 and 1130 there were probably twenty plantations in England and Wales; between 1150 and 1170 perhaps eighteen. But between 1130 and 1150, the broad period of the upheaval, only seven. Since the rate picked up sharply once more after the wars, and remained high for another two centuries, it seems safe to blame the wars alone for this lapse.

After the wars we are clearly beyond the period of Conquest (save in Wales) and thereafter the proportion of foundations with castles drops rapidly, as does the proportion in which the King took a direct part. Military plantations, if successful, are inevitably self-destructive: once a castle has imposed peace and order on the countryside, it ceases to be necessary. In fact, the interesting phenomenon of the post-war generations is that the towns in which the King is interested are largely commercial (or tax-gathering) ventures rather than strategic ones; and Kings were, furthermore, glad to sell charters and concessions to other projectors and their boroughs.

Henry II's contribution to urban history, for example, seems largely to have consisted of granting and confirming charters, status and liberties to the foundations of others – for cash. Richard and John's reigns cover one of the most active bouts of plantation of all, yet they themselves were only involved in Portsmouth and Liverpool, obviously immensely successful foundations,

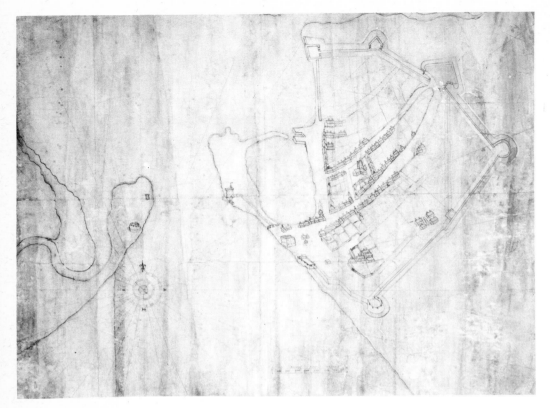

Portsmouth: a Plan of about 1545. The many empty insulæ within the Town Walls can be seen, looking rather as if the inhabitants of this plantation of 1194 had taken to farming them. Portsmouth remained a subordinate part of the Port of Southampton until the 18th century.

Salisbury in 1751. The regular street-plan of the New Salisbury created by the Bishop when he moved his Cathedral in 1219 stands out clearly.

St Augustine's Church, Hedon, E.R., Yorks. This port foundation of 1138 once had three great Churches, of which only St Augustine's now survives, known as 'The King of Holderness' and clearly the relic of the days before Ravenserodd and Hull took Hedon's trade away.

Hedon. The contracted size of the present town can be seen easily from the air; as can the shrunken width of the creek which originally brought the ships up from the Humber.

but still only two out of a possible forty. Richard clearly had other distractions, and expensive ones, but John's equally severe need for revenue failed to stimulate him to take a lead in the spate of town-founding that was in progress. The investment cost of a plantation, especially if it did not require a castle, was small, and the royal lands were extensive. Nor were Richard and John, like their successors, pre-occupied by building French bastides; Richard did plant Marmande in Gascony and St Rémy and Petit Andelys in the older English holdings to the North, but John was equally inactive in France.

Their subjects, however, were intensely busy. Amongst the foundations of the two reigns were Stratford-upon-Avon, Barnet, Bawtry, Royston and Leeds; and no less than six in Cornwall, a county whose quite apparent otherness provoked generations of landlords into attempting its conquest by urbanisation, with the result that it ended up with thirty-eight towns (more than all save one other county – Devon) of which nineteen were plantations *de novo*.

The distribution of new towns by county raises a number of questions, to most of which no answer of immediate conviction yet exists. Royston, for example, reminds one that Cambridgeshire is ringed with plantations – its eight neighbouring counties contain over twenty, from Newmarket right on the border to more distant King's Lynn, Baldock, Chelmsford, Dunstable and so on – but itself has not only no plantations at all, but a bare three organic towns. Since the very similar terrain of Essex supports four plantations, and Hertford has seven, this is distinctly puzzling.

Baldock, one of the Hertford foundations, is worth a moment's special notice, partly because its founder was an Order, the Knights Templar, who were granted the land in about 1148, and partly because of its arrantly commercial plan, despite the military planners. The Templars diverted the Great North Road which ran along the boundary of their land so that it looped right through Baldock market place, may well have also bent the Icknield Way to do the same, and called their town Baudoc, the mediæval corruption of Baghdad, because their aspirations for it were on a grand scale. Its consistent failure to live up to those aspirations may stem from the already crowded competition at its foundation – it has always been surrounded. As a general rule, the densities of planned towns before industrialisation, which introduced its own distinctive criteria of site and placement, are in close relation to the degree of wilderness – of nature and of men. Cornwall and Devon are remote, as are Northumberland and Westmorland, both with a high proportion, while the highest proportions of all are in Wales and on the Welsh border: eleven Welsh counties have nothing but planted towns.

Henry III was a great deal more active than his immediate predecessors: not in England, however, where his sole direct intervention, at Warenmouth, Northumberland, failed, but in Wales and in Gascony. The inference is plain: the king was most active where the threat to his control was greatest. As has been pointed out by E. A. Lewis, and reaffirmed recently by Harold Carter, 'there are no towns of purely Welsh origin'. Within certain limits – allowing for the expansion of organic sites – it is true to say that the towns of Wales have been put there by the Kings of England – or by their mighty tenants. Henry III's reign saw the founding of eleven Welsh (and nine Gascon)

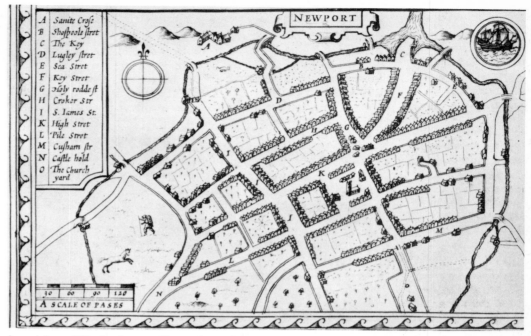

Newport, now the capital of the Isle of Wight, shown by John Speed in 1611. Founded between 1174–84, it was originally called Novus Burgus de Medina. The Medina forms the boundary to the north and east.

A   Sanite Croſe
B   Shoſhoole ſtret
C   The Key
D   Lugley ſtret
E   Sea Stret
F   Key Stret
G   Holy rodde ſt
H   Croker Str
I   S. Iames St.
K   High stret
L   Pile Stret
M   Cuſham ſtr
N   Caſtle hold
O   The Church yard

A SCALE OF PASES

bastides. Their immediate function was oppressive (the Welsh were there first) and their placement[1] and morphology reflect their origin. King John had, incidentally, planned such a spate of Welsh plantations, but, like a number of his projects, it was still-born.

From our point of view, there is not much to be said about these strategic – at times, almost tactical – plantations. None of them were of the first or second rank of importance after the conquest of the Welsh was completed, unlike some earlier foundations (Brecon, Carmarthen, Haverford West) and their immediate successors (Denbigh, Caernarvon, Beaumaris), and none can be distinguished for any particular ingenuity of plan or amenity. Their great charm – the charm of so many Welsh foundations – is that nowhere else do we find such a concentration of sites which have remained in use without being wholly overwhelmed by subsequent growth. At Caerphilly, for example, the lake-sheltered castle remains the centre of the town, and it is perfectly possible to ignore the declining pits and look up the Rhymney valley from the slight eminence of the market as though to see Llewelyn's army.

Nevertheless, there is little we can discover or deduce about their origins – intellectual or structural – that does not quickly descend to conjecture. From the time of the Conquest until the death of Henry III, it is perfectly possible to discuss any English king in the role of town-builder, or promoter, and to discuss here and there the detail of that building – purpose, scale, shape, amenity, aspiration, influence – but neither the kings, nor their subjects, can be considered to have left any real evidence that town-building either inspired them, or they it. With the accession of Edward I, a king who can be written of as much in terms of architecture as in terms of war, the story becomes infinitely more rewarding. Sufficiently so for this first great English town-builder to occupy a chapter to himself.

[1] The effective borders of the principalities of both Llewelyn the Great and Llewelyn ap Griffydd were defined by English foundations of this period – Painscastle, Hay, New Montgomery, Deganwy, Cefnllys, Welshpool, Dyserth and Caerphilly are all English responses to a Welsh challenge.

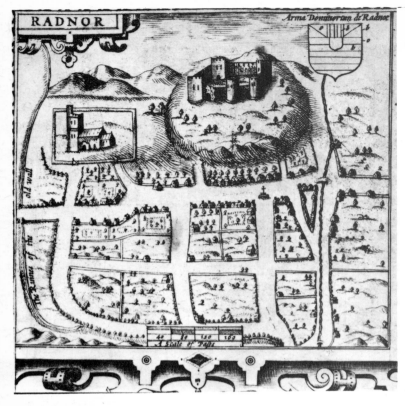

Edward I

Opposite page
Upper left
New Radnor. It seems probable that this is a 13th century rebuilding of the Norman site of Old Radnor in order to strengthen and enlarge the defences.

Lower left
New Radnor from the air: it is not noticeably any more populous than when Speed was there. It still comes nowhere near reaching the Wall on the left.

Right
Edward I: from the Tomb of John of Eltham, Westminster Abbey.

[1]The others were Stephen Penshurst, Prior of Angouleme, and Bishop Kirkby of Ely.

Edward I has every right to be considered by the English as one of their greatest Kings. In the course of a thirty-five-year reign, rarely interrupted by mere peace, he enthusiastically defeated Scots, Welsh, French, Popes and Saracens, his feudal tenants and his feudal overlord, successfully extending the power of the English throne throughout the British Isles, maintaining its French empire, and binding to his house by marriage much of the European monarchy and the English aristocracy. Many of his actual triumphs, when analysed, seem thin – he vanquished ill-matched enemies like the English Jews, and the civil populations of Berwick and Ghent – but there is no doubt that his unceasing zeal brought long-term rewards. In every way, from his incessant superstitious piety to his illiterate devotion to the ideals of chivalry (which did not preclude raising taxes or Papal blessings by effective fraud, nor marrying off his children to advantage before they left the breast, nor evading solemn promises – evasion being preferable to unchivalrous breach) he was a ruthless, militaristic philistine. He had all the virtues of mediæval Kingship, and the greatest of those was, of course, success.

In pursuit of his ambitions, which might justly be called despotic, he attacked and overthrew not only barons and the neighbouring monarchs, but towns and their civil liberties. When the City of London attempted to maintain its ancient privileges against his Justices, he imposed direct monarchical rule upon it for thirteen years. He seized the liberties of York and charged the citizens one thousand Marks for their restoration; he trumped up issues to seize the liberties of Norwich, and to fine the people of Bristol £500. By and large, he avoided actually entering towns – whether because, as an obsessional huntsman, he found them restricting, or because he rightly mistrusted the welcome given such a high-taxing King, one cannot be sure. At any rate, few Kings can have spent so few nights under city roofs, and few have shown such consistent contempt for urban concerns and values. Edward was patently committed to the open country.

Having said that, one must continue to say that during his reign there were nearly forty new foundations in England and Wales (and over fifty in Edward's French territories) – and that the King played a greater part in this surge of plantation than any other. Indeed, Edward I far outstrips any other English King in the attention he gave not only to the siting and chartering of new towns, but to their planning and colonisation. The implication is clear: few Kings have had such a sustained need to maximise revenue, and to impose strategic control, and, given Edward's total distaste for the urban way of life (and urban subjects), his plantation policy proves beyond doubt that in terms of revenue and strategy, towns are essential techniques of government. Edward I's endorsement of the proposition proves it far better than that of any other, less objective, founder. Indeed, the King's total pragmatism could not be better illustrated than by his appointing Henry le Waleys and Gregory de Rokesle to be two of the commissioners empowered to lay out the New Winchelsea made necessary by the inundation of the original Cinque Port[1]. Both were, during the course of their commission, Lord Mayors of London the last two before Edward suspended the position for thirteen years. Indeed, de Rokesle was the Mayor whose refusal to submit, in his position as Mayor, to the summons of the King's Justices at the Tower, provoked the withdrawal of the City's liberties. Edward was not prepared to brook any argument from existing towns – but nor was he prepared to deny himself the advice of those best experienced in the administration of towns.

Edward was of course responsible for Aquitaine before he became King of England, his father, Henry III, having endowed his heir with the revenues of the great Dukedom at the age of four, and with the title itself on his marriage at fifteen. And as we have seen, all English Kings who retained great interests in France were bastidors – founders of new towns. Even those who played no part in urban settlement at home (if England can be called the home of Kings who habitually spoke French), like Richard Cœur-de-Lion, had to use plantations to protect, and enrich, their lands across the Channel. Edward I certainly had wide experience of plantation in Gascony before he ever came to the English throne. Nearly thirty bastides were founded there between his assumption of the Dukedom and his accession as King: nearly all of them placed so as to suggest that trade (markets, tolls and taxes) mattered more than defence.

The connection between England and France extended far beyond the ruling house; and before one assigns the distinct 'Gascon' pattern of Winchelsea to Edward's experience alone, one should recall that le Waleys, frequently Lord Mayor of London, had also been Mayor of Bordeaux. His prominence was unusual, but not his background. Probably the great majority of both the territorial aristocracy and the leading merchants shared this intimate involvement with both countries.

It is with England and Wales that we are concerned, however. And in those countries Edward I was responsible for foundations (and re-foundations) or every size, success and function. He takes direct responsibility for only two completely new English foundations – the immense success of Kingston upon Hull and the utter failure of Newton (Dorset) – but was, of course, also

Prospect of Conway in 1749. The typical union of Town with Castle stands out.

responsible for the complete rebuilding of New Winchelsea and the substantial rebuilding of Berwick (as well he should have been), and managed to remove from its original patron, the Bishop of Winchester, Newtown (or Francheville), in the Isle of Wight. But he aided and abetted many other English foundations from his enthusiasm for selling charters. Nether Knutsford, Wavermouth, Skinburgh, Newton Arlosh, all had market rights from the King, although Wavermouth and Skinburgh plunged into the Solway Firth almost as soon as they began. But Edward's real legacy is in Wales; despite the evidence that he understood the commercial charm of town-foundation, it was the conquest of the Welsh that summoned forth his greatest efforts, and one can understand how his wholly mercenary projects – like poor Newton, altogether too close to thriving Poole – have been obscured in memory by his mighty chain of urban forts in Wales. During his reign there were founded, in the wake of English armies, nearly thirty towns. They range from Bangor and Caernarvon to Llawhaden and Trefnant (which only lasted four years). The greater ones, nine of the ten founded by the King himself, were of course centred on huge castles, and populated by French and English settlers attracted by all manner of royal inducement. All were designed to combine strategic site, tactical defence, and long-term anglicising influence. In the circumstances, it seems fair – having admitted that some Welsh plantations, like Templeton and Trefnant, lacked castles – to discuss a military site, Caernarvon, as an example of Edward's Welsh strategic planning, and then to take commercial Winchelsea (for contemporaries, one of the most important ventures of them all) to illustrate his more pacific English style. For our purposes it is of course distinctly helpful that these two should have neither slipped beneath the waves, nor beneath a tide of subsequent development. It is still possible to walk the bounds of Edward's Caernarvon and Edward's Winchelsea, and to summon up a vision of what he built with merely ordinary powers of imagination: Edwardian Hull would undoubtedly require extraordinary powers, and Newton, necromancy.

John Taylor, who published a 'Short Relation' of his 'Long Journey' (whether from consideration or indolence one cannot guess) in 1652, paid Edward's scheme for Caernarvon great tribute. Nearly four hundred years after it was built, he wrote of his arrival at Caernarvon: 'I thought to have seen a Town and a Castle, or a Castle and a Town; but I saw both to be one, and one to be both; for indeed a man can hardly divide them in judgment or apprehension; and I have seen many gallant fabrics and fortifications, but for compactness and completeness of Caernarvon, I never yet saw a parallel. And it is by Art and Nature so fitted and seated, that it stands impregnable, and if it be well manned, victualled, and ammunitioned, it is invincible, except fraud or famine do assault, or conspire against it.' In fact, during the Civil War it had been besieged, successfully, and Madoc's Revolt in 1294 over-ran it before it was complete, but it remains true that it *looks* impregnable. In 1660, in a fit of general mistrust of such fortification, the Government ordered its destruction – both Castle proper and the walls which it extends about its town – but the order seems not to have been proceeded with, quite possibly because it became apparent that the necessary effort would be too expensive.

The immense strength of Caernarvon is not simply one of structure (although some walls are nearly twenty feet thick at their base – twenty feet of solid stone) but of site. There had been a Roman fort there – the town is named for the Roman camp in the land opposite the isle of Anglesey (Y Gaer yn Arfon): the Latin name, Segontium, recognises the river Seiont which flows into the Menai Strait at this point. There may have been a fortification there even before the Romans: there certainly was an additional Roman fort after the first – an anti-Irish measure of the 4th century A.D., overlooking the first century original. In time there was a Norman castle too: Hugh, first Earl of Chester, erected a classic motte-and-bailey (on the present, or Edwardian, site) in 1090. By 1115, Gwynedd, the last Northern stronghold of the Welsh, had passed back once more into their hands, and both Llewelyn the Great and Llewelyn ap Gruffydd used Caernarvon as a base. When Edward took it finally for the Anglo-Normans, in 1283, and began his castle and his town, he was merely following sound precedent.

Caernarvon is on a promontory, and the town/castle site itself is further sheltered by lying between the rivers Seiont and Cadnant where they flow through the slight promontory to the Menai Strait. Thus, although the site is not raised above the surrounding ground (like Criccieth or Harlech, both Edwardian), it can only be approached unimpeded from the one direction – directly to the landward, from Beddgelert. Not only do the two rivers help to shelter the site, they make it also a natural trading centre for the surrounding countryside. Not only does the Strait shield one side of the town, the town controls the Strait. Throughout its history, Caernarvon has been among the most important towns in Wales: the link between Conway and Harlech, guarding the entrance to Anglesey, one of the four regional capitals designated by the Act of Union in 1536 (with Carmarthen, Brecon and Denbigh, the last another Edwardian foundation), the fourth most populous town in Wales at the 1831 Census (after Swansea, Newport and Carmarthen, but still above Cardiff), and still within the top ten Welsh towns by administrative and commercial significance. It required no great originality or percipience by Edward to place one of his major foundations on such a favoured site.

The plan itself, and its fulfilment, are entirely laudable. Caernarvon is a splendid example of the bastide, in which the Castle takes the place of motte and the high-walled town is one great bailey. A simple grid-pattern of streets, running north from the Castle (parallel to the sea-wall) and east-west across, filling the ground between the Castle Ditch and the mouth of the Cadnant (the Seiont guarding the Castle's southern wall). It scarcely needs description, let alone praise, since we can fortunately still see most of the original Castle and Town Walls, even if the houses lining the original streets date from much later times.

Edward was fully aware that isolated military emplacements are ultimately vulnerable – long periods of peace erode their strength just as sieges reduce it in the shorter run. He always, therefore, strove to protect his military investment with a source of civil wealth. From the moment work began on his Caernarvon, in June 1283, there was simultaneous work on Castle, Town and Quay.

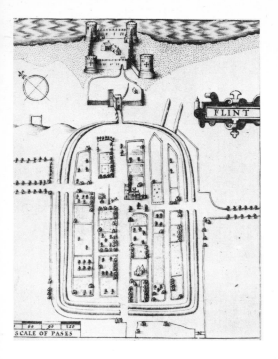

FLINT

SCALE OF PASES

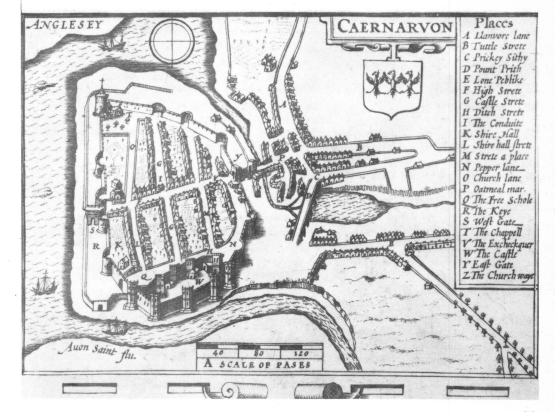

BEAUMARIS

A The Castell
B Castell stret
C Wexam stret
D Water Gate
E Wall stret
F Rotten Row
G Clay pitt lane
H Free Schole
I Market House
K Britons mills
L Britons Hill
M The Friery

A SCALE OF PASES

ANGLESEY

CAERNARVON

Auon Saint flu.

A SCALE OF PASES

Places

A Llanvore lane
B Tuttle Strete
C Prickey Sithy
D Pount Prith
E Lone Peblike
F High Strete
G Castle Strete
H Ditch Strete
I The Conduite
K Shire Hall
L Shire hall strete
M Strete a place
N Pepper lane
O Church lane
P Oatmeal mar.
Q The Free Schole
R The Keye
S West Gate
T The Chappell
V The Excheckquer
W The Castle
Y East Gate
Z The Church waye

Speed's Plans of 1611: Flint, Beaumaris, Caernarvon. Their relative fortunes in the three centuries since their foundation can be seen from the tree-covered insulæ *of the first two, and the extra houses outside the Walls of the last.*

Flint from the air: the insulæ *are just as plain now as in 1611, or in 1277, when Edward planted it.*

Caernarvon in 1750.

Caernarvon from the air.

The Castle, which has justly been placed alongside Alnwick as the finest in Britain, and which Dr Johnson called 'an edifice of stupendous magnitude and strength . . . I did not think there had been such buildings', took from 1283 till 1330 to complete. Its cost seems to have been a little under £25,000, which might reasonably be converted to about £2½ million in our slightly inflated currency. The cost was high enough in money, but the labour and materials demanded by such a project (and Edward I had Conway, Caernarvon and Harlech all started within weeks of each other) must have imposed an even greater strain on the resources of the time – already stretched by war, and by the remoteness of the site. Flint, which had only a ditch and wooden palisade to shield the perfect grid-plan town beneath the Castle, employed nearly two thousand men a week for the first five weeks, and cost all told about £7,000. When one takes into consideration the greater cost and complexity of Conway, Caernarvon and Harlech, it seems likely that during the summer of 1283 there must have been an army of builders at least as large as the army with which Edward had defeated Llewelyn, all working on his castles. Even 3,000 men, a not unlikely figure, would have represented the largest

peace-time concentration of human beings to be found outside the half-a-dozen greatest towns in all of Britain. Administration and supply of such a labour force, so far from established civilisation, must have taken quite remarkable managerial talent, and a large proportion of the national product. Edward's annual revenue was probably around £80,000 and his army on most campaigns (shorter by far than the time taken to build a bastide) seldom exceeded 12,000 men and frequently fell far below that – while still winning battles. Indeed, on the only occasion when the English army rose to 20,000 strong, in 1298, it proved so unmanageable and undisciplined that it was rapidly disbanded. And finally, it should be borne in mind that when a great castle was completed, its permanent garrison was unlikely to exceed a hundred men. Building Caernarvon today would be a significant national investment: for the 13th century, Edward's nine great Welsh bastides must be ranked as quite phenomenal sacrifices to posterity.

The materials were not, as one might rashly think, lying there to hand. The quay (on the Menai Strait side of the Castle, not where the 19th century slate-quay lies, on the Seiont side) was essential because to it came the ships

Caernarvon: the market from the Castle.

Caernarvon: into the walled town from the sea-front.

bearing timber from Conway, Rhuddlan and Liverpool (plantations all) and the incessant flow of ferry-boats bearing stone from Anglesey. The stone and wood of the Welsh homes, wrecked to make way for the conqueror's new town, was undoubtedly re-used, but in the main, everything that was needed came in by ship – neither the condition of the roads, of road-transport, nor the attitude of the inhabitants encouraged any other means.

The town-walls were erected hand-in-hand with the other work, not merely to give shelter to the builders and their shanty-town, but because the whole principle of the bastide is to supply a military installation with its own supporting market-community – and to further the process of pacification by increasing trade. Within the walls, probably completed by 1285, Edward intended to settle a reliable population of traders and smallholders and craftsmen. He offered ten years rent-free on the sixty-three burgage plots squeezed into the narrow island, cheap masonry left over from the Castle, and assigned the new town some 1300 acres beyond its walls for town-fields. No Jews (in any case, on the verge of total expulsion from England for three-and-a-half centuries) and no Welsh, but every encouragement to ambitious

Englishmen capable of building on their plot.

The project was far too large to be left to haphazard supervision, by ordinary soldiers or workmen, and Edward's great abilities included that of delegation. Sometime late in the 'seventies he had managed to seduce from the service of Count Philip of Savoy a master mason known as James of St George. James had already had sixteen years' experience both building and maintaining palaces and fortifications, and Edward found plenty of work for his expensive new recruit. James of St George served as architect, director and mobile foreman for Caernarvon, Conway, Harlech and Beaumaris, for certain, almost certainly for Flint, Rhuddlan, Aberystwyth and Builth, and may well have borne general responsibility for Hope, Denbigh, Ruthin, Holt, Hawarden and Chirk as well. As we shall see later, when we turn to Edward's plans for Berwick, one of the King's greatest contributions to town planning was his respect for expertise; he realised, like Alexander the Great, that however strong the military incentive, making towns is a civil art, and one requiring proper application.

James himself bore the fundamental responsibility for Caernarvon, but by the time it was re-taken after Madoc's rising, in 1295, the work was well in hand, and the plans for what was still unfinished were presumably settled. Thereafter, the supervision was taken over by Walter of Hereford, an architect with largely ecclesiastical experience, who remained in charge until his death in 1309. He was succeeded by his deputy, Henry of Ellerton, a burgess of Caernarvon. There is no doubt that, in the early stages, many of the most

Caernarvon: Castle and town from the seaward side.

Caernarvon: looking West along the sea-front.

skilled men were French – but that deserves no especial comment now, nor would have excited it at the time, since the King and the territorial aristocracy were themselves as much French as English. What is more remarkable is that the great bulk of the workers, at Caernarvon and elsewhere in Wales, were English, drawn from all over England, and kept at work far from their homes in a land arguably more foreign to them than Gascony. Many of those craftsmen we may assume stayed on to become the first burgesses of the towns they built.

None of those first houses have survived; Caernarvon's oldest house is probably no older than the 16th century. But the lay-out of the town, like the Walls themselves, remains essentially as Edward knew it. For the first twenty years of its existence, the new foundation had not even a Church of its own, using instead the ancient Parish Church of Llanbeblig, out beyond the Roman site of Segontium on the road to Beddgelert; then, in 1303, Edward, Prince of Wales, born so fortuitously in the incompleted Castle in 1284, issued orders for the building of a garrison chapel, St Mary's. The work was carried out by Henry of Ellerton, and there is a tradition that he seized his chance for immortality by posing with his wife for the carvings of a man and woman still to be seen in one of the spandrels. St Mary's was then, and still remains, a chapel of ease to the mother Church of Llanbeblig.[2]

The Chapel apart, Caernarvon's early plan called for few amenities. From the earliest times there seem to have been both suburban housing, outside the Walls, and a market at the Gate rather than inside. Although Edward intended that the town should be the administrative centre for the three new counties on the English pattern, Caernarvonshire, Anglesey and Merionethshire, and the particular magnificence of the Castle bears out his military intention, he saw no need to make its civil stature equally apparent. To all intents, it comprised but three streets at right-angles to the main street from East (landward) Gate through to West (Quayside) Gate, its sixty-three plots crammed in to fill every inch: nor were the plots large, measuring sixty feet by eight. However, its very congestion may have helped to keep the inhabitants' morale high in the face of alien neighbours, and at a distance from their protecting Power. Certainly, Caernarvon never seemed to have great difficulty in making its way, although it lacked, until the slate-trade of the 19th century, any particular industry of its own. This unexceptional prosperity, and civic moderation, has not produced a town of self-generated splendour – what is best about Caernarvon is what has survived unaltered from the 13th century – but it has equally not produced such great expansion or self-confidence that the later burgesses have chosen to obliterate the plan originally given them. The Town was in fact quite happy to see the Castle razed in 1660, but when the Government gave up the scheme, the people of Caernarvon did not volunteer to carry it out themselves. Camden's impression, almost four centuries ago, would still stand today: he found the buildings (that is, those built after the foundation period) 'for the manner of the country are sightly enough'. Caernarvon remains a town of distinct importance to its surrounding counties, but nothing it has done, built for itself, none of its people, has ever matched up to the magnificent self-confidence of its foundation. Its Castle

[2]Llanbeblig means Peblig's Church, and Peblig (Publicus) is said to have been the uncle of the Emperor Constantine the Great, allegedly born in Segontium while his father, Constantine Chlorus, and mother, the Welsh-born Helena, were stationed there.

Beaumaris: the main street of the town seen from the Castle.

Beaumaris: the end of the town, sharply breaking off at the old wall-line, seen from the Castle.

Square has statues of Sir Hugh Owen and of Lloyd George – who invented the bogus ceremonial with which modern Princes of Wales, of another foreign line, are invested at Caernarvon – but there is nothing else within the town that might remotely be considered to compete with the Castle and the Walls.

Despite its grandeur, and that of so many other Edwardian Welsh plantations, none have been completely over-grown by later progress and expansion; indeed, the reverse is true of Bere, which has been more literally over-grown. Caernarvon was primarily founded to meet strategic need, and built no larger than military wisdom would suggest. Edward's capacity for the larger vision is better illustrated in England: with Wyke upon Hull, a Cistercian foundation of the 12th century, which he took over in 1293 and enlarged into Kingston upon Hull, with three new approach roads, new Quay, new Water Mill and fifty new building plots on a rectangular pattern. With Newton, Edward's grand project of 1286 for a port to handle the Purbeck marble: the King's commissioners were instructed to lay out this splendid rival to Poole with market place, Church, harbour, and a promised charter granting two market days, a Fair, and the rights of London. Unfortunately, partly no doubt because the deep-water channel does not run to the conjectured site, no-one ever seems to have taken up any of the offered plots. Newton never really started, and has now disappeared completely.

Edward's long experience of town-foundation, and his firm confidence in the consultative and delegation processes, are shown at their best in January 1297, when he summoned to him, at the old (c.1229) foundation of Harwich, experts in town-planning and administration from twenty-one English towns. The object was to advise the King on the necessary rebuilding of the sacked port of Berwick. The conference itself was a sequel to the discussions of the Parliament held the previous autumn at Bury St Edmunds (which of course had been extended to a Plan two centuries before) which had led to twenty-four English towns being summoned to elect delegates who knew 'Best how to devise, order and array a new town to the greatest profit of Ourselves and of merchants.' The other arguments of that Parliament – the clergy produced Pope Boniface's Bull, *Clericis Laicos*, to justify refusal of the King's demand for a tax of one-fifth on all their movables – prevented much progress being made on Berwick's problems, but the Harwich conference was supposed to remedy that omission. At Harwich, the King could draw upon the advice of named men, rather than the freely chosen representatives of towns, and among the men he named were, of course, le Waleys, who had served him at the foundation of New Winchelsea, and the greatest citizen of that plantation, Thomas Alard. The conference, as though called yesterday, delegated its real work to a sub-committee, which it packed off to the ruins of Berwick to get on with the planning. Obviously, from the surviving evidence, the town they produced, and which Edward chartered in 1302, was similar in scheme to Caernarvon – castle and town, on this other turbulent border, linked together. Like the Welsh foundations, it was meant to offer stern resistance to any future insurrection or invasion, and to flourish by its trade as well: as port and market, it flourished rather better than most such frontier settlements.

Winchelsea: from the air, flying over INSULA XVI and looking towards St Thomas's Church.

Below
Winchelsea: as it is now on the O.S., with the insulæ *marked overprinted.*
Below right
Winchelsea: the original plan probably looked like this. The numbers of the insulæ *are those of the rent-roll of 1292; B is St Thomas's, K the King's Green, D the Old Market.*

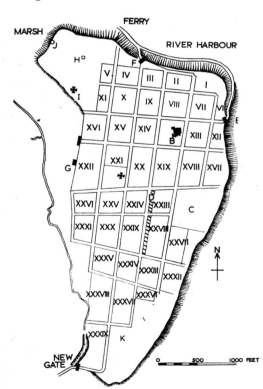

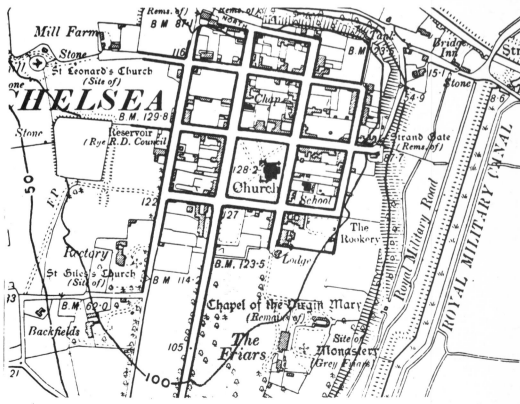

Alard may well have resented the call upon his time, however; no doubt he shared the King's concern for the peace of the realm, but he may have felt that the greatest profit of merchants, especially himself, was better served by being left to get on with business in thriving Winchelsea.

Celia Fiennes in 1697 arrived in Winchelsea and remarked that it 'looks not of any great circuite of ground by the first view, being high, but in the middle you see it has been a fine place for there were 36 large squares of buildings; the remains of pieces of walls in most places you see or else a hedge supplys that you see the streets were very broad and long and divided these squares, the cross streetes the same; I rode up a middle streete and saw the others run across of equal breadth, remaines of Churches and halls are to be seen, but else grass grows where Winchelsea was, as was once said of Troy.' The modern guide-book, on the defensive for ancient civic pride, has for its third sentence: 'In fact, Winchelsea is not a village but a town and one of the Cinque Ports.' Since the end of the 15th century it has been necessary for the surviving inhabitants of this, arguably the quietest of English towns, to make quite clear to visitors that it is a greater grave they walk on than they see. To Thomas Alard, as to his relatives Nicholas, Gervase, Reginald, Gervase senior, all of whom had property on the same street as he, there was no call for such protestation: the Alards were the greatest family in one of the nation's greatest ports. A port so respected for its wealth and naval vigour by the King that he had taken the lead in building it all over again when its original site began to sink beneath the sea. Defoe, in the 18th century, showed perhaps a proper realisation of what he saw when he called Winchelsea 'rather the Skeleton of an Ancient City than a real Town'. An Ancient City, which one might now mistake for a hill-top village, unless one looked again, and wondered about those 'large squares' and regular streets, 'very broad and long'.

Old Winchelsea was probably built upon a shingle spit jutting from the Fairlight Cliffs into the sea opposite the surviving site of Camber. The sea ran past it, and on to Rye, and yet beyond, to Oxney Island. Nowadays, of course, the sea stops respectably s rt at Camber, and shrinks to an unpretentious creek before venturing up to Rye; but before it began to retreat, it made one last onslaught on the land, in the 12th and 13th centuries, and succeeded in first isolating, and then inundating, Old Winchelsea.

The Town first applied for Royal help in 1236. Although it was already, with the neighbouring foundation of Rye (probably laid out on its grid shortly after the Conquest), a full member of the Cinque Ports Confederation, and therefore undoubtedly important, that first petition drew no response. After several more requests, each more pressing than the last, since the sea had reached the market place by 1262, and its importance had been endorsed by compulsory Royal purchase in 1247, Edward I decided in 1280 to appoint a commission of inspection. The commission, despite the conservative requests of some burgesses for mere assistance with sea-walls, decided that wholesale removal was the only answer. The King, both landlord of the town and beneficiary of its trading profit, accepted the decision, and acquired the Manor of Iham, where a high plateau above the marshes fronted the River Brede on two sides, as a new site. The last resistance of the optimistic faction in the town vanished, like the nearby town of Broomhill, with the storms of winter 1287. Up the hill from the disappearing remnants of Old Winchelsea there came the burgesses, including not only the living Alards but their family tombs. The last series of storms had breached the shingle causeway, making the old town an island at high tide, and by 1291 the old town had been abandoned to the water. Edward's new town was laid out on a spacious grid. Despite its hill-top site, New Winchelsea had room for 716 building plots of varying sizes, on a total site of 150 acres. As well as house-plots, the commissioners had to provide land for a market place, two Churches, a cemetery and the Kings Green, twelve acres of open space by the New Gate at the narrowest section of the plateau. The regularity of the grid, designed to produce thirty-

The tomb of Gervase Alard, St Thomas's, Winchelsea.

nine *insulæ*, or Quarters, was recognised by the street-names: the east-west streets were methodically called First, Second, Third, and so on up to Ninth Street. First, Second, Third, Fourth and parts of Seventh and Ninth still survive; but there is now open ground where once there lay twenty-seven Quarters.

The grandness of Winchelsea's scale – and it appears to have been designed for a population three or four times the average 13th century town[3] – did not reflect any anachronistic royal concepts of amenity in general. Caernarvon's cramped streets are far more typical than are Winchelsea's broad avenues. The object of the exercise was to make this most important town both attractive and efficient: Edward even offered seven years rent-free (an offer he seems to have forgotten rather quickly) in his eagerness to restore the fortunes of the port. It was a fishing port, of course, and provision for the fishing boats was made at the new Town Quay beneath the North Cliff, and its seamen and ships formed part of that Cinque Ports fleet which was not only capable of thrashing a much larger French fleet at St Mahé in 1293, but of working off traditional grievances against the Yarmouth fleet at Sluys in 1297 – an unhappy prelude to an English campaign in which thirty-two ships were burned and two hundred seamen killed in a pitched internecine battle. But Winchelsea was also a great trading port, particularly prominent in the thriving wine-trade. The magnificent cellars, arched and vaulted with Caen stone, which can still be found beneath later houses, and the grass, were, as was remarked in 1570, 'meet for famous merchants', and the cargo they were meant to store was probably the wines of the King's lands in the Gironde and Garonne. Furthermore, Winchelsea was in the front line of England's land defences: part of its eventual decline can be attributed to the effects of French attacks in the 14th and 15th centuries. There were seven principal assaults, every one with attendant damage and destruction (St Thomas's Church still bears vivid scars), and innumerable minor attempts. For the French, Winchelsea represented not only a dangerous source of English sea-power, but a vital English frontier fortress, controlling the gateway to much of south-eastern England. Royal concern for the welfare of the town did not stem from Royal ownership – rather, it was taken into Royal ownership because of its real importance.

Some cellars, and St Thomas's apart, there is not much left of Winchelsea's original building. The withdrawal of the sea – the free shingle which had slipped away from under Old Winchelsea came back to build a bar across the Brede – ended Winchelsea's great trading days, so that by the end of the 15th century the last merchant had left the town, but what the sea left behind was splendid farming land. Although infinitely reduced in size, the town therefore retained enough prosperity to indulge the great re-building passions of the 16th, 18th and 20th centuries. There is the Strand Gate, the ruins of the Grey Friars' chapel, questionable fragments of the Court Hall, a gable of St John's Hospital (like Holy Cross and St Bartholomew, an almshouse, not a medical foundation), the New Gate – now far into the fields – and some rubble that once was the Black Friars' house. Otherwise, one needs strong imagination to recreate the noise and squalor of a mediæval market town from the gracious

[3]At its peak it may have had 6000 inhabitants: as many as Bristol and twice the size of Oxford.

cleanliness of this well-ventilated village. Streets made wide for heavy traffic – horses, oxen and rough sleds, operating on unmetalled roads, need ample space to dodge the ruts and mud – are now unsettling in the absence of any great street-activity. Building plots intended to accommodate merchants' houses, stores, shops and working gardens are now occupied, if at all, by white-painted country homes for commuters and the elderly. St Giles's has gone, struck by lightning in 1413, and not thought worth re-building: in 1359, the French besieged many of the townsfolk there, and butchered them in what is still sometimes called Dead Man's Lane. St Thomas's remains visibly too large for the population, although itself drastically reduced in size by French assault.

Even so, it is possible to grasp something of this 'apotheosis of urban geometry' as it was built to Edward's order. Its firm contempt for the natural strictures of the site – laid out as nearly rectilinear as ropes and sticks could make it – and its imperious position, overlooking the reclaimed fields that

once were marsh and sea, safe from flood and on the lookout at all times for invasion; the obvious grandeur of its Church, and the charitable foundations it was capable of supporting, all this one can recapture. Should the sea once more change its mind (and there is no reason why it shouldn't – the movements of the shingle on that coast continue to exercise geographers), one can imagine Winchelsea regaining something of its power; and in that event, it is doubtful whether the ensuing changes would 'spoil' a town designed by man for bustle, not for somnolence.

The general bustle of Edward's reign represented one final fling of the mediæval genius for town-foundation. Afterwards, there was not only a sharp reduction in the number of new towns, but a virtual abandonment of Royal leadership. While Edward had been pre-occupied in Wales, a number of his greater subjects had been busily improving the value of their lands by urban development. No really successful foundations date from this reign – apart that is from the King's own – and it has been convincingly argued that the market for new towns was, in terms of the mediæval economy, approaching saturation, but nevertheless Edward's subjects were responsible for a dozen or more plantations in England. The decline in the town-founding habit after the end of the 13th century is quite plain to see; for the next three centuries, we can only find half-a-dozen Welsh, and about the same number of English, foundations (the imprecision stems from the difficulty of assigning some foundations more accurately than by generation, and of course from the ever-present risk that there were foundations we have not yet identified). The reasons – at least those we may conjecture in hindsight – are equally plain: the conquest of the three countries, insofar as it could be furthered by plantations, was complete. The commercial colonisation had reached the stage where numbers of existing towns were visibly failing – Newton is merely an extreme example of the over-crowding that had taken place in a number of counties. Debilitating competition existed between two Looes, Polruan and Fowey, Hedon and Hull, and indeed wherever over-optimistic founders had attempted to share the success of existing ports or markets. And finally, the 14th century was one of profound decrease in population: recurrent waves of the Plague, between 1348 and 1400, reduced the population by as much as a third. The great expansion of the towns had coincided with a steady growth of the population, and of the land under cultivation. After the Black Death, it took a century or more for the population to climb back to its previous level, and the land under cultivation shrank in proportion, leaving behind, on what became once more the waste, or passed from arable to the less labour-demanding sheep-walk, both deserted villages and abandoned plantations. The last expiring gasp of the mediæval tradition came with the foundation of Queenborough, Edward III's reconstruction of Calais falling outside our scope, of course, in 1368. Edward III, having decided to provide a fortress on the Isle of Sheppey to protect the Medway estuary, seems to have aped instinctively the techniques of his predecessors, and provided his Castle with a town, and the town with helpful privileges. Even so, Queenborough can hardly be counted a great success.

After Queenborough, there are no more direct Royal foundations: Coleraine and Londonderry and other less successful 'bastides' in Ulster, e.g. Salterstown, were foisted upon an unenthusiastic City of London by James I, and the Crown – a rather different concept from the King, particularly from King Edward I – is responsible theoretically for various Scottish bastides of the 18th century, but never again do we find an English King summoning a town into being purely by the Royal fiat. It may perhaps follow that henceforth we seldom meet a new foundation inspired by a concern for the national interest. The tradition that survives is that of the particularist feudal landowner, improving his rents by development, regardless of the wider consequences, and not that of the occasionally disinterested monarch, planning for the economy as a whole.

The long pause in practical town-building between Queenborough (1368), Falmouth (1613) and Londonderry (1610), although it may be taken as ample evidence of profound change in the economic and strategic aspirations of English government and English landowners, should not be taken to suggest a loss of interest in the theory of town-planning by English thinkers. Indeed, it was during this fallow period that the best-known of all English idealist schemes, Sir Thomas More's *Utopia*, was written, as was Francis Bacon's *New Atlantis*, with its equally perfectionist vision of Bensalem.

Both More and Bacon were writing in the tradition of Plato – and of Christian millennarianism: the nature of their ideal cities was very different from those of Edward I, and brings us to a crucial division in the history of British town-foundation. The difference between Londonderry and Bensalem, intellectually as well as actually, is the difference we shall meet again and again – between Wren and Winstanley, Pantisocracy and Nash, New Lanark and New Harmony (a fine, but vital difference, this), James Silk Buckingham and Titus Salt. It is a distinction that is sometimes very plain, occasionally almost imperceptible, and that finally almost disappears, with the combination in Ebenezer Howard of both traditions: the Garden City unites the desire to improve men's characters, or souls, and to give practical expression to certain spiritual convictions, with the mundane desire to build pleasant and efficient towns. The two themes, both of which can be found throughout this history, are the moral and the practical; and whether the planned community is for the Elect, or for profit, the originators tend to borrow freely from the notions of the other side.

If we confine ourselves for the moment to the moralists, we must immediately be struck with the paucity of their physical invention: the Utopians lived in square cities, divided into four regular quarters, in unbroken terrace houses (with 'large gardens' behind every one), which they changed by the drawing of lots every tenth year. The only distinction between their homes, where even the contents were held in common (a very frequent characteristic of all subsequent Utopias), lay in the gardens: 'their studie and deligence herin commeth not onely of pleasure, but also of a certen strife and contention that is betwene strete and strete, concerning the trimming, husbanding, and furnishing of their gardens' – the authentic note of English planning from Silchester via Saltaire to Letchworth. Whatever the objectives of the moralists, Christian, communist or anarchist, they seldom show any greater originality than the jobbing builder, plumping for the right-angled grid in the great majority of cases: Owen's parallelograms, Richardson's Hygeia, Buckingham's Victoria, are all based on the perfection of the right-angle, whether in the grid or in the marginally more adventurous radial pattern. There is perhaps one extra reason – additional that is to the simplicity and authoritarian obedience of the grid – why utopians should favour it: for those obsessed with egalitarian notions, it offers insurance against any given street or house seeming preferable to another.

Despite this lack of architectural inspiration, or perhaps in the intellectual climate of England, because of it, the moralists (most of them might justly be defined as chiliasts as well) have had at least as much influence on post-mediæval town-planning as have the practical, and inventive, architects. England is surely one of the very few countries where the influence of Andreæ's Christianopolis was as strong as that of Scamozzi, Alessi, or Palladio's plans and buildings; and the long history of Antilia, Macaria, and the Rosicrucians testify to Andreæ's influence. In fact, most of the apostles of utopia have

Utopia: the frontispiece – it does not bear out More's own statement about the Utopians, 'he that knows one of their towns knows them all'.

proceeded to detail their schemes on the basis of prolonged exposure to the Bible, and little, if any, knowledge of building. There are innumerable examples in English history of societies and subscription lists fired with zeal for projects to build Zion on the principles of Spence, St Simon or Emanuel Swedenborg, but very few whose inspiration came from Wren or Jones.

Perhaps in consequence, when we do discover schemes inspired, or occasioned, by material needs, they are often justified by claims of likely spiritual benefits. Doxiadis regards utopianism as the product of experience in planning, on the grounds that any artificial shaping of the environment according to a plan is inevitably idealist to some degree, and inevitably suggests the prospect of planning for total perfection. It might equally be said that it is only by reference to a complete ideal that even piecemeal planning can take place – that each and every architect and builder must have some notion of

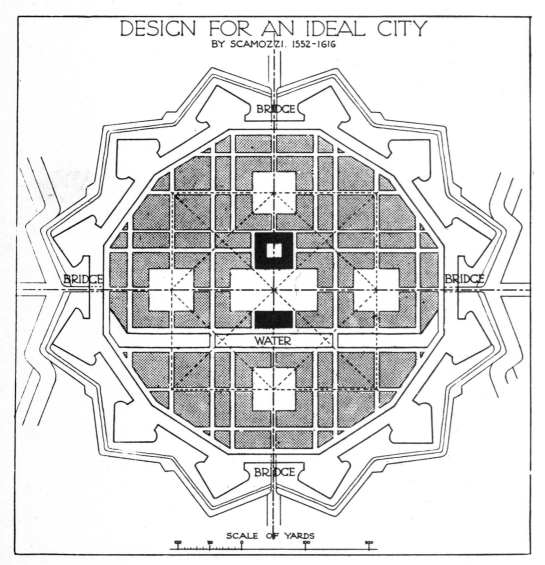

DESIGN FOR AN IDEAL CITY
BY SCAMOZZI. 1552-1616

Scamozzi's Ideal City: like those of Cataneo and Perret, similar in shape and lay-out to that of Vitruvius.

One of Vitruvius's Town Plans (from the 1511 edition) showing his basic attachment to the radial plan of octagonal shape.

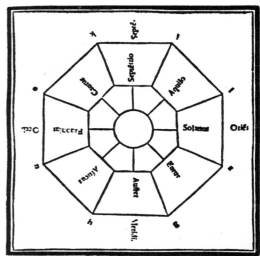

utopia before he can produce its fragments. There is no hypothetical situation in which we can regard the builder as free from choice, and every choice which is made for reasons in which the physical, spiritual, æsthetic, political or economic welfare of the proposed inhabitants plays some part, as opposed to that of the planner, is in that restricted sense an utopian choice. In either case, planners who might be supposed to be concerned merely with the provision of cheap and tolerable accommodation for factory workers very often turn out to consider that what they propose will also eliminate crime, improve health, and inspire an artistic renaissance, if it does not also accelerate the Second Coming. The crucial division in town-planning, though it must be made, allows for cross-benches and cross-fertilisation. After all, both the most extreme social, and the most pragmatic civil, engineers share in this context a faith in the importance of environment, and each can give the other ammunition.

To return once more to the rebirth of the town-founding habit, at the beginning of the 17th century, the Ulster plantations show little evidence that between their building, and that of their predecessors in North Wales, three hundred years, and the Renaissance, had passed. The Corporation of London were assigned by the King the land (4,000 acres at Londonderry, 3,000 at Coleraine, renting at 53s 4d an acre per annum), and left to get on with making the best of their investment. Walled – the plantations followed after all upon the heels of the final conquest of the O'Neil and the O'Donnel – and laid out on straightforward grids, they could as easily have been built by James of St George as in the reign of James VI and I.

Londonderry in 1622.

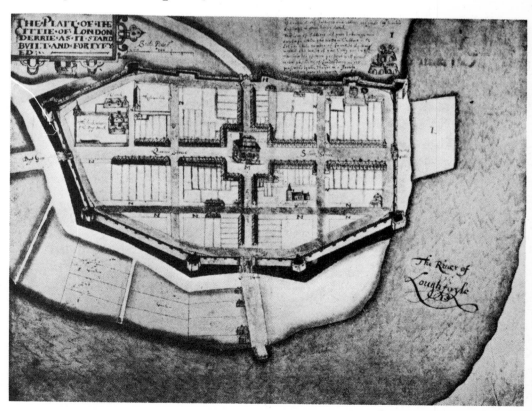

There were at this time some other foundations, or developments, which do show signs of change, and which presage far greater changes in the ensuing years. In 1608, Lord North discovered the properties of the waters on the heath at what became Tunbridge Wells; the growth of the watering places during the next three centuries is dealt with at length later on, as there were to be so many. And Falmouth, which again belongs to a class of town deserving of a special section, represents, in the person of its projector Sir John Killigrew, who aided his foundation by securing for it the market which had formerly been at Penryn (and the Customs House followed) the rise of the commercially-adept Stuart gentry. Killigrew's spiritual heirs can be found all over Britain in the ensuing generations – busily founding ports, milltowns, canal and railway towns upon their lands, and exerting their political influence to aid the projects.

However, the most important, and imposing, project of the century was of a very different order: in conception, it showed every evidence that a renaissance of taste and confidence had taken place, coincidentally with that of knowledge; and in execution, it showed quite disastrously that the business of the 17th century was already business, not the greater glories. Wren's London was on a scale of magnificence unequalled in any single building since the cathedrals of three centuries and more before, and unequalled as a coherent family of buildings since the downfall of Rome. Obviously, although we have the plan and many specimens of Wren's building, we do not have Wren's London. It was altogether too magnificent for the King, the Privy Council, and the citizens.

The opportunity which Wren, John Evelyn and Dr Hooke all seized, and which the capital and the nation refused, was of course presented by the Great Fire. It began on Sunday, September 2, 1666, in Pudding Lane, two hundred yards north of London Bridge. It ended on the Wednesday, September 5, having spread east to the Tower, west to Temple Bar, and as far north as Smithfield. Altogether 373 acres within the City walls – about eighty per cent of the City – and another 63 acres outside the walls had been burned down. 13,200 houses had been destroyed, 84 Churches, including St Paul's, and the Guildhall, Baynard's Castle, the Steelyard, the ancient Livery Halls and the Temple, the brothels of Alsatia and the merchants' premises in Lombard Street. Mediæval London had been razed, leaving behind smoking rubble and blockaded streets.

Eight days after the fire burned out, a citizen in Blackfriars began to rebuild on the site of his old home. The King immediately summoned the Privy Council and announced that no-one should attempt to rebuild until this opportunity to re-plan the capital had been properly considered. Plans had already been started by Evelyn, appointed in 1662 as one of the Commissioners 'for reforming the buildings, wayes, streetes, and incumbrances, and regulating the hackney coaches in the Citty of London', and by Wren, one of the Commissioners appointed to survey old St Paul's, as well as by Hooke, who presented a discourse and a 'plot for a new Citty' to the King on September 13, and a model to the Common Council on September 21.

The Lord Mayor and the Aldermen preferred Hooke's plan to those of Wren and Evelyn, but they may have been swayed by his immense intellectual

London: the light area is the extent of the Great Fire.

reputation. Robert Hooke, fellow and Secretary of the Royal Society, was without doubt one of the most catholic geniuses that even that fertile age produced. He invented the marine barometer, the spiral watch-spring, built the first Gregorian telescope, discovered the fifth star in Orion, calculated the rotation of Jupiter, published the theories of elasticity, of the kinetic hypothesis of gases, of combustion and of the principle of the arch, and was acknowledged by Newton to have materially aided him in his work on optics and with the law of Inverse Squares. He was appointed to be one of the three Surveyors of the City of London (with Peter Mills and Edward Jerman) after the Fire (an appointment 'by which he hath gott a great Estate' according to his friend John Aubrey) and built the Bethlehem Hospital (Bedlam), Montague House, and the College of Physicians, in addition to setting out the street-lines and private house-plots.

However, the Plan prepared by this practical mathematician, chemist, physicist, engineer, astronomer, instrument-maker, architect, and god-father of the theory of gravitation failed to get official approval. It was a perfect grid, its streets running absolutely straight from east to west, north to south, and, unlike those of his rival planners, bore no sign that the Italian renaissance of architecture had impinged on England at all. Hooke may have lacked either the knowledge, or the talent, necessary for town-planning – hardly unjust, in the

Wren's Plan for London: 'approv'd of by King and Parliament, but unhappily defeated by faction'.

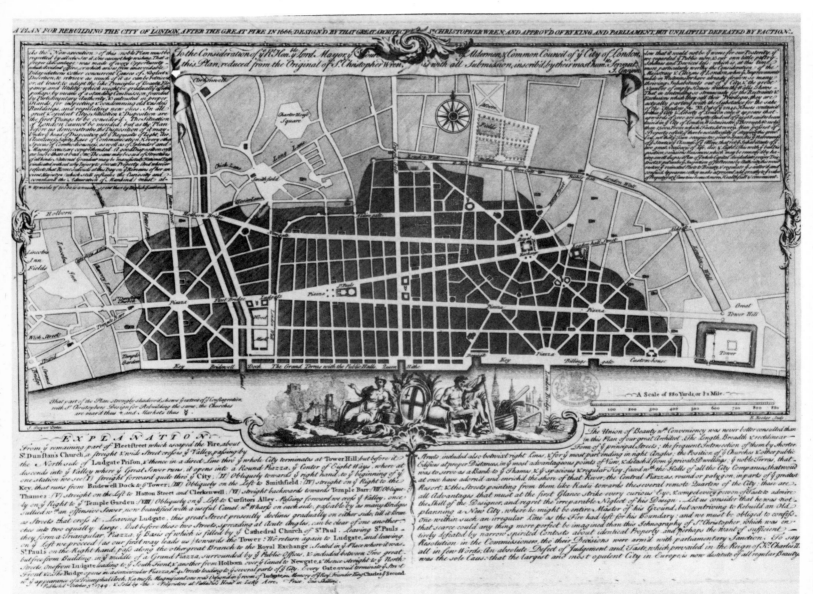

Evelyn's Plan for London: note the similarities in the treatment of Fleet Street, St Paul's, and the other island-sites and fora to Wren.

circumstances. His 'great Estate', incidentally, which Aubrey characteristically implied to have been got by taking bribes (and they would have been offered) turned up after Hooke's death, locked in an iron chest that the busy scientist had not opened for thirty years.

Wren's and Evelyn's plans are more remarkable. Not the least astonishing aspect of them being their very great similarity in surprising detail, as well as general scheme. From them both, it is quite obvious that some powerful new movement had begun to infiltrate English ideas about the city. The language of their plan – piazzas, triumphal avenues, interlocking *fora*, tensions created by magnificence and resolved by dramatic punctuation – is the language derived from Rome, via Vitruvius's *De Architectura Libri Decem*, and used in the ideal

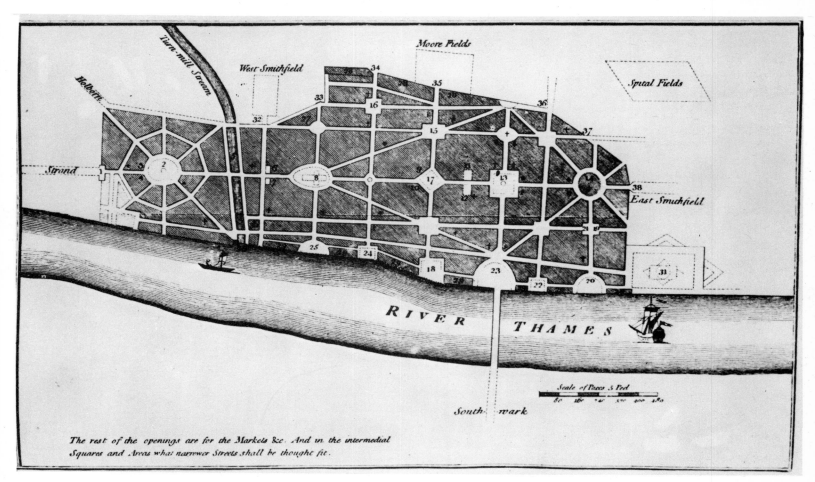

schemes of Alberti, Filarete, and Scamozzi.

Vitruvius, an earnest and apparently unoriginal compiler of prevailing styles and rules in Augustan Rome, had laid down rules for the imposing city designed for grandeur and the rich, founded on the geometry of the circle: his exhaustive handbook of Imperial building had been republished in 1511. Alberti (1404-1472), in his *De Re Aedificatoria*, reprinted a number of times in the 16th century, argued for streets 'in the manner of rivers' save where great dignity was required, when straight streets were best, and for the use of piazzas. Filarete (Antonio Averlino, *c*.1400–*c*.1469) who dedicated his ideal city of Sforzinda to Francesco Sforza, provided not only a great central square, but sixteen lesser squares, and alternated radial avenues with radial canals: the peripheral shape was that of an eight-pointed star. Scamozzi, finally, in his *L'Idea della Architettura Universale*, published the year before his death, 1615, when he was sixty-three, distilled Roman practice and renaissance elaboration into one textbook of ideal city building.

All this impassioned theory, at large in Europe for two hundred years, surges up in Wren's and Evelyn's plans. Piazzas, above all; and the most curious coincidence of many is that both Plans site their most imposing piazza of all in Fleet Street, approximately where Chancery Lane now enters it. Indeed, looking at the two together, in which a great Fleet Street piazza completes a vista beginning at the steps of St Paul's, set itself in similar triangular sites, and in which innumerable other streets are designed to resolve into other squares and circuses, one might almost hypothesise some common rubric to which both men were confined by the rules of an imaginary competition. What has gone, despite signs of Evelyn at least still feeling its temptations, is the grid: in its place there is the Baroque city, with Vitruvian geometry and Augustan magnificence.

The grid can create immense tension, but often cannot satisfactorily resolve it (only the distant horizons redeem New York's oppressive power); the radial scheme can all too easily lean on one central feature for all its drama. Wren's plan, more than that of Evelyn, since it gave infinite attention to every street and every intersection, constantly aims at the combination of self-contained vistas with the suggestion of continuity. For example, innumerable Wren streets were aimed at Churches – in such a way that the eye could both rest on the Church, and anticipate the other views to come when the Church was reached. Both Cities would have been monumental, but Evelyn's, with its eighteen open spaces (Wren had half-a-dozen) might well have been altogether arid – their mutual passion for the piazza, although shared by untold other and later planners, is one of these stylistic conceits which we should mistrust. It might be argued that if London had had such features for three hundred years, we would have learned how to live with them, but the observable fact is that most piazzas built in Britain turn into urban cemeteries; designed as oases in the busy City, they become instead isolated patches of desert. Neither the climate nor the temperament – which may be related – of the British favours piazza life: the warm pub is more suitable than the sidewalk café. There is a case to be made that the planned evacuation of Covent Garden, Inigo Jones's great piazza of 1631, far from giving London a great new architectural asset, will merely remove the life and leave behind a parking lot.

Part at least of this argument is that Wren's London would have been an international architectural masterpiece, a place of pilgrimage for centuries to come, but would have anticipated the dehumanisation of the City by two hundred and fifty years, creating an empty shell of public and commercial monuments instead of making the centre once again a place to live as well as work. Neither Wren nor Evelyn allowed for streets to curve: even their piazzas in Fleet Street, magnificent octagonal rotunda, were made up of straight lengths and sharp corners. And both, of course, since that was the central point of the style they sought, capped every view with something important. Curved streets and unimportant views are traditionally beneath the dignity of architects, but there is evidence to suggest that living becomes uncomfortable in an environment of sustained PERFECTION. Wren's open spaces, whatever their primary purpose (and we take the view that it was æsthetic rather than sanitary) would of course have given the City lungs. His vision included one great sward of open garden from St Paul's down to the Thames (one can see at Greenwich that Wren's use of nature would have been distinctly disciplined) and that would undoubtedly have been an asset. However, it is a great deal less certain that the grouping of all twelve main Halls of the Livery Companies in one great Square, rather than their distribution about the town, as with Evelyn, would have been successful: no Company would accept a building markedly less grand than that of any other, and the effect would surely have been that of a massive prison exercise-yard.

The greatest problem with this scale and type of plan – the problem of all baroque cities – is that although it demands geometric unity, unfaltering grandiloquence for every sentence, and can thus give a very powerful impression as a whole, it automatically precludes planning for the neighbourhood. Each street in the scheme is conceived as an important statement, and since it is involved with the importance of the intersecting streets, there is no room for the smaller scale, the milder tone. London has managed to over-grow the firm grid of Soho, but no City could have over-grown Wren's plan: there would have been no room for humble buildings, humble trades, or humble men. Within the context of the plan, ordinary life would have been untidy, trivial, a source of congestion; like many other plans, it ignores the prime function of the city, as a place for short and cluttered lives to be lived through, and elevates instead the autocratic vision of the city as a manifestation of supreme power – intellectual, political or military – as the highest form of commemorative statuary. The city becomes a cenotaph in several senses: both empty grave, symbol of dead grandeurs and dead causes, and focus of society only at its moments of supreme formality. In any case, neither Wren's nor Evelyn's London were accepted. The complete re-making of the centre of what was already the greatest city in the world was quite naturally a major political issue; and each difficulty that was encountered took time that the Government felt could not be spared. Their case was not that the Plan, or any objections to it, must be examined, but that London and its citizens must get back to work. The capital, the greatest port, the greatest market, the greatest source of revenue, simply could not be allowed to stand idle while the merits of a rebuilding scheme were debated. Uninsured merchants and craftsmen were eager to be back at work – or else to leave in search of opportunities elsewhere. The rebuilding plan enacted in February, 1667, fell far short of the aspirations voiced in the first few days after the fire, because the people of London refused to go unhoused and unemployed while the greater plan was argued out.

The objections to the plans therefore mattered most in that they existed: any objections at all meant wasted time, and lost income for both citizens and

Crown – a Crown which far from being able to subsidise such delay, depended constantly on subsidies from the City. However, the main objections were to the proposal that all land be temporarily given up to public trustees before redistribution. Given Aubrey's comment on Hooke's profit from his Public Surveyorship, one can see one reason why any freeholder would have been reluctant to put his trust in officials. The need for the surrender arose from the plan to widen streets, provide public open spaces, and set Churches and public buildings on 'conspicuous and insular' sites. Although it was officially announced that all this extra space would be created overall by removing churchyards and gardens (one of the rare English schemes which proposed to remove gardens rather than supply them) and that when the land was handed back everyone would get as much as before, the citizens showed understandable mistrust. They wanted the land they had had before, where it had been before, and on the same frontage as before, practical shopkeepers having a very different view of the relative value of varying sites from that of theorising planners. Within two months of the Fire, the King had given up hope of persuading the City to cooperate without protracted negotiation, and had therefore effectively given up hope of implementing any great re-planning at all.

Nevertheless, although it had to be accepted that Londoners would rebuild on their old sites, and that most street-lines would remain as they had been, the Government did impose some improvements on the capital. Instead of a profound reconstruction *de novo*, London got permission to restore itself according to a building code. Wider streets (the citizens conceded much of their gardens without the struggle one might be led to believe any Englishman would make), uniform frontages, no overhanging eaves (not that anyone presumably wished to rebuild in the jettied style that had by then been superseded), Commissioners for Paving and for Sewers. Houses, in brick or stone – a fire-control measure that had been promulgated, but not enforced, for centuries, but now carried special conviction – were to be four storeys in main streets, three in streets 'of note' and two in the back lanes. To oversee all this, and particularly to adjudicate between landlords and tenants 'of houses destroyed in the late dreadfull fire', a Court of Fire Judges was appointed. And to help get the building done, craftsmen in the building trades were encouraged to come to London (which the market pressure would have aided anyway) by the removal for seven years of the various restrictions to which they would otherwise have been subject.

'By the prudent vigilance of all parties, London, to the amazement of all Europe, was in four years' time rebuilt in so different a style from what it was before the Fire, that those who saw it in both states could not reflect without wonder at the wealth that could sustain the loss, and bear so prodigious an expense as was laid out in restoring it.' The speed of the rebuilding was remarkable, if the style was merely different: by the summer of 1668, thirteen hundred houses had been rebuilt (ten per cent of the losses), and the rate of reconstruction rose sharply in the ensuing years. By 1670, attention and capital were able to be diverted to the replacement of the Churches, and Wren was of course commissioned to build fifty-one in place of the eighty-four which had been destroyed. He had been hoping for much more no doubt, when on

September 13, 1666, he was appointed to the Commission which was to produce the plan. But, like Hugh May, Sir Roger Pratt, Robert Hooke, Peter Mills and Edward Jerman, the rejection of the whole did not prevent him working with enthusiasm on the parts. In retrospect, one may perhaps be happier to be left with his Churches (we still have sixteen substantially as he built them) than to have inherited a wholly monumental City. The Victorians, after all, demolished, neglected or throttled more than thirty of his Churches in the course of killing off the residential City, and might have achieved even more remarkable flights of philistinism had they had an already dehumanised canvas on which to work – one need only look at what we have done with the corpse handed down to us in our turn to understand what happens to a City without life.

Wren's unbuilt City, although the most important example of Renaissance influence on British town-building, was not the only one. The beginning of the development of Tunbridge Wells came after Jones's Covent Garden, and showed its influence; and much of the urban renewal and expansion of the time naturally reflected the prevailing taste of Europe and of sophisticated London. But in the main, partly no doubt because there was no substantial new foundation until the 18th century, British towns do not demonstrate the theories of this period very well. To get some impression of the City that Wren would have built (or Evelyn for that matter) one has to combine knowledge of Wren's buildings – themselves all buildings of importance by intention and function, as well as effect – with the completed towns of Renaissance Europe: Richelieu, Karlsruhe, Palma Nuova.

London: the view from what is now the Northern end of Waterloo Bridge, showing Wren's Churches dominating the sky-line. No Embankment, buildings still on London Bridge, boatmen plying between City and Southwark sides.

The rebuilding of great Cities to great standards has occasionally happened, despite the wretched examples of the Fire and of the Blitz. London, Edinburgh and Newcastle have all benefited from fortunate coincidences of capital, demand, and taste. Of them, only Edinburgh can really show a whole New City, planned and carried out consistently, but the great estates of London, Nash's scheme, and the remodelling of Newcastle's heart by Dobson and Grainger (whose Grey Street stands comparison – or stood – with Regent Street), all constitute, like the Woods's Bath, major statements about the City. They have in common, of course, that they were built for a confident and privileged class, whose numbers and wealth were being rapidly augmented by the dramatic expansion of the economy as a whole, and that (excepting Newcastle's special case) they were built to baroque street-plans, but in classical detail. And there is little argument that Bath, the Squares of London, and Edinburgh's New Town comprise the most important, influential and successful body of urban architecture in Britain, examples of such power, unfortunately, that they have emasculated much of the planning and building of later generations, who have consistently taken the view that it does not matter if you rip down real Adam so long as you put up in its place ersatz Kent.

The development of Bath is dealt with in its place as the first among spas, so may be passed over here save to say that the Woods's use of natural contour, of the sweeping composition concealing within its detail quite unspectacular houses, of unifying classical decoration, was immensely influential – not least in Edinburgh, and on Nash's London. London, however, must be given due consideration as the first among British cities by size, and, for a brief time, by grace.

Long before the City proper had been rebuilt, London of the late 17th century was spreading in every direction. It was already the largest city in the world, and probably the richest. It had already seen, in the Covent Garden built by Inigo Jones for the 4th Earl of Bedford in 1630, the introduction of advanced Italian ideas in conjunction with the commercial exploitation of a great aristocratic estate; and much of the most important development that took place for the ensuing two hundred years derived from Covent Garden in both respects. Indeed, shortly before the Fire, in 1661, the 4th Earl of Southampton had emulated the neighbouring Bedford estate with Bloomsbury Square, which has the distinction of being the first of those archetypal London compositions to be called a Square.

Bloomsbury Square is significant for other reasons: it was built by the method of selling 'building leases', thus paving the way for the entry of the speculator, whilst keeping his rapacity within some bounds of uniformity and decency, and it included from the start provision for a market, and for subsidiary streets. Evelyn called it a 'little town', simply because the new residents of Bloomsbury would not be dependent on the existing city for everything save their houses.

Lord St Albans's development of St James's Square, with its own Church of St James's, Piccadilly, after 1665, followed similar lines. Once again, the speculator was responsible for actually building the houses, and hand in hand with the peers whose names, subsidiary titles, and country homes are preserved in the streets and squares of central London, go the speculators – Sir Thomas Bond of Bond Street, Storey of Storey's Gate, Frith of Frith Street, Downing of Downing Street, Gregory King, the pioneer demographer, whose King's Square has ended up as Soho Square.

Amongst the long line of speculators, two stand out. At the end of the 17th century, the wholly unprincipled Nicholas Barbon, whose lifelong lack of probity culminated in his Will, which stipulated that none of his debts should be paid, and at the end of the 18th, Sir James Burton, father of Decimus.

Barbon, son of Praise-God, and, in his spare time from practical experimentation in the theory of credit, author of the remarkably intelligent *Discourse of Trade*, was responsible for a number of developments: Essex Street, Red Lion Square, Buckingham and Villiers Streets, Bedford Row, Great Ormonde Street, and many more. His contemporary, Roger North, said of him that he was 'the inventor of this new method of building by casting of ground into streets and small houses, and to augment their number with as little front as possible, and selling the ground to workmen by so much per front foot, and what he could not sell build himself.' Whether he did in fact invent this technique, responsible ever since for the high rate of bankruptcy among small builders persuaded to seek independence through speculative sub-contracting, he could have learnt little from the property sharks of modern times, not merely in matters of crude business chicanery, but in self-justifying public relations: his written work sets out the case for building's social value as primer for the economy as a whole.

Burton was less blatantly unscrupulous. A Scot, he arrived on the London scene in 1792 when, as a small builder in Southwark, he managed to get a toehold on the Foundling Hospital estate with the south side of Brunswick Square. Ten years later, he had built six hundred houses on the Hospital estate alone. Before he retired to the final, unprofitable speculation of St Leonard's on Sea, he had built some £2,000,000 worth of houses on the estates of the Duke of Bedford, the Skinners' Company, and the Crown, among others, incidentally saving Regent Street for Nash, reviving the fortunes of Tunbridge Wells, and launching Decimus Burton via his own projects. Bloomsbury, beyond the 17th century beginnings of Bloomsbury Square, is largely Burton: Russell Square, and all its surrounding streets until one reaches the next interval – i.e., Bedford Square on the west, Tavistock Square to the north, the extension to Burton Crescent and beyond in the north-east, and Brunswick Square in the east. The borders are with Cubitt's later Bloomsbury, and with Cockerell's work for the Foundling Hospital – Brunswick Square and Mecklenburgh Square.

The Foundling Hospital estate (it centres on Coram's Fields, the small park named after the Hospital's founder which now occupies the site of the great Orphanage itself) was developed on the lines laid down in the previous century by the Earl of Southampton. Cockerell's Report in 1790 made clear that the new Squares should have 'subordinate parts . . . so calculated as to comprise all Classes of Building from the first Class down to Houses of Twenty-five pound pr. annum without the lower Classes interfering with and diminishing the Character of those above them'. There was from the beginning the intention of producing a community, not just a select ghetto, although it must be said that this principle, apparently so liberal, would have in its time had the perfectly pragmatic justification that the first Class needed handy stabling for their servants and tradespeople, who might otherwise be too far away for an un-mechanised age. These principles – partnership of Estate and speculators, overall provision for an integrated sub-community – can be found throughout 18th century London: the Grosvenor Estate's huge Grosvenor Square, the Cavendish-Harley plans of 1719 for the expanded village of St Marylebone, the Portman Estate's Portman Square, the Southampton Estate's Euston Square, and the Eyre Estate's most significant St John's Wood. St John's Wood, erected between a first Plan of 1794 and 1830, was a suburb, comprising both detached and *semi-detached* villas, with gardens. It marks, in practical com-mercial terms what Nash's Regent's Park does on the grander scale of fantasy – the end of the expansion of central London, a city built in city-style, and the beginnings of outer suburbia for the middle classes.

All these private developments, however large, and the later giant scheme on the Grosvenor Estate for Belgravia, represent piecemeal additions to the span of London. Because of the almost invariable use of the Square as the heart of each fresh development, flanked with great houses and supported in depth by lesser streets and houses, the overall effect had been to add new neighbour-hoods to the city, without losing the continuity of the city-feeling. Although built up by private ventures, one by one, the vast new area of north-central London, viewed as a ground-plan, or an aerial photograph, could almost pass as one autocratic scheme, imposed by government. There were quite as many open spaces, of great formal power, as any baroque planner could have wished, and the symbolic magnificence of London was quite equal to its actual importance, without anything but the free play of the market and a happy primacy of appropriate taste to thank. Nevertheless, it had been a piecemeal process, and was beginning to show it – if only because there were not the avenues to match the squares, and the in-filling between great projects fell disastrously short of Cockerell's enlightened hope that 'the Stile of the Buildings at the several Boundaries be . . . as respectable as possible con-sistent with their situations'.

Planning on the larger scale had not been lost – merely not carried out. In fact, between Wren and Nash, the next architect to get anything like an autocratic opportunity, there had been one brilliant proposal published, which, although unsponsored and unadopted, has influenced London development ever since. John Gwynn's *London and Westminster Improved*, published in 1766, was fired by the belief (quite accurate) that 'the finest part of the town is left to the mercy of ignorant and capricious persons'. What Gwynn wanted was for the capital to be treated as a whole, and his extremely detailed suggestions for improvements included the embanking of the Thames, another bridge near Waterloo, a vista down the Haymarket, and a Palace in Green Park, as well as a great piazza at the junction of Whitehall and the Strand.

However, nobody was in a mood, or indeed a position, to tackle the political struggle necessary to impose new order on the existing city. Those with a mind to betterment could seek opportunities on the expanding perimeter, where there was a choice, for owner, speculator and builder/architect, between the thorough decency of Finsbury Square (built 1777–91, but anticipated by Gwynn) and the muddled squalor of Stepney and Southwark.

The first man with any likelihood of influencing events towards some broader re-examination of the capital was John Fordyce, Surveyor-General of His Majesty's Land Revenue. In 1793, realising that the Marylebone Farm north of Portland Place was due to revert to the Crown in 1811, Fordyce persuaded the department to offer £1,000 for the best proposed development of this valuable parkland. In 1797 he followed this up (nobody had submitted a scheme, nor did they by the time the Department itself was merged in 1809) by advising that an architect be consulted on drawing up a long-term policy for all the London estates of the Crown. Fordyce did not seem to be making any headway by the time of his death, in 1809, but if London was to have any real unified plan, he was right in believing that only the Crown Estate could carry it through.

When Fordyce died, and his Department was merged with that of Woods and Forests, the reversion of the Farm was almost upon the Crown; since there were no other architects to turn to, the Crown could only consult its own. Land Revenue had had two, T. Leverton and T. Chawner, and Woods and Forests had another two, John Nash and his assistant, James Morgan. Leverton and Chawner produced a plan no different from the prevailing *ad hoc* methods of London growth; it would have launched from the northern end of Portland Place a further series of checker-board squares, packed in layerings of smaller streets. Leverton's great work had been Bedford Square in 1775, and thirty years' experience had not suggested any need for change.

Nash, of course, produced a very different vision; he had grasped Fordyce's original point about the desirability of uniting distant park with Carlton House, by providing a new triumphal avenue in a London already surfeited with impressive fora. His scheme drove a grand new street from Palace to park – for he proposed to keep the Marylebone Farm semi-rural, and, in place of heavy terraces, to scatter country villas in a variety of picturesque styles among the trees, gently reclaiming this sylvan scene for the great Town of which it was a part by binding in the Park with terraces in the urban style.

Nash was a peculiar man, with an odd career behind him; it is really very difficult to assess his worth in our generation, because he stands at present very high in contemporary esteem – higher, perhaps, than at any time. His work has the important quality that it combines many elements of orthodox, received, good taste, with liberal additions of camp. It is possible to like Nash and Wood, Nash and Hawksmoor, Nash and Pugin, Scott, Mackintosh, Wright. His own jovial unconcern for consistency, accuracy, for the text-books of either architecture or business, confuses the problem even further. Park Crescent is almost irreconcilable with Sussex Place, let alone with Blaise Hamlet or the gargantuan King's Cottage at Windsor.

Nor is his private life safer ground. It is normally much simpler to establish facts about a man's career than criteria of taste, but in Nash's case we seem unlikely to discover whether his Royal patronage stemmed from the Prince Regent's sleeping with Mrs Nash or not. That is, we cannot be sure if he did

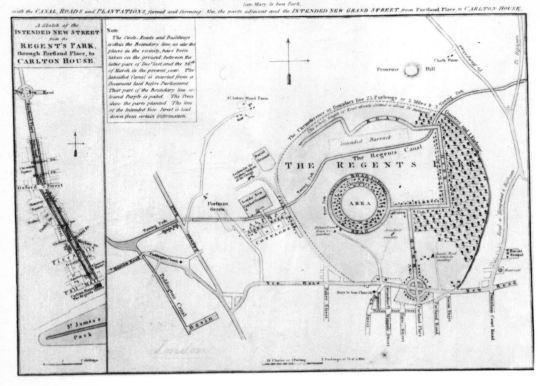

THE REGENT'S PARK.

The Regent's Park Plan as it stood in April, 1812, with a full circus at Park Crescent, canal going through the Park, and large barrack 'intended' – which actually went up by the Park Villages on the East.

Right
Nash's London: apart from all the dark-shaded areas on this plan, he was also responsible for the area to the east of Suffolk Street, in Trafalgar Square.

1. The Regent's Canal
2. Gloucester Gate
3. Park Village East
4. Park Village West
5. Hanover and Kent Terraces
6. Sussex Place
7. Cumberland Terrace
8. Chester Terrace
9. Cambridge Terrace
10. Clarence Terrace
11. Cornwall Terrace
12. Someries House
13. York Terrace
14. York Gate
15. Doric Villa
16. Ulster Terrace
17. St Andrew's Place
18. Park Square
19. Park Crescent
20. All Souls' Church
21. Oxford Circus
22. 29, Dover Street
23. The Quadrant
24. Piccadilly Circus
25. Theatre Royal and Suffolk Place
26. Suffolk Street
27. Waterloo Place
28. United Service Club
29. Carlton House Terrace
30. Clarence House
31. The Marble Arch
32. Buckingham Palace
Nash also planned the area to the east of the Suffolk Street developments; i.e., Trafalgar Square and improvements to the Strand.

have an affair with her, or if the great brood of 'adopted' Pennethorne children were actually royal bastards, or if, supposing one or both those suppositions to be true, that this had Nash's complaisant approval in exchange for sustained employment. We cannot even be sure that Nash was cuckolded (if he was) by the Prince, or if he obligingly married one of the existing royal mistresses to provide a cloak. And it has been suggested that Nash would not have been able to consummate the marriage, if it had begun as an ordinary one (which would presumably commend him to the Prince as an 'official' husband), again without any real hope of our proving or disproving the theory. The strongest single argument for this general theory of Nash's advancement, popular scandal apart (and the populace sang a song about the Prince whose refrain went 'With N–sh have a Smash, singing yo heave ho'), is that all documents which could possibly illuminate the problem have been conscientiously destroyed.

All that is clear is that after 1798, when Nash married Mary Ann Bradley, at twenty-five twenty-one years his junior, his standard of living rose quite markedly; and Miss Bradley, the daughter of a failed coal-merchant, brought no great dowry. Furthermore, Nash, whose previous successes had been provincial, became thereafter an increasingly important London architect, receiving his Crown appointment in 1806; the same year he added the Manor of Ningwood to his house and land in the Isle of Wight, and his London home. The notional salary from the Crown for Nash and Morgan both was only £200 p.a., so it is clear that Nash had other expectations. It may be that those

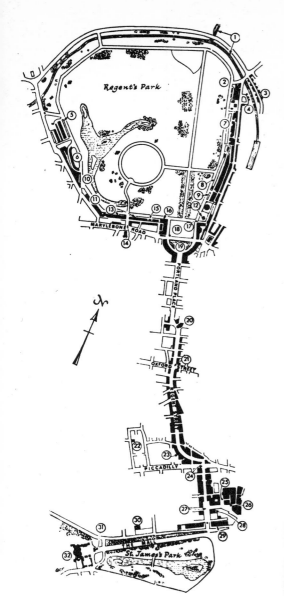

other expectations proved justified when the Crown Estate showed no hesitation in choosing his plan, rather than that of Leverton & Chawner, in July, 1811. He was asked to reduce the number of villas in the Park, but, conditional on that alteration, Nash was able to enter upon twenty years of continuous, if highly-criticised, work for the Crown, culminating in the drawn-out misery of the enquiries into his work at Buckingham Palace, and his eventual withdrawal, in unproven disgrace, to his East Cowes home in 1831.

From the viewpoint of the town-planner, Nash's strange flaws as an architect are insignificant; what matters is his sustained vision of the new spine he planned for London. Regent Street, the link between Waterloo Place (that is, the forecourt of Carlton House) and Portland Place (to become the final

broad entry to what was to have been Park Circus, and is Park Crescent) was not to be smashed in one straight line through the existing property, but to follow the natural curve of the division between Soho and Mayfair. It would, said Nash, supply a 'boundary and complete separation between the Streets and Squares occupied by the Nobility and Gentry, and the narrow Streets and meaner Houses occupied by mechanics and the trading part of the community'. He foresaw it becoming an extended piazza, where 'those who have nothing to do but walk about and amuse themselves may do so', and, even with the gross intrusion of endless streams of crawling motor-cars, his placement of the street remains successful. It does provide a satisfying approach to the quieter splendour of Portland Place, it is one of London's more walked-

Hanover Terrace from the South-West: Nash.

Sussex Place: Nash.

upon streets – idle, shop-window gazing, walkers, not hurrying ones – and it does delineate the natural border of two districts with strong personalities of their own. His own buildings for it have all gone, but its shape, and something of the Regency piazza character, have survived.

The Park at the head of his processional avenue naturally suggests, strongly in his original plan, a little less so as it was completed, the garden suburb. Nash wanted lots of villas, a canal through the Park, a central double-circus containing a National Valhalla, Park Circus, and satellite accommodation for workers, tradesmen and so forth to the east. What he got was eight villas, a canal round the Park, no double-circus (derived from Gwynn), no Valhalla, but Park Crescent, York Square (Munster Square), and the streets between it and Park Village East and Park Village West. In fact, there were no longer enough plutocrats housed in the Park to support the colony of helots provided for to the east, and the Park Villages, late additions to Nash's plan, are the bourgeois quarter of what was originally planned to be a proletarian neighbourhood.

It is interesting that Nash, despite his strong grasp of the unifying force of proper urban planning, nevertheless saw the Park district, including the surrounding terraces, as part of the vista of Regent Street, but not necessarily part of the neighbourhood of it; that he foresaw his villa-dwellers and crescent-dwellers shopping on their own side of the New Road (the Marylebone Road) despite his attempts, with Park Crescent and Park Square, to bridge the gulf that it caused. And it is perhaps relevant to this that his style in the Park Villages is flagrantly picturesque, mock-rural, the other extreme from the rather pompous imperial rhetoric of Carlton House Terrace. Nash was not taking the City out into the country, but drawing the two together on a continuum. Not, of course, that the motley assembly of styles and buildings ranged along Regent Street followed any even progress in manner or importance; but Nash was only too eager to find takers for most sites capable of

financing any development at all – even Burton ran out of ready capital by the time the Quadrant came along, and Nash cobbled together an alliance of craftsmen and capitalised the project with risk labour, rather than hard cash.

Despite the hair-raising quality of most of the transactions involved, and the great suspicion of his contemporaries, Nash's eventual contribution dominated London then, and has continued to provide a core for the West End until today. Regent's Park, Regent Street, Pall Mall East and Trafalgar Square, St James's Park, Carlton House Terrace and Buckingham Palace – one could reasonably show a tourist Nash's London, and no more, if time were pressing. If the money on the taxi-meter went too high, and the tour could not be finished, Nash would understand, and forgive.

Long before Nash was let loose upon the growing confusion of London, and stamped down upon potential chaos the cohesive mark of genius, the Kingdom's other capital had recognised that its condition was unworthy of a great City. Edinburgh had its corporate attention drawn to its shortcomings by a pamphlet of 1752: *Proposals for carrying on certain Public Works in the City of Edinburgh.* It was written by Sir Gilbert Elliott, strongly influenced by George Drummond, and commanded by the Convention of Royal Burghs. 7,500 words long, it drew some very severe comparisons between London, and its 'delightful prospect' closely associated with a 'spirit of industry and improvement', and Edinburgh: 'but . . . one good street . . . and even this is tolerably accessible only from one quarter. The narrow lanes . . . by reason of their steepness, narrowness and dirtiness, can only be considered as so many unavoidable nuisances. Confined by the small compass of the walls, and the narrow limits of the royalty, which scarcely extends beyond the walls, the houses stand more crowded than in any other town in Europe.' The interest of the Royal Burghs in the problem to begin with had been aroused because these crowded, rickety sky-scrapers had started to collapse.

Edinburgh remained an overwhelmingly mediæval city, perched on a

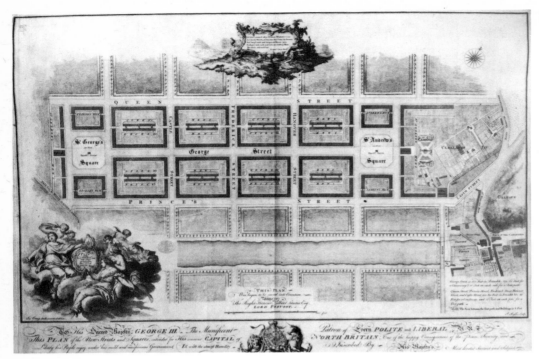

rock, made up of warrens, closes, wynds, courts, its houses teetering blocks of flats, its only decent street, the High Street, 'incumbered with the herb-market, the fruit-market, and several others', with 'no exchange for our merchants; no safe repository for our public and private records; no place of meeting for our magistrates and town-council; none for the convention of our boroughs'. Beneath the rock, cutting it off from the empty fields of Barefoot's Parks, was the North Loch, 'what was originally an ornament of the Town, a most insufferable nuisance', full of sewage and offal from the shambles.

What the pamphlet proposed, having lambasted existing Edinburgh, was that an Exchange be built upon the ruins on the north side of the High Street (where ramshackle houses had been torn down for safety's sake), that a 'building for law courts, the town council . . . &c' be erected on the similar ruins in the Parliament-close, and that an act of Parliament be obtained for extending the royalty (Edinburgh's limits), 'to enlarge and beautify the town, by opening new streets to the north and south, removing the markets and shambles, and turning the North Loch into a canal, with walks and terraces on each side' – all of which should be paid for by a national contribution.

The pamphlet, supported by 'the magistrates and town council, the college of justice, and several persons of rank who happened to be in the neighborhood of this place', merely fuelled a grievance that had been simmering for a hundred years. As Drummond, Lord Provost of Edinburgh in 1725, 1746, 1750, 1754, 1758 and 1762, was to remark in 1763 to Thomas Somerville: 'Look at these fields (Barefoot's Parks) . . . you, Mr Somerville, are a young man, and may probably live, though I will not, to see all these fields covered with houses, forming a splendid and magnificent city. To the accomplishment

Edinburgh: the New Town from the Castle. The park in the foreground was once the North Loch.

of this, nothing more is necessary than draining the North Loch, and providing a proper access from the old town. I have never lost sight of this object since the year 1725 . . .' And the promise of the North bank of the Loch had been discussed, promoted, debated, since 1688.

By the middle of the century, however, there was a great deal more money, as well as increasing incentive to escape the squalor of the old town; the failure of the 1745 meant many things, among them the final victory of Protestant capital and Protestant ethic over the gentler inefficiency of the old order.

Edinburgh: the Old Town from the New; early 19th century.

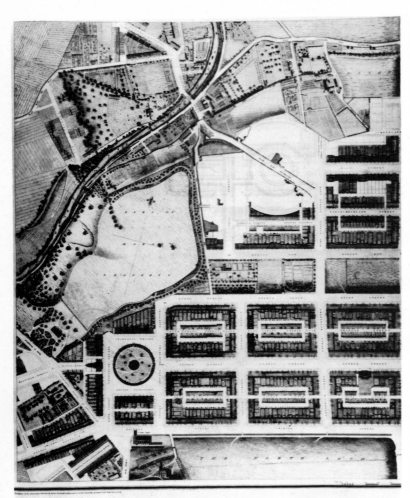

Linen and wool, if not yet coal and iron, cotton and beef, were beginning to bring in large incomes from the South, and the cities of Scotland were eager to share in the visible affluence of South Britain. As the *Proposals* pointed out, 'so necessary and so considerable an improvement of the capital cannot fail to have the greatest influence on the general prosperity of the nation.'

Thus, almost as soon as the message had been digested, a subscription opened for the building of the Exchange. Nearly £6,000 had been promised before the close of 1752, and the following September the foundation stone of a design by John Adam was laid, a further £5,000 overdraft at both the Bank of Scotland and the Royal Bank having been arranged. Although the whole venture seems to have been as financially confused and unprofitable as any Nash development, the building was finished by 1760, a year after the beginning was made on the draining of the North Loch.

The object of the exercise, for the real instigators like Drummond, was to open up the opposite bank, not just to remove the giant cess-pit. Accordingly, in 1763, tenders were sought for the building of a bridge (even with the water gone, there still remained a gulf between old town and open park): a foundation

Edinburgh: 1819, and the New Town already spreading North and East, although the Moray estates to the West are unbuilt.

Opposite page
Above left
Edinburgh: 26 St Andrew's Square, by Sir William Chambers, 1770.

Above right
Edinburgh: 8 Queen Street, by Robert Adam, 1771.

Lower left
Edinburgh: 66 Queen Street, 1780.

Lower right
Edinburgh: Rose Street, rear, the backs did not pretend to the formal dignity of the fronts.

stone was laid, a subscription opened – and nothing happened. In January 1765, another notice appeared, inviting 'all Architects and others' to submit schemes. A Bridge Committee examined them, decided that David Henderson's was best, but sought estimates for both his, and one by William Mylne, a member of the Committee. In August, 1765, having given Henderson the

Edinburgh: Sir William Chambers's house for Sir Laurence Dundas, St Andrew's Square – now the Royal Bank of Scotland. 1772.

prize (thirty guineas), the Committee agreed to build Mylne's bridge.

Work began and progressed rapidly (it was, after all, 1,134 feet long, so to have one of the arches out of three complete by 1768 was commendable) until, in August, 1769, the virtually completed bridge collapsed at the southern end, killing five people. Although the contract had called for completion by

Edinburgh: George Street looking West, with Kay's St Andrew's Church (1785) on right.

November, 1769, the delay this caused, and the problems of finding extra money and labour, meant that the bridge did not open until 1772. Even then, it had continual problems, some of which were still being put right in 1784 by David Henderson.

The bridge had all along been seen by the Council as the key to the new and better city that they sought; and so, once it was under way, they issued another notice, calling this time for 'Architects and others to give in Plans of a New Town', dated April, 1766. By May, the Town Council had received six such plans – a most remarkable instance of Edinburgh's intellectual fertility at the time – and by August, had chosen that of James Craig as the best. During the course of the following year, Craig seems to have spent a great deal of time listening to the ideas and amendments of a sub-Committee of the Council, and putting into practice the advice they gave; but by July, 1767, everyone appears to have agreed upon the Plan, and Craig's overall scheme was endorsed, with a stringent list of supporting regulations. Pavements were to be ten feet wide, the building line adhered to strictly, with no overhanging projections, and a sewer provided in George Street.

Craig's plan has suggested to various critics at various times the influence of Wood, of Gwynn, of Héré de Corny's Nancy, of Richelieu, of Vitruvius. The real point is that it was in a style generally accepted, in theory, but not previously tried on such a scale in practice. Many of the gayer, more delicate, figures of rococo Nancy are missing from Craig's rather leaden-footed Edinburgh; but Nancy is markedly further south than Edinburgh, and inhabited by Frenchmen. Looked at as a Plan, Craig's undoubtedly pales beside many others of the century, but walked through to this day, Edinburgh New Town is magnificent. Whether Craig was sufficiently perceptive to appreciate his countrymen's need for something less ornate, or whether he was insufficiently able to provide anything more decorative, the results are to the good: Edinburgh is not, and could never be, until the wind changes its direction, a bouffant, charming city.

The skeleton of the Plan is straightforward: two Squares, joined by a central avenue, itself the spine of a simple grid. The houses on the north side of Princes Street look back over the North Loch, those on the south of Queen Street down towards the Forth. The very simple plan sits comfortably on the plateau, balancing the spiky mediæval city across the ravine quite easily.

Craig did not have any real control over what was built on his ground-plan, and at first the Council seem to have been so eager to attract customers that they disclaimed any intention of enforcing æsthetic standards – 'as people's taste in building is so different'. It was not until the 1780's that attempts were made to impose any uniformity, by which time St Andrew's Square was complete, and the builders were at work on various sites between there and Hanover Street. But at this juncture a series of ordinances laid down that none of the buildings in the principal streets should exceed three storeys, that those in Rose Street and Thistle Street should be restricted to two storeys, that there should be no dormer-windows, and that anyone taking a site should start building within a year. As a short walk along Rose Street, or a quick glance at the roof-line virtually anywhere in the New Town, will confirm, mere regulation did not necessarily reform the bad habits of speculative builders.

It was at this juncture, too, that the Town Council decided it should provide the New Town with a Church. Craig's Plan had marked in two, facing each other at the extremities of his axis, but by 1781, the site on St Andrew's Square was already occupied by Sir Laurence Dundas's mansion (now the

Edinburgh: lamp standard, Queen Street.

74

Edinburgh: Queen Street.

Edinburgh: Hanover Street looking North.

Edinburgh: Charlotte Square, looking North to Adam's North side, completed 1793.

Royal Bank of Scotland) which Sir Laurence had erected in an atmosphere of curious vagueness about site and specification, such as to suggest that part at least of his enormous wealth had gone to quell the conscience of the Town Council's clerks. Instead, the Council had to persuade a Mr Young to let them have back a site on George Street, into which they squeezed David Kay's St Andrew's.

Again at this time, the Town Council had to be sued as far as the House of Lords by a group of public-spirited New Townsfolk to establish that the open view across the Loch, shewn on Craig's Plan, meant what it had implied, for a number of buildings had begun to rise on the south side of Princes Street. Fortunately, the feu-holders won, and the Council, having been berated for its

Edinburgh: North side, Charlotte Square, Robert Adam.

lack of honour and of wisdom by Lord Mansfield (to anyone familiar with the capacities of Edinburgh Town Councils for sustained unwisdom, the fact that up till then they had behaved with foresight is incredible) was forced to agree that the view would remain as first planned: open.

The progress of the Town continued. By 1790, Hanover Street was largely full, by the middle 'nineties, Frederick Street as well. At this juncture, with Charlotte Square (Craig's St George's Square) coming into view, Robert Adam was commissioned to design it as a whole – a departure from the piecemeal practice up to date, and one apparently occasioned by the embarrassment of the Council at the criticism they had suffered over the Princes Street affair, the missing site of St Andrew's, and the erratic quality of much independent

Edinburgh: North side, Charlotte Square.

Edinburgh: North side, Charlotte Square, detail.

building. Adam gave them a stunning specimen of the finest urban architecture: Charlotte Square is indisputably amongst the most splendid groupings in the whole progress of British townscaping. Yet even here, illicit dormers have crept in, as have parking meters and a one-way system.

After Charlotte Square, which was not filled up until 1820, the boundaries of Craig's Plan were complete, but the pressure on expanding Edinburgh, which had faltered, much to the anguish of the over-extended Council, several times, now took off into sustained growth. As anyone who goes to Edinburgh will see, the New Town manner extends far beyond Craig's limits; and that, too, is the measure of its excellence, for when the neighbouring estates of the Earl of Moray, of Heriot's Hospital, of Sir Francis Walker and of Henry Raeburn were developed, they were developed in New Town style – increasingly infected by Robert Adam (or John Wood) styling. Like the 19th century history of the London estates, 19th century Edinburgh must be left to observation: in both cases, the great period has passed, but indelibly shaped its successors. If one should seek to know what urban scenery is like, and ought to be, then Charlotte Square and Regent Street must be part of any answer.

Edinburgh: North side, Charlotte Square, detail.

*Edinburgh: the Moray estate, Moray Place,
1822 onwards.*

Edinburgh: the Moray estate, Ainslie Place.

Places of Resort

For the greater part of human history, mankind has been divided into two main classes: those for whom life, whatever its notional responsibilities of State and estates, was one long holiday, and those for whom the only holidays have been prescribed religious festivals on which no work was done – but on which proper behaviour was no more a matter of choice than on working days.

Neither class accordingly understood in the word anything like our meaning, which normally contains the idea of voluntary travel away from home with no end in view but that which is non-work. Indeed, for the poor (and we should emphasise that one remained poor in this sense unless and until actual money had also brought recognised independent status: a labourer with savings could not safely assume freedom of movement on that ground alone) travel at all was a rare, and strictly circumscribed, experience. The easiest exceptions to the successive controls of villeinage and the Settlement Acts, for extreme example, were travel with, or on behalf of, one's master, travel to or from the armed service of the King, and travel on pilgrimage or in search of treatment for illness or disability. But the last two were by no means absolute rights, guaranteeing exemption from Parish Officers, Justices' inquiries, press gangs – or bandits. A crippled pauper on the way to a shrine or healing springs was just as likely to be bundled back to his home Parish as a sturdy pauper, as it was generally felt that Christian charity was quite sufficiently strained by the Poor Rate on behalf of local needs, without accepting the charges of other parishes.

However, it is true that to travel in search of spiritual or physical medication was felt to be distinctly less dangerous or reprehensible than straightforward wandering abroad (in search of work or liberty, both highly peripatetic luxuries for the poor). The two were commonly associated, as they always have been; the intimate correspondence of water and divinity can be remarked as much in Greece or Rome as in pagan Gaul, or at modern Lourdes. The behaviour and inferred beliefs we assume for the shrine of Aesculapius of Corinth and for that of Sequana (the source of the Seine) is not far from that we may observe by the Ganges, the Jordan, or at the Cloutie Well in the Black Isle. And the relationship of water and spirit can only be intensified if the magical spring or well actually does do people good – by its mineral content, masquerading as divine intervention.

All this may help to explain why the story of holiday towns is very largely a continuation of the story of what we now call spas. What starts as a place to which it is respectable to travel for the cure gradually becomes a place to which one repairs for general relaxation. And it should not be forgotten that the vogue for seaside holidays began because it came to be said that bathing in the sea, or drinking sea-water, was of specific medicinal value – not just because the seaside 'did you good'. Even today, there is a great deal of common conversational justification for the obviously guilt-ridden indulgence of a holiday – all on the lines that a holiday, or the particular place or activity of the holiday, improve the physical or mental health. Analyse any normal exchange on the subject, and one realises just how seldom either party produces plain hedonism as a reason for taking, or enjoying, a holiday.

The British spa, or holiday-place, with the longest history, and the greatest influence, is of course Bath. Aquæ Sulis or Aquæ Calidæ to the Romans, it was not only already a spa (having, like Buxton, a swimming pool as well as magnificent public baths) but the most sophisticated and cosmopolitan of Romano-British towns. The town's fame survived the departure of the Romans, and Bath was well known for the curative properties of its waters in the Middle Ages. At that period, the waters, as Bath's most important asset, were strictly under the proprietorship of the Abbey, but at the dissolution, the town itself managed to secure the ownership. It is clear that the title already mattered, not only because both monks and town in their turn proved eager to possess it, but because Bath (with Buxton) is given the peculiar

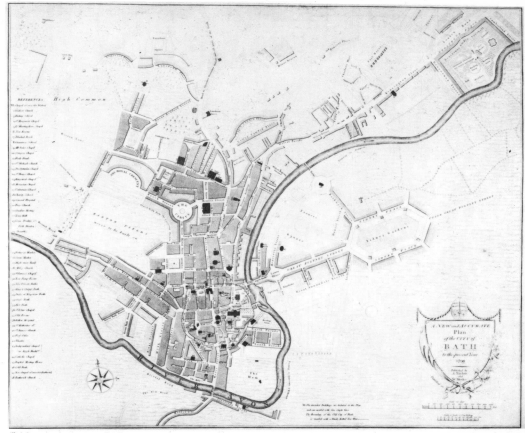

endorsement of the 1572 Poor Law, which specifically laid down that the sick, even though poor and potentially a charge upon the Rates, were to be allowed to travel there.

The hot springs, the mythological discovery of King Bladud, were not Bath's only asset: apart from the wool trade, in which Bath, like many other Western towns, was prominent in the later Middle Ages, the citizens seem very early on to have realised that their water could be made but the centrepiece for a full-scale entertainment industry. There were musicians employed by the 16th century, actors probably before the Civil War (James VI & I's Queen, Anne, visited the town in 1613) and certainly by the Restoration, in addition to a large number of inns, taverns and dealers in consumer trivia. By the 1680's according to Celia Fiennes, 'the town and all of its accommodations is adapted to the batheing and drinking of the waters and to nothing else' and as a classic example of the particular kind of behaviour engendered by the service industries, one might cite her description of the 'Serjeant belonging to the Baths that all the bathing tyme walkes in galleryes and takes notice order is observed, and punishes the rude, and most people of fashion sends to him when they begin to bathe, then he takes particular care of them and complements you every morning, which deserves its reward at the end of the Season.'

The Restoration and after was the beginning of the real heyday, not merely

83

of Bath, the first among spas, but of spas in general. The increasing demand of the rich for leisure cloaked as medicine sparked the discovery of more than a hundred different sources between 1660 and 1714; it is the time when Epsom, the Clifton Hotwells, Islington (like Hampstead, Dulwich, Streatham, a London suburb once visited from choice in order to take the waters, incredible as that now seems), Tunbridge Wells, Cheltenham and Scarborough come to .prominence. Celia Fiennes, incidentally, reached Scarborough in 1697 (it had been a spa of sorts for about seventy years by then) and observed of its waters that they were of a 'brackish and saltness which make it purge pretty much'.

The economic and social (let alone medical) developments which explain this sudden passion of the English for drinking tainted water are outside the confines of this book, but their product was naturally to create new towns wherever springs were found and exploited. At Bath itself, the most important development of this period was probably the consequence of Queen Anne's visits of 1702 and 1703. The Corporation, seeking to ensure the best possible show for its royal visitor, hired a certain Captain Webster, gambler, duellist and bon viveur, as Master of Ceremonies – a post more that of Artistic Director of the Festival than compère – and decided after the Queen had gone that the job should stay. Captain Webster fought his first losing duel in 1705, and as his successor, the Corporation appointed a bizarre young (thirty-one) man called Richard Nash. Beau Nash during the ensuing forty years virtually invented the holiday industry, and provided the incentive to Ralph Allen and the architect John Wood to make Bath the very epitome of the handsome spa.

Nash was born in Swansea in 1674, the son of a glass-maker. A very successful glass-maker, who was able to send his son to Jesus, Oxford – where he failed to take a degree; to buy him a Commission – but 'the profession of arms required attendance and duty, and often encroached upon those hours he could have wished to dedicate to softer purposes'; and finally to the Temple – where the Beau did so little work, wore such fine clothes, and entertained so lavishly, that his friends suspected he must be a highwayman.

Whilst at the Temple, Nash staged his first entertainment, being entrusted with the amusements for a visit from King William in 1695: it is said that the King was sufficiently delighted to offer Nash a knighthood, which was refused. Having failed to become a lawyer, Nash became instead a gambler, but he remained grateful to his father for trying; when, in later years, it was rumoured that he was a bastard, Nash explained his reticence thus: 'I seldom mention my father in company, not because I have any reason to be ashamed of him, but because he has some reason to be ashamed of me.'

As a gambler, Nash favoured the expensive dare: he once won fifty guineas by standing at the great door of York Minster as the congregation filed by, clad only in a blanket. He had a reputation as a winner at the tables, which he seems to have augmented during his reign at Bath by exacting commission from the gaming-house proprietors. Indeed, the eventual downfall of this social despot came with the Acts of 1740 and 1745 which clamped down on gambling, and meant the end of the Nash-style in Bath.

However, when he first arrived in the city, Nash imposed an immediate

domination upon it. As early as 1706 he was capable of convincing the inhabitants that their city was their livelihood, to the extent of raising £18,000 amongst them for improvements to the roads. Throughout his career there, Nash combined a meticulous care for the ephemeral activities of the visitors of the day with this sure grasp of the long-term interests of the holiday-machine. He gave equal attention to the maintenance of polite behaviour, of proper dress, and to the need for decent roads, good lodgings, the permanent appointments of the gracious city. After his fall from power, the Corporation voted him £10 a month (small gratitude for what he had done) and eventually buried him in Bath Abbey at a cost of £50.

But Nash's zeal for getting things done properly would not in itself have

Bath: the Circus in 1784.

THE CIRCUS AT BATH.

Bath: the Crescent in 1788. Despite its felicity as an urban design, this demonstrates how much it was a frontier station of the town amid the country.

THE CRESCENT AT BATH.

succeeded in transforming Bath, and his efforts were augmented by those of the philanthropic Ralph Allen, and those of the Woods, father and son. Like Nash, Allen deserves description. Twenty years younger than Nash, Allen made his first impression upon the city as postmaster in 1720, when he devised a system of cross-posts which avoided the necessity for all mail to be routed via London. In those generous days, he was able to operate his scheme as a private fief, and it has been estimated that from 1720 until his death in 1764, Allen made an average of £12,000 a year out of the posts – ample supply for a man with an appetite for generous giving.

Nash's idiosyncrasies included an immense cream-coloured beaver hat, worn at all times, and justified on the grounds that it was too distinctive to be

Bath : interior, 15 Queen Square (John Wood I).

stolen; Allen's included the commissioning of a Sham Castle from Sanderson Miller, and the invention of a novel bathing machine, which he first tested, personally, at the age of sixty-nine: 'a treatment so extreme and so strange that it savoured of madness'. Incidentally, just as we meet Nash again at Tunbridge Wells, it so happens that Allen tried his bathing-machine at Weymouth, and effectively founded that resort. Nash's flair, and Allen's money, both found expression in the buildings of John Wood the first; he was probably a Yorkshireman who settled permanently in Bath in 1727, having been commissioned to build (at the age of twenty-two) both a house for Allen, and Queen Square. Wood was less colourful than his patron, but quite as busy. Allen, whose interests by then included the improvement of the Avon navigation and the Bath stone quarries on Combe Down, put Wood in charge of the quarry, and the use of as much of its product as he could justify.

Wood's ambition was, as the briefest examination of his work reveals, to create monumental compositions, to transform simple houses into parts of a brilliant, coherent, whole – to make Bath another Rome. His Queen Square (1728-36) is already totally assured, in the Palladian style which Bath helped to spread all over Britain during the ensuing eighty years. The Parades (1740 onwards) were intended to frame a sunken garden – a Forum for the Imperial City – and his Circus (begun 1754, the year Wood died) is a unique example of unhesitating Grand Style: a circle, divided into three segments of eleven terraced houses each, with the incoming roads arranged so that they do not continue across the line. Around the circle, along the concave façade, the unity

Bath: the Pump Room, a print of 1820 showing a surviving pre-war life.

88

is maintained by the layering of the Orders – Doric for the ground floors, Ionic for the first floors, Corinthian for the second. It is a magnificent work of art, and desirable housing on those grounds alone, but it reveals the principles upon which Bath was built, principles of grandeur and beauty for the visitor, for the appreciative eye, not principles of residents' convenience. Indeed, the kind of building which went on under Wood, and his son (who was responsible for the splendour of Royal Crescent [1765/75], in which the provision of a mere thirty houses is turned into a definitive statement about what Cities should aspire to), was building designed to create a need, not answer one. It had a vital part to play in making Bath successful, not merely at the obvious level – Assembly Rooms, Pump Room, hotels and lodging houses – but at the highest level of artistic achievement. Nash, in enforcing standards of fastidious behaviour and gallantry, and the Woods, in building on the highest plane, were consciously investing capital for the future, as well as coping with the problems of the present.

Bath's importance can scarcely be overestimated: it created the yardstick against which all other resorts were judged, and, incidentally, provided too an exemplar of urban style which can be recognised at work again not only in Brighton, Buxton, Weymouth, but in Regent's Park and Edinburgh. Nevertheless, there were other spas, and other styles.

Bath's oldest rival was, as we have seen, Buxton; but despite the unwilling visit there of Mary Queen of Scots while in the custody of the Earl of Shrewsbury, and the expansion of the Old Hall in 1670, Buxton was never able to keep up with Bath after Nash. Indeed, in 1781 John Carr (architect of Harewood House) built there for the Duke of Devonshire a new assembly room and library in a monumental Crescent, a most sincere piece of flattery. But much greater competition was offered Bath by Clifton, Cheltenham, Harrogate, Leamington, Malvern, Scarborough, Epsom, Tunbridge, all of which claimed at differing times large sections of the relatively small market.

The Hot Springs of Clifton were first noticed in 1480 by William of Worcester, but they did not attain any general celebrity until about 1632, when they were recorded to be beneficial for cancer and scrofula, applied externally, and for inflammation, dysentery and hæmorrhage, applied internally. Incidentally, the great majority of English mineral waters appear to have had purgative effects: a most curious medication for dysentery and colic, but commonly employed in such cases. Despite the closeness of Bristol, and the enthusiasm of the local tradesmen, Clifton did not, however, grow really large until late in the 18th century. A new well, 320 feet deep, was sunk (at immense expense) in 1772, possibly an aftermath of the Lisbon earthquake twenty years earlier, when 'the water became so red and turbid for some days as to be unfit for use', and at about that time the development of 'piles of stately edifices of Bath stone' began. It seems to have grown haphazardly, if strongly influenced by Bath and Wood, as a result of the increasing wealth of Bristol.

Harrogate's springs were also of some antiquity, the first, the Tewit Well, having been discovered by Captain William Slingsby in 1571. But again their, development and exploitation took time: in 1656 the spring was surrounded by a terrace, sixty yards square, and it was not until 1786 that Lord Loughborough paid for it to be domed over. At this period Harrogate, like so many other ambitious spas, provided itself with theatre and library; but, despite the fact that Timothy Bright had called it 'the English Spa' in 1598, thus importing from Belgium a new English noun, as late as 1821 it was said that Harrogate 'hardly exists'. The full development of Harrogate's unique patchwork quilting of grassy spaces – the Stray, West Park (Prospect Row as it was in 1821) and so on – took place in the 19th century.

Shortly after Captain Slingsby's discovery in Yorkshire, Dudley, Lord North, returning from a visit to the Earl of Abergavenny at Eridge, observed a spring which had 'on its surface a shiny scum, and left in its course down a neighbouring brook a ruddy, ochreous track'. It says something for the established reputation of Bath, Buxton and Spa at the time that Lord North's reaction in 1606 to this sight was to leap down from his horse and bottle a sample, rather than to spur away from the unnatural brook. His Lordship's physician analysed the sample and pronounced it most medicinal. Shortly afterwards, two wells were built on Bishop's Down, near Tonbridge in Kent, and the single cottage there was joined by several others – and, in the season, by numbers of tents. Indeed, it was in tents that Queen Henrietta Maria's party camped in 1629 when Tunbridge Wells received their first royal visit. Mrs Humphreys from the old cottage, created chief Water Dipper, was at that time the spa's only employee and the cure (twenty pints at a sitting was commonly prescribed) its only amenity or purpose. Tunbridge's popularity, naturally enhanced by the Queen's stay, was increased still further in 1632 by the publication of a treatise on the waters by a Doctor Rowzee of Ashford. Dr Rowzee, like his colleagues, was all for the use of mineral springs, just so long as the patients did not conclude they could dispense with the services of the doctors, and he intelligently proceeded to expatiate at length on the importance of proper advice before resorting to the wells. 'The remedy must be used with reason, discretion and circumspection, otherwise hurt rather than good will follow the use of it' he insisted; but discretion and circumspection seemed to include doses of fifteen pints or more, and Sir Dudley North, grandson of the discoverer of the wells, experienced some difficulty getting through his dose. 'Such an Explosion was a Crisis the Doctors said they had never known before.'

In 1638, Tunbridge's first major physical expansion took place: a promenade known at the time as the Walks, but subsequently as the Pantiles, was laid out, and there rapidly developed that distinctive division remarked by Celia Fiennes in 1697, and visible in Kip's engraving of 1718: 'the Gentry takes as a diversion while drinking the waters to go and buy their dinners it being every day's market and runs the whole length of the Walke which is between high trees on the market side for shade, and secured with a row of buildings on the right side which are shopps full of all sorts of toys, silver, china, milliners and all sorts of curious wooden ware.' The shops on the right (as one strolled away from the triangular Well enclosure) were arcaded (what Celia Fiennes and her contemporaries called piazza, from a confusion of terms founded in Inigo Jones's Covent Garden).

Tunbridge really came into its own with the Restoration. Although the promenade was followed in 1639 by the erection of two groups of wooden cottages (at Southborough on the road to Tonbridge and at Rusthall, a mile in the other direction), there was not another marked expansion until, the Court having taken up rustic Tunbridge, the Lord of the Manor in 1676 hired the tenants' rights on the common under the pretence of needing extra

Tunbridge Wells: Kip's engraving of 1718 shows the Pantiles looking towards the Wells (B).

Bird's Eye View of Tunbridge Wells in 1718.

grazing, and proceeded to put up houses and shops round the Pantiles. A subsequent lawsuit was won by the aggrieved freeholders, who received in compensation a part of the estate which included the Assembly Rooms.

Thereafter, in the hey-day of Tunbridge, development proceeded dangerously quickly: so much so that, in 1740, an Act of Parliament was procured to forbid further building on the Heath. That was five years after the eager beneficiaries of the boom had secured the summertime services of Beau Nash, who left Bath between its Spring and Autumn seasons to the unfashionable few, and processed across southern England in a 'post chariot and six greys, with outriders, footmen, French horns and every other appendage of expensive parade'. Nash found at Tunbridge a society not only similar to that which he had shaped at Bath, but largely made up of the same people; and Hamilton's judgment of Tunbridge Company – 'though always numerous is always select; since those who repair thither for diversion ever exceed the number of those who go thither for health' – would have fitted Bath quite as closely. The style that was being set depended on fine walks, theatres, shops, libraries, not merely on the provision of chemical draughts.

The grander period of Tunbridge architecture came after that of Bath, of course. The peculiarly rustic appeal of the Kent spa, often remarked upon, although reinforced by urban amenities, did not demand so much attention to monumental grandeur. Decimus Burton's Calverley Park estate, for Mr Ward, dates from 1828-48, and the prevailing style of the town today reflects the gradual transition of the early 19th century from resort town to residential town, a transition which took place at many of its rival spas as well, including Bath, Malvern, Leamington, all of which abandoned the gaiety, and risks, of the Season, for the security of the genteel old.

The other 17th century spas – Epsom (springs discovered in 1620), Scarborough (about 1626), Leamington (1688) and so on – all conformed very largely to the pattern if not the timing, of growth of Tunbridge. Epsom was in fact declining as a spa by the early 18th century, though fortunately it had already established itself as a place for horse-races, and had in consequence a short season (the Derby and the Oaks) but a rich one. Scarborough was many things besides a spa, but the significance of the waters to the economy of this port can be gauged from the fact that the town financed a rapid and diligent search for the spring after a cliff-fall in 1737 had buried it; and at the end of the 18th century, Scarborough had all the standard amenities of a superior resort – theatre, library, reading room, assembly rooms, and, since its 'Spaw' was fortunately beside the formerly unregarded sea, bathing machines. Leamington – officially Leamington-Priors, not yet Leamington Spa – although its waters were recorded by Camden, Speed and Dugdale, and were first analysed in 1688, did not really rise to prominence until the end of the 18th century, after Mr Abbots discovered a second spring, and the Earl of Aylesford enclosed the first. Lewis in 1835 remarked of this 'fashionable watering-place' that 'from an inconsiderable hamlet, consisting only of a few cottages, and containing only 543 inhabitants, it has . . . risen with unprecedented rapidity, within the last twenty-three years, into a large and populous town, containing . . . nearly 1,200 houses.' Another late developer was Malvern, of which Lewis observed 'the more ancient portion of the village is irregularly built, and consists of houses scattered on the declivity of the mountain; but since the celebrity of the springs and the purity of the air have made it a place of fashionable resort, handsome ranges of modern houses have been erected.' In fact, the description here, and the process in nearly every case, is that of Tunbridge: what we are discussing is the phenomenon of fashion. Discovery alone is not enough – that produces tents, or 'irregularly built', 'scattered' houses. But as soon as some portion of Society alights upon the particular charms, or claims, of a given spa, then it grows up very quickly indeed, usually with public subscription by astute businessmen to finance libraries, assembly rooms and the like, and with good-quality villa or terrace houses going up as a speculation, but a speculation which can only work if the houses are appropriate to the tastes of the holiday-making class.

The effect of sudden smartness – the beneficial effect of royal endorsement – can be seen quite vividly at Cheltenham. The first spring there was found in 1716, enclosed in 1721, and in 1738 Captain Henry Skillicorn erected over it a pavilion, with pump-room and surrounding walks. Nevertheless, Cheltenham remained small, and relatively unsmart, until the 1780's. In 1780, there were only thirty lodging houses, whereas by 1830, there were to be several hundred. The turning point seems to have been the visit, in 1788, of King, Queen and Princesses; and shortly thereafter, the suburb of Montpellier was added to the now-fashionable town. This was followed in its turn by Pittville, laid out as a speculation by Joseph Pitt, M.P., on land that was part of the Town Field until the Enclosure of 1806. A contemporary observer allowed himself what in retrospect seems a slight exaggeration: 'a new town has been planned on a magnificent scale', he claimed in 1835, and went on to call the Pump Room (1825) 'a splendid edifice, erected at an expense of more than £20,000'. In 1836, the Queen's Hotel was built, and that cost £50,000. The stakes were naturally rising with the growing prizes brought by improved transport, and rapidly-increasing national income.

Cheltenham's style is Bath-derivative, with terraces and crescents, but already at some remove: grandeur has weakened to tastefulness, stone to stucco, the sweeping grace of the classic orders given way to the prettiness of wrought-iron balconies. It is as if Bath had been filtered through Brighton. But another difference which is relevant to our theme is that Cheltenham – late Regency, early Victorian Cheltenham – like Leamington and Tunbridge at this very period, is beginning to build for residence, as well as visits. The speculators, like Pitt, still put up hotels and lodging-houses, but they also embark on whole estates of villas, with gardens, verandahs and an atmosphere of provincial cosiness totally opposed to the proud sophistication of Wood's Bath. The shapes of the streets, the pillars and porticos, still suggest the city, but the houses increasingly belong to the outskirts of the quiet country town.

The change is symptomatic of two wider changes of this time. In the first place, the great towns and cities themselves were rapidly becoming too expensive, too crowded, too dirty and noisy, for their centres any longer to be lived in by the gentility, who began increasingly to retire to the old spas from the

Fashionable Dresses in the Rooms at Weymouth
1774.

Weymouth: after Ralph Allen had demonstrated his bathing-machine there in 1763, it rose into fashion steadily, reaching its peak after 1789, when George III took to staying there – prudently bringing supplies with him from Windsor, to evade the high prices charged by seaside shopkeepers.

Sea-bathing:

Your prudent grandmammas, ye modern belles,
Content with Bristol, Bath and Tunbridge Wells,
When health required it would consent to roam,
Else more attached to pleasures found at home.
But now alike, gay widow, virgin, wife,
Ingenious to diversify dull life,
In coaches, chaises, caravans and hoys,
Fly to the coast for daily, nightly joys,
And all, impatient of dry land agree
With one consent to rush into the sea.

 Cowper, in 'Retirement', 1782.

work-dominated hearts of London, Liverpool, Birmingham, Manchester. Industry was clearly making these great cities, and many more, engines of production and commerce, rather than complete cultures in themselves: the dreadful partnership of rising land-values and declining amenity was well on the way to killing the cities, and creating the dormitories. And on the other hand, just as the demand for all-the-year-round homes in Cheltenham and Tunbridge rose, so the holiday traffic left them in search of the new fashion – the seaside.

The rise of the sea-bathing resort is often attributed to Dr Russell, whose *Dissertation concerning the Uses of Sea Water in Diseases of the Glands* was published, first in Latin in 1750, and subsequently translated into English in 1753.

95

This treatise, extolling the virtues of a mineral water available in inexhaustible supply wherever there was a handy coast, coupled with Dr Russell's own choice of the Steine at Brighton for his home and surgery in 1754, is frequently credited with the fashion as a whole, and the rise of Brighton in particular. However, there is no doubt that people were bathing in the sea rather earlier than this, and were occasionally swigging sea-water for their health as well – and not merely at Scarborough, the established spa which happened to be beside the sea.[1] Blackpool's site appears on an early 18th century map, when it was known as 'Mr Forshaw's bathing place', and Sir John Floyer's *History of Cold Bathing*, the testament of a dedicated apostle of the practice who thought rickets stemmed from inadequate drenching at Baptism, was published in 1702. It has been proved that bathing in the sea for fun, as well as for melancholia, gout, hydrophobia and rickets, took place in the first half of the 18th century at Deal, Eastbourne, Portsmouth and Exmouth, as well as at Brighton and Scarborough.

However, since Brighton stands in much the same relationship to other seaside towns that Bath does to the spas, Dr Russell's claims need not be totally disproved. The fact is that Brighton was the first really successful coastal resort, and that its rise does stem from the middle of the 18th century. What Dr Russell had actually said was, in his own summary, 'I distinguish sea-bathing into *general* and *topical*: by the former I mean, when the whole body is immersed; by the latter, when sea water is applied to some particular part of the body only. We will begin with the consideration of the first: and that nat-

[1]*Scarborough Spa*, published in 1667 by Dr Robert Wittie, advised sea-bathing for gout. Incidentally, many resorts founded on the sea also took the trouble to find and publicise fresh-water springs as well: Brighton's chalybeate spring was found in 1760, and both East Bourne and Whitby made much of their chalybeate waters.

Bathing Machines: as seen by Rowlandson in 1790.

BATHING MACHINES

urally suggests the situation of the place; which, I think, should be clean and neat, at some distance from the opening of a river; that the water may be as highly loaded with sea-salt, and the other riches of the ocean as possible, and not weakened by the mixing of fresh water with its waves. In the next place one would choose the shore to be sandy and flat; for the convenience of going into the sea in a bathing chariot. And lastly, that the sea shore should be bounded by lively cliffs, and downs; to add to the chearfulness of the place, and give the person that has bathed an opportunity of mounting on horseback dry and clean; to pursue such exercises as may be advised by his physician, after he comes out of the bath.' Having ordained the site so clearly, Russell presumably confused his patients by choosing Brighton, where the beach could hardly be called 'sandy and flat', but numbers of other resorts, including Scarborough, promptly claimed that the description fitted them, usually with some promoter's licence.

Brighton was of course a town well before Dr Russell came. It was quite old enough (Bristelmestune in Domesday Book) to have lost its earliest development, the lower town below the cliffs, to the sea, and the substantial fishing village petitioned the King in 1685 for incorporation as a borough, without success. Curiously enough, the oldest surviving area of the town, the 'upper town' on the cliffs (bounded by the sea, East Street, North Street and West Street) appears to have been laid out on a grid pattern some time in the late 13th or early 14th century. It might possibly be that the coincidence of shape, period, and cause (erosion of the coast) between this and Winchelsea is not all that coincidental, and that Edward I's influence can be found here too; but it must be said that there is no evidence apart from the street-plan for this.

Post-Russell Brighton is not by any means as regular, not only because it grew by private speculation, but because the street-lines had to follow the boundaries of the town's open fields – the Laines – and the access-baulks (leakways) and strips (paul-pieces). In other words, the town has been gradually built up on shapes imposed by the way the land was parcelled out before sale, the way it was for agriculture, however inappropriate that was for urban development. The only planned parts of the new Brighton, laid out as entities, did not come until the great boom of the 1820's, when the number of houses in the town doubled, and it showed the highest percentage growth of population of any English town. In that period, Kemptown and Brunswick Town were properly planned, both by the architects Amon Wild, his brother Amon Henry Wild, and C. A. Busby.

Before discussing these projects, however, one can hardly ignore completely the building of Regency Brighton. It may not strictly have anything to do with planned towns, but it is important in the development of the resort-style. In the first place, then, the transition from inland spa to seaside resort might be dated with hindsight to Brighton's first royal visits – those of the Duke of Gloucester in 1765 and the Duke of York in 1766. Although from this time onwards houses of the better sort began to be built, it remained true in 1775 that Brighthelmstone, as it still was, was a village of unpaved streets and houses of cobble-nogging. It was not until 1784 that the Prince of Wales arrived, and took a house (Grove House) on the Steine; but although this was clearly outside the eastern edge of the town, the resort already had a theatre and a library. It was still a port, declined, but with a Customs House, and yet already on the way to becoming a spa. The influx of fashionable society brought about by the Prince's liking for the place merely accelerated the transformation. There had been 650 houses in 1770; by 1801 there were 1,282, and chief amongst the additions was the Prince's Marine Pavilion, built for him in 1787 by Henry Holland (it went on growing, and being remodelled, until John Nash completed this 'oriental palace, combining the characteristics of a Turkish Harem and a Russian Cremlin' between 1815 and 1820).

By 1820 there were over three thousand houses in Brighton, the great majority of the additions being on the east side, around the focus of 'Florizel's Folly'. The population, 2,000 in 1760, had risen to 24,429, and the number of visitors in a year from four hundred to over ten thousand. The process seemed sufficiently irreversible for T. R. Kemp, M.P., one of the Lords of the Manor, to decide that what Brighton needed was housing for residents – seasonal residents, perhaps, but people wanting greater space, both in their houses and around them, than was available in the crowded centre. He hired the Wilds and Busby to design Kemptown, well out into the fields to the east of the existing town, but naturally overlooking the sea. It is incidentally worth stating the obvious at this point: at a very early stage in the growth of seaside towns, people decided it was pleasant to look at the sea, as well as to bathe in it and, perhaps, drink it.[2] As a result, seaside towns grow along the coast, and are typically rather thin – the commercial centre being perhaps central on the strip, but reached rather quickly from the landward. The Promenade as a feature, simultaneously for walking and driving along, and enabling large numbers of hotels to claim that they overlook the sea, reaches quite astonishing proportions, and on the South Coast now there is more ribbon-development, more growing-together, than practically anywhere else in the country. Brighton and Hove, Bournemouth and Poole, Hastings and St Leonard's, are not pairs of resorts, but single conurbations, plastered along the rim of the land.

Kemptown was directly influenced by Nash's work in Regent's Park, and, at a remove, by Edinburgh and thus, ultimately, by Bath; which is to say that it is in the tradition of Roman urban composition. Its centre, Lewes Crescent and Sussex Square, is shaped to funnel in as much of the sea-view as possible to the houses: Lewes Crescent, the bell of the horn, spans 840 feet, 200 feet more than Bath's Royal Crescent, and Sussex Square, one hundred yards wide from east to west, is larger than Grosvenor Square in London. The Crescent's arms, where they reach the front, are carried round to form Chichester Terrace and Arundel Terrace. The select nature of the plan is typified by the provision of its own Church, St George's, which was built in 1824, four years before the whole scheme was completed (in a sense it never has been; the original plan provided for two additional flanking squares set behind the sea-front terraces). The houses were meant for the rich, with large families and several servants; apart from Church, grassed central area, and view, the amenities were left to existing Brighton, so that although Kemptown is a very successful piece of design in the grander Regency manner, it is not truly a Town in intention.[3]

[2]By 1857, when Mrs Merrifield wrote *Brighton, Past & Present*, she knew visitors 'went to the sea determined to see as much of it as they could, and increased their sea-view by inserting bow-windows', a very typical feature of guest-house architecture. There were also ships to be looked at – a bull point in the promotion of the Mersey resorts, and the piers at Channel ports.

[3]In 1833, J. D. Parry observed that the 'sea line of houses in Brighton now extends from the eastern extremity of Kemp Town, to the Adelaide-terrace . . . full three miles; a range of piles of buildings, alone to be equalled at St Petersburgh'.

Brighton: Kemptown. Even now, Brighton proper has not completely hemmed it in, and there are tennis courts where Kemp originally hoped for a further square and streets.

Brunswick Town, on the west, where Brighton was already nudging up against Hove, is to a degree more of a town: it has not only a Church (St Andrew's, 1828, by the young Charles Barry), but a market, so that the residents did not need to go into old Brighton for their shopping. Brunswick Town is less grand than Kemptown, although in the same manner, and is really only Brunswick Square, a rectangle perpendicular to the front (Brunswick Terrace) with attendant mews, back-street and market area. Built in 1824, it was already over two miles from Kemptown – that is, the front, which was to be paved all the way from Marine Parade to West Street in 1829, was more than twice the depth of the town at its most built-up section.[3]

After Brunswick Town (in those peculiarly loyal times, this minor fief of

Brighton: Kemptown, Lewes Crescent.

99

the House of Hanover was commemorated time and time again – for example, at Weymouth, and in London) and its neighbour to the west, Adelaide Crescent, begun in 1830 and not completed until 1860, Brighton's growth continued, not least after the arrival of the railway in 1841 which made Brighton's propinquity to London even more significant, but it reverted to the in-filling pattern, unplanned and unremarkable. What had been established quite firmly, was the general pattern of the seaside town: long front, or promenade, central amenities (theatre, library, aquarium, and so forth – growing steadily more plebeian with the expansion of the resort's market), and residential property combining something of the now unchallenged 'good taste' of Georgian style with the comforts of the country villa. Piers – Brighton's chain-pier, aimed at least as much at strolling voyeurs as at potential passengers on board ship, was promoted in 1821, six years after Margate had built her new pier with provision for bands as well as ships – were only the finishing touch to the proper seaside town. Without a pier, a resort is not in the classic mode, but before the pier, there must be a promenade.

The progress of Brighton was not of course entirely unaccompanied, although much of it can be regarded as trail-blazing. Margate's pier was only one symptom of a nation-wide phenomenon. It is worth extracting from the invaluable Samuel Lewis's *Topographical Dictionary* of 1835 a few instances of this amazing transformation of the English coast.

Broadstairs: 'a small sea port and hamlet . . . an inconsiderable village, inhabited only by a few fishermen, it has lately risen into celebrity as a place of fashionable resort for sea-bathing.'

Bognor: 'prior to 1709, an insignificant village, inhabited only by a few labourers and fishermen.'

Blackpool: 'was, until well within the last eighty years, an inconsiderable hamlet.'

Budleigh Salterton: 'that hamlet is rising into repute as a watering place.'

Cromer: 'the town was formerly inhabited only by a few fishermen but, from the excellence of its beach, the salubrity of its air, and the beauty of its scenery, it has become a bathing place of some celebrity.'

East Bourne: (*sic* – and so for some time afterwards) 'recently resorted to as a bathing place.'

Margate: 'This place, formerly a small fishing village . . . about the middle of the last century it became much frequented as a bathing place.'

Rhyl: 'This place . . . prior to the year 1820, consisted only of a few scattered dwellings; but since that time, from the pleasantness of its situation on the coast of the Irish sea . . . it has become a place of favourite resort for sea-bathing, and is frequented by numerous visitors.'

Sidmouth: 'to its great attractions as a watering place is its present prosperity owing, the extent of which may be estimated by the circumstances of the population having increased more than 1,000 since 1821.' (Its population then approximately 3,000 – i.e., having risen by fifty per cent in ten years.)

Torquay: 'this place, about forty years since, was an insignificant fishing hamlet, but is now a fashionable and attractive watering place.'

Weston-super-Mare: 'has within the last few years more than doubled its population, from the construction of a bathing establishment at Knightstone, since which time it has become a fashionable and well-frequented watering place.'

Worthing: 'This fashionable and attractive watering place is comparatively of recent growth, having risen within a few years, from a small fishing village to its present size and importance.'

The repetition is effective: and these were all instances of rapid growth from small beginnings. There were plenty of other coastal towns, of the greatest antiquity and importance, which had desperately clambered on the bandwagon. Great Yarmouth built its theatre in 1778, and installed bathing machines; Plymouth added the Union Sea Baths in the 1820's to the attractions of its £50,000 theatre of 1811 and the library of 1812; Cowes brought in bathing machines, as did Ilfracombe, Lowestoft and Lyme Regis, ancient ports fallen into some decay; and Hastings, adapting to the changing role of the Cinque Ports, built a theatre, introduced horse-racing (in 1827), laid out terrace walks, and invested in the Pelham Baths. Weymouth, whose flagging fortunes began to revive as soon as Ralph Allen demonstrated his bathing-machine there in 1763, attracted the patronage of George III, who was a regular visitor from 1789 to 1805 (while his son was holding rival Court at Brighton). It grew into one resort with Melcombe Regis in the process of erecting theatre, assembly rooms, Belvedere, the Crescent, Gloucester Row, Royal Terrace, Chesterfield Place, York Buildings – a rapid speculative boom at the close of the century and shortly thereafter which has left it architecturally much richer than nearly any other resort save Brighton.

And there were of course some towns that came into prominence from nothing – not even the 'insignificant fishing hamlet' – resorts like Southport, New Brighton and Blackpool, Southend, St Leonards and Bournemouth. These were the new towns of the industrial revolution, just as much as the great manufacturing cities, or the mill villages. Their prosperity depended on the chain of speculators, expanding leisured class, and eventual flow of proletarian trippers, particularly by railway; and they no longer had any real connection with the cure, Society, or the Season – they invented their own Season, and have ever since attempted to prolong it with illuminations.

Southend, for example, began when the growing frequency of sea-bathing visitors from London caused a row of cottages, Pleasant Row, to be erected in 1767 in the Parish of Prittlewell. A plain red-brick terrace of two-storey cottages, it could have as easily been intended for the fishermen who sailed out of the estuary as for a nascent holiday industry. Shortly afterwards, the Ship Hotel and Marine Parade were built, and in 1791 a distinctly more adventurous row, Royal Terrace. In 1803 the Princess of Wales stayed at what was still the South End of Prittlewell – and by 1835 Lewis had spotted the exact reason for the town's rapid growth: 'being the nearest watering-place to London, [it] is rapidly rising into importance'.

Although the resort was well-established, and well supplied with both residential and resort accommodation by 1859, it was the investment of the London, Tilbury & Southend Railway in its future which finally converted it into the East End's riviera. Sir Morton Petre, with Brassey and the Lucas brothers, not only launched the railway, they invested in the town with the project for the Cliff Town. The population of the resort rose from about four thousand in 1859 to twenty thousand in 1901, and Southend is now, with Westcliff and Shoeburyness, the centre of a coastal conurbation of more than 150,000 – capable of entertaining six million visitors a season.

Brighton apart, Southend's competition, most particularly for the working class excursionists, came from Margate above all others; indeed, before the railway reached Southend and Brighton, Margate dominated this trade, thanks to the steam packets which ran from London to Margate from 1815 onwards (taking over the existing traffic of the sailing 'hoys'). In their first year they brought 23,500 visitors, and by 1830 they were ferrying one hundred thousand trippers a year. It was observed that 'the trade of the town is almost entirely connected with the resort of visitors'.

Bognor, although vaguely related to an existing village, Bersted, grew much more rationally – that is, intentionally – than Southend and Margate. It was descended upon in the 1780's by a wealthy Southwark hatter, Sir Richard Hotham, who had decided to found a spa. Hotham was not however sufficiently prescient: he attempted to found his Hothampton between Bersted and the sea, not really by the sea, and his ambitions for it were still too firmly rooted in the grandeur and style of Bath. Hothampton House and the Dome, in Hothampton Crescent, dating from the end of the 1780's, demonstrate the high standard of design – and of visitor – to which Sir Richard clung, as he spent some £60,000 attempting to found a resort for which there was no demand. Seaside Bognor did not begin to grow until the end of the War, in 1816, although *The Beauties of England & Wales* in 1813 observed that 'it consists of several rows of elegant brick structures, but so detached that the place is at least a mile in length, erected with the professed design of making Bognor the resort of more select company than is to be found at other bathing places.' But even the new building of the 1820's still conformed to this vague conviction of Bognor's social superiority and it never became a serious competitor for the mass traffic.

There was naturally some competition for the richer custom: it remained after all much more significant this early in the century. Sir Lawrence Palk acted as the philanthropic sponsor of Torquay, deliberately aimed at the villa market, as Richard Parsley took the lead in Weston-super-Mare. Sidmouth's bid for the primacy among aristocratic resorts, apparently succeeding when, in December 1819, it attracted the Duke and Duchess of Kent with their infant daughter, Victoria, whose health it was thought Sidmouth would improve, experienced a sharp set-back. In January, 1820, the Duke himself caught cold whilst admiring the view of Tor Bay, and died – in Sidmouth.

Not all this early development was in the South, round the arc of London: William Sutton, an inn-keeper of Churchtown in Lancashire, put up the first beach-hut (reputedly built of driftwood) at South Hawes, a sandy bathing-place near the fishing village of North Meols, in 1792. Known as 'The Duke's Folly', Sutton himself being 'The Duke', it had to be substantially extended in 1798, the year after a Mrs Walmsley had put up the first villa nearby, and at the party to celebrate this addition (The Sutton Hotel), the new resort was christened Southport. In 1805 a second hotel was built, and in 1807 Wellington Terrace, a row of houses largely intended for the accommodation of staff and servants, began what was to become Lord Street.

From the very beginning, Southport enjoyed one immense advantage: the land, with very little exception, has, throughout its growth, had to be leased from the Lords of the Manor, and the Lords responsible at the beginning of the 19th century, Madam Bold of Bold and her nephew, Bold Fleetwood Hesketh, imposed a firm control on development, forbidding factories, laying down street widths (they procured an Act of Parliament to ensure that Lord Street itself, the town's magnificent natural boulevard between the sand hills, be no less than eighty-eight yards wide), and effectively preventing the building of any 'courts and slums, every house, however small, having garden plots at front and back'. Southport today prides itself on being a Garden City, and the claim is not unreasonable. Its street-plan, a very flexible grid based on the long spine of Lord Street – Albert Road (which provides a level straight of a mile and a half), has plenty of room for parks, and for side-walk flower beds, and the resort is now of course distinguished for its six golf-courses. Although in early plan and appearance Southport was up to the æsthetic standards of Weymouth or Brighton, it managed always to attract trade from the working class of industrial Lancashire, brought by packet boat on the Leeds & Liverpool Canal to Scarisbrick Bridge at first, and, after 1848, on the Liverpool, Crosby & Southport Railway. Its population, 100 in 1809, was 4,766 by 1851, 10,097 by 1861.

Southport was very lucky, of course: Sutton was just an innkeeper with ambition, not a ruthless speculator, and the Lords of the Manor were incorruptible by easy profits. The plan that arose, and was endorsed by the private Act of 1825, represented an intelligent and tasteful response to a growing demand. By and large, resorts that ended up as pleasantly airy and healthy as Southport required firm direction from the start by committed promoters, if they were not to sink beneath a speculative jungle.

The southern equivalent of Southport is probably Bournemouth. Once again, it began with just one man building, and grew because of the interest of the traditional landowners. At the beginning of the 19th century, the resort of the district was Mudeford, east of Christchurch, which George III visited, and it was to Mudeford that Lewis Dymoke Grosvenor Tregonwell took his wife in 1810 to recover from the death of their infant son. Mrs Tregonwell, on an excursion they made to the mouth of the river Bourne, fell in love with the site (after the enclosure of 1802 Sir George Tapps had planted two hundred acres of pine woods on the East Cliff) and asked her husband to build a house there. Largely to humour her – he was 'anxious to do anything to distract her mind from Trouble' – Tregonwell bought land from Tapps, and had built there a mansion for themselves, which they stayed at for the first time on April 24, 1812.

The Tregonwells became the centre of a small colony, of servants (the Butler, Symes, had a cottage which is now Portman Lodge), relatives, friends, and invalids. Tregonwell, in the words of Dr Granville, Bournemouth's first historian in 1840, 'delighted with the sheltered situation, the genial temperature that prevailed here at all seasons, the magnificent seaward prospects and tranquil retirement that might be successfully sought, created a mansion which became his favourite residence surrounded with shrubberies and plantations. He also built an Inn by the side of the road, then little frequented, and a few cottages which were occasionally resorted to in the bathing season by invalids desirous of availing themselves of the advantages offered by the natural peculiarities of the spot'.

Nothing more than this took place until after the deaths of both Tregonwell (in 1834) and Sir George Tapps (in 1835); and it was the succession to the estate (which had retained control of all the sea-front) of Sir George Tapps-Gervis which produced the Bournemouth Plan. The new owner employed an architect, Mr Ferrey, to plan him a 'marine village of Bourne' on the east side of the river valley – Tregonwell's colony lay on the west. The theme of the plan was to be nothing but detached villas, each with its own grounds. Westover Villas were immediately proceeded with, the first being leased to Mr David Tuck at a ground-rent of £8 per annum. The social aspirations of the estate were made quite clear to Mr Tuck: not only must his house cost at least £500 to build – more than it cost to build semi-detached suburban houses in the 1930's, and five times the cost of a respectable cottage at the time – but he must pay 'one pound sterling as rent for the use of a pew'.

The Plan also included the Bath Hotel (1838), a Crescent, Baths, Library and Reading Room, and 'Greek, Italian, Elizabethan and Gothic villas to be erected along the cliff-front'. It was not carried out in its entirety, but the dominance of the estate was maintained after Sir George's death in 1842 by his Trustees, who joined Tunbridge and St Leonard's in hiring the services of Decimus Burton. Dr Granville had already reported on Bournemouth, which 'possesses so many capabilities of being made the very first invalid sea-watering place in England', and had sternly advised the landowners that 'you must not let in strangers and brick-and-mortar contractors, to build up whole streets of lodging-houses', and Burton's report for the Trustees in 1845 concurred. 'The wooded valley through which the Bourne rivulet flows to the sea is and must always constitute the principal object in the landscape . . . as a general principle in designing a building plan for Bournemouth, formality should be carefully avoided.' As a result, Bournemouth has always managed to maintain both its amenities (notably of course, the trees) and its tone, despite the vast increase in its traffic after the railway from the Midlands arrived in 1870 – not entirely to the satisfaction of all 2,000 of its inhabitants, one of whom declaimed:

'But let not Bournemouth, health's approved abode,
Court the near presence of the iron road.'

Of course, the prevailing spirit of Bournemouth is a long way from the metropolitan charm of Brighton, let alone the classic urbanity of Bath: it is the victory of the picturesque, of stockbroker villas, over the self-confident town. As such, and particularly because of the social pattern this imposes, it is a type of resort, not the type of the resort, and not one on whose general principles we can usefully draw save in very restricted cases. Much of the architecture is in itself delightful, but the whole, particularly now that it has spread to enclose Poole and become the dominant element in a solid line of middle-class resorts from Christchurch right round to the Swanage side of Poole Harbour, is unsatisfactory.

From the same period, but aimed at a much more vigorous clientele, is St

Louis Tregonwell, whose house at the mouth of the Bourne, built in 1811–12, founded the resort of Bourne Mouth.

Leonard's. Decimus Burton's work here stems from the fact that the estate on which the town arose was bought in 1828 by his father, Sir James Burton, the hugely successful London builder, who had the intention from the beginning of laying out a watering place on the lines of Brighton. Having learned from the experience of existing resorts, the Burtons provided the longest possible frontage on the sea, two-thirds of a mile, and broke up the villas and public buildings, in stuccoed brick, with liberal use of gardens. The speculation, which was what it was, although Decimus Burton actually built himself a house there, was not profitable, although the aim of attracting aristocratic residents was rapidly achieved (the widowed Duchess of Kent and the Princess Victoria took the villa at the West End of the Marina for the winter of 1835), and Dr Granville thought the Marina itself was surpassed only by the crescents of Bath and Bristol. Since the estate lay only a mile from Hastings, and the plan concentrated on developing the front to the utmost, St Leonard's rapidly grew into the older town, and in 1872 the two became a joint municipality. Sir James Burton died there in 1837, having lost much of his Bloomsbury fortune.

Apart from Southport in the North, there was Blackpool, which had grown from a 'bathing place' named after a boggy pool at the end of the hamlet, in 1730, to fifty houses by 1788. It really began to expand, by the usual organic and selfish methods, after the Railway arrived in 1846, to augment the influx of Manchester and Bolton trippers brought by the thrice-daily coach service introduced in 1825. And there was Whitley Bay, Scarborough, Whitby, but the parallel to St Leonard's was quite blatantly New Brighton. James Atherton, a Liverpool merchant, who had already made a great deal of money by speculative development in Everton, bought in 1830 an estate of 170 acres of sandhills and heath near Wallasey. On this flat stretch, handily opposite Liverpool but still as much a seaside as a Merseyside resort, he planned New Brighton.

[4]his 'PLAN for forming a new Watering Place at Leasowe Castle' was remarkably close to a modern Holiday Camp.

Wallasey itself had already begun to benefit from the holiday-making of Liverpool: Colonel Edward Cust had converted Leasowe Castle – sometimes known as Mockbeggar Hall – into an hotel,[4] and a large number of 'handsome houses and marine villas' had sprung up since the War. The site as a whole, which now includes Seacombe and Egremont as well as Wallasey and New Brighton, was eminently suitable for the new fashion: its front now boasts a four-mile Promenade, and those who grew bored with sea-bathing and horse-riding could always watch the wealth of Liverpool steaming by. At any rate, Atherton issued a prospectus in 1832 which explained in detail why there was an 'Eligible Investment at New Brighton, Cheshire'. 'As New Brighton is likely to become a favourite and fashionable Watering Place', it began, 'several Gentlemen have proposed to erect there a handsome Hotel, and a convenient Dock or Ferry to be called "The Royal Light House Hotel and Ferry", and to establish a communication by Steam packets between that place and Liverpool. The expense of this undertaking is estimated at £12,000, and it is intended to raise this sum in shares of £100 each . . .' The prospectus went on to promise 'at least 20 per cent' and to detail the advantages of the site: 'commands from all points the most interesting and extensive Views,' 'the most beautiful Beach, the Sands are hard and clean, free from Mud, Gravel or Quicksands'. And, no slight consideration at the mouth of the Mersey, 'the Tide never recedes more than 200 yards . . . prevents those disagreeable exhalations so common on other shores'. All in all, 'the proprietors intend to avail

The Liverpool Ferry "Sir John Moore", off New Brighton, 1836. The sandhills and still sparse building can be seen quite plainly in this painting by Samuel Walters.

themselves of the natural advantages . . . to erect all Villas on such sites that one shall not intercept the view of another . . . to erect a Church, Market Place, Shops and Buildings that will include a Reading Room, Baths, Billiard room, Post Office, etc., etc., and indeed nothing will be left undone to make it a most attractive and fashionable watering place.'

Seduced by such enthusiasm, it must have come as something of a shock to prospective settlers and investors when they left the Ferry and found that the cab required two horses to draw it up the steep incline of Victoria Road, as the sand came up to the axles; indeed, to see that all the north side of the road was sandhills, hopefully planted with shrubs to keep it from blowing away, and that the view from the first development, St George's Mount, was of nothing but sandhills to the sea. However, the undoubted pressure from Liverpool for bathing, and for detached villas, as Atherton had foreseen, overcame these deficiencies, and the site filled up steadily although the New Brighton Aquarium, Baths and Hotel Company, with its Salt Water Baths of 1881 and Variety entertainment from 1882, and the Pier Pavilion and Tower Theatre, of the 'nineties, did not complete the transformation from scattered villas to successful holiday-machine until the turn of the century.

New Brighton had its Ferry from the start (it only ran in the summer until the 1850's, when enough permanent residents had arrived to sustain commuter traffic), but the immense holiday-making potential of Lancashire people could not really be exploited until the railways had spread. When they did, they did not simply bring increased business to existing resorts, they created new ones. They brought North Wales within the reach of Lancashire, Lincoln close to the Yorkshire towns. Llandudno and Colwyn Bay, Mablethorpe, Cleethorpes and Skegness, were all the beneficiaries of the 'iron road' that Bournemouth so mistrusted – and which killed off the holiday traffic of Beaumaris.

Llandudno, noted before the 1840's only for 'gulls, razorbills, guillemots, cormorants, herons, falcons, puffins and copper mines', was already experiencing an increase of holiday traffic by 1849, the year the railway ran from Chester to Holyhead, but ten years before it extended to Llandudno itself. Accordingly, one of the most prominent landowners in the district, The Hon. E. M. L. Mostyn, drew up a plan for a new town on his Gloddaeth estate, and marked off the 179 lots of land he was prepared to sell. The next stage was to procure a private Act in 1854 which appointed Town Commissioners to carry out development, and inaugurated the period of actual building. The building plan stipulated that 'the town that is to be, shall resemble, as far as is practicable the "country", securing at the same time in the laying out of the various plots of ground order and uniformity'. What it meant was a garden suburb, on a grid scheme which is still perfectly clear. There were stringent regulations for street and pavement widths, house sizes, and 'no court or courts of houses will be permitted to be erected for habitation, no cellar shall be let as a distinct and separate habitation.' Since there was also firm zoning of larger and smaller house-lots, the shape of Llandudno was never susceptible to crude market pressure, and grew up on the now classic resort pattern, with maximised promenade, backed up by shopping district and shading off into residential building all round. It is not particularly distinguished for any one architectural feature, but it is a very good example of the inevitable compromise between Bournemouth and Brighton. Where New Brighton attempted to cling to the pure Bournemouth ideal – every house its own secluded sea-front villa – Llandudno manages to be a town while keeping open space and decent building intervals, although falling far short of the real urban standards of Brighton, which, on economic grounds, it could hardly justify.

Colwyn Bay is an even more extreme example of this 'opening up'. Where Llandudno had just existed, as a few cottages and two small Inns, in the 1830's, Colwyn Bay was still an empty tract of land, the Pwllcrochan Estate, on which were only Lady Erskine's mansion, and the Cursing Well of St Elian, to which angry pilgrims from all over North Wales used to come intent on fixing some dreadful penalty on their enemies. The entire Parish had only one hundred and seventy inhabitants in 1831. The Holyhead railway, however, in 1848, taking a direct line between the hills and the sea, went straight along the coast at Pwllcrochan, by Old Colwyn; and to this day, the antecedents of the town, like those of Skegness, are easily deduced from the placing of the Station, immediately behind the Promenade at the entrance to the Pier. The railway separates the town from its sea-front, in fact. The Estate and the Railway exercised mild discretion rather than conscious and determined planning, but the result, like that at Llandudno, was to produce a garden-resort, distinguished particularly for the well-wooded backdrop to the town provided by the 'dingles' and the Pwllcrochan Wood. The social character of both these towns may be guessed from the fact that, at the 1961 Census, both had more than twenty-five per cent of their population made up of those of pensionable age.

The railways did more than bring new life to sleepy villages, and new hope to ambitious landowners. In the case of Cleethorpes, for example, the railway virtually built a town to go with its station. In 1791, Lord Torrington described Cleethorpes as 'three miles of boggy turf to Grimsby', and it was still only a fishing hamlet with occasional visitors for bathing in the 1840's. The Manchester, Sheffield and Lincolnshire Railway changed all that: they bought large tracts around their rail-head, and built sea-wall, promenade, pier, and ornamental gardens. The town was really begun by the Station, which one might infer from the fact that it occupies a highly desirable site *on* the Promenade, completed in 1863; and the Railway Company's enthusiasm for their resort (apart from the excursion tickets they could sell, they used Cleethorpes as a rest and rehabilitation centre for their own employees) reached its peak in 1885, when they put up a sham ruin, their very own sea-front Folly, called Ross Castle after the then Secretary of the Company.

The Great Northern Railway wrought similar changes at Skegness, which Leland had reported as early as 1540 'clene consumid and eten up with the se', and which counted a population of just 185 in 1831, when the Southern Wash resort of Cromer had 1,232, a library, newsroom, and regular regatta.[5] Under the benevolent patronage of the railway, between 1873 and 1881 the hamlet

[5]Middle-class visitors from Nottingham stayed at the Georgian Inn at Frieston, although the prescient Byng in the 1790's had observed that 'if a good house was built here (Skegness), with a clever landlord, it would draw much company'.

was transformed. A grid plan for the main streets was drawn up, with a central circus, in the middle of which James Fowler was commissioned to build St Matthew's Church (Skegness lost its first Parish Church to the sea some time before Leland), and the order in which the main buildings opened is instructive: Station (1875), St Matthew's (1880), Pier, with glazed dome (1881), and Lumley Hotel in 1883.[6] Cleethorpes, incidentally, got its main civic building, the Council House, forty-one years after the Railway Station.

In fact, of course, almost any resort today, if it could re-plan itself for its main function, would like to bring railway line (and six-lane motorway) right into its heart from every major centre of population, so that one should hardly criticize the Railway Companies for doing just that with their own invented spas. It is one of the great principles of the resort, apart from maximisation of the sea-frontage, that it should be easily accessible to its market; and even today it is thought perfectly unremarkable that resorts spend large sums on posters at inland railway stations, although most of their patrons long ago switched to motor transport, and are hardly likely, in any case, to make a sudden impulse decision, whilst waiting for a local commuter train, to dash instead to the booking office for a ticket to sunny Clacton.

It is probably true to say that the process of travelling to the resort is indissolubly part of the entire magical quality of the seaside tradition, and naturally railways play a major part in this mythology, although paddle-steamers and charabancs (not motor-coaches – far too unromantic) are also involved in the glorious memories of excursions past. And if it was railways that made the seaside viable as a mass industry, it was the seaside that gave the working class somewhere to go, an objective within their purse, and within the range of a day's brief holiday. The seaside resort was the spa, and the riviera, of the poor; its Variety their theatre, its Pier their Casino, its promenade their boulevard, and its rise, by no coincidence, the period when the inland towns became too grim and authoritarian to tolerate the annual Fairs and semi-pagan Festivals of the poor.

Holiday towns can perhaps be divided into three types: classic Spa, where Society moves *en bloc* to lead a slightly less formal version of its London life – a broad group which would include Bath and Brighton, and towns where the better race-meetings, regattas, even agricultural shows, take place; picturesque retirement – towns as much like the country as possible, all separate villas, stucco and bougainvillea; and Fun City, the fairground by the sea. Naturally, many resorts combine elements of more than one type: Brighton is very much the first and the last, Southport the second and the last, Leamington and Cheltenham combine the first with elements of the second. What is unfortunately true is that the tendency since the middle of the 19th century, at the latest, has been away from the first alone – unfortunate merely because it is only the first that erects as an objective the creation of the rounded urban whole, as pleasant to look at and live in when the Season's past as when the noise and colour are at their height. One can visit Brighton in the winter, but there is something unbearably desolate and desperate about conventioneers at Blackpool when the mighty promenade is abandoned to the Irish sea. Fun City is as disastrous as Work City: both represent a breakdown of true civilisation.

[6] It is also relevant to note that the Nottingham half-day Saturday dates, like the Bank Holiday Act, from 1871, or just before.

Transport Towns

Towns and roads, towns and bridges, towns and rivers, have always gone together. The relationship between transport and trade, and between transport and administration, is of primary importance, and it is often impossible to judge whether a town exists to guard and supply the through-traffic on its road, or whether the road is there to feed the town. Is such a town the father or the child of its bridge? Is such another on the road, or is the road by it?

These are classical problems of urban history, posing the same kind of question as some fortified or castellar towns – is the castle protecting the town, or is the town there to supply the castle? Military priorities are usually rather easier to judge, however, and are often better recorded at the time than nice considerations of trade.

The delicacy of this symbiotic relationship of town, trade and traffic, pronounced for Roman, Anglo-Saxon, Norman and later mediæval foundations, becomes more blunt when we deal in coastal shipping. Inland fords and bridges, docks and jetties, can be either causes or effects; coastal ports, founded as such, have a plainer causal relation with the sea.

The simplicity lies in the obvious fact that the town followed the sea. Nothing bears this out more plainly than the history of Winchelsea, or of Hastings, Hythe or Hull. Boroughbridge followed the bridge, just as the Mersey Tunnel followed Liverpool and Birkenhead: but there must always remain a small doubt about London and the ford at Southwark, about innumerable settlements on the great North and Western roads where the road itself does not absolutely follow the path of greatest ease.

So far as new towns go, we could list dozens whose purpose and prosperity depend on the existing lines of communication; and certainly, if we cling to the coastal foundations, some of the very greatest ports are plantations – Portsmouth, Liverpool, Hull, Boston, King's Lynn, Harwich, North and South Shields, Falmouth, Devonport, Port Glasgow. Equally, if we take a list of notable failures among plantations, new towns that have sunk to hamlets or even disappeared, the ports include Ravenserodd, Skinburgh, Warenmouth, Wavermouth, Hedon, the Looes and Newton (Dorset). On the margin there would be Queenborough, Yarmouth (I.O.W.) and those ports whose prosperity now depends on holidays – Penzance, Poole, Weymouth and, indeed, most of the Cinque Ports, so many of which were foundations or re-foundations. None of these lists is exhaustive: ports and fishing harbours are the largest single class of British plantations, from Penzance and Milford Haven in the South and West to Ullapool and Pultneytown in the North. Generation after generation has had to occupy itself with building ports, not only to cope with the increasing demands of trade and population, but to stay abreast of the sea's unpredictability.

But ports, like towns at fords or bridges, are virtually traditional: the difference between Winchelsea and the new docks at Tilbury is only one of scale. Both had to be designed to accommodate the size of ship in common use, but that aside, they are merely coastal havens for ships sailing on the sea, or up the river. The beginnings of the commercial revolution in the 17th century revived the practice of town-building, and first of all, of port-building, with Falmouth, Whitehaven, Devonport and Port Glasgow, but it required the industrial revolution proper to produce two entirely new classes of transport town: towns we can firmly say came after the road, and not conjecturally before. The road was either a canal, or a railway, and a number of our most important modern towns, however muddled they may now appear, sprang up with sudden speed at the order of one man, or one company, less than two centuries ago.

Both canals and railways – in the sense of trucks running on fixed lines – antedated the Industrial Revolution, however generously one casts that imprecise event back into history. But if we concern ourselves strictly with the canal age and the railway age, the frenzied periods when every investor, every engineer, and many landowners, were devoting the greater part of their energies to the transport revolution, the phenomenon began in the middle of the 18th, and lasted until just beyond the middle of the 19th century.

The incentives for this transformation were innumerable, or at least, inextricable one from another. Certainly, an expansion of industrial production demands, and depends upon, an accelerating flow of raw materials in, and finished goods out; it also concentrates population in urban circumstances, simultaneously denying them land and the freedom to dispose of their own time – rendering them dependent on produce for the market, which again requires transport. The greater the complexity of economic society, the greater its sensitivity to national and international policies, the more pronounced and polarised the political and social differences, the more the government needs rapid transport for its writ, and its troops.

All these factors, like the internal pressures – that is, the steady accumulation of both capital and the joint-stock habit which took place, producing for the projector and the inventor a seller's market – were at work on the traditional methods as well. The first beneficiary of the commercial revolution of the 16th and 17th centuries was sea-transport, both deep-water and coastal; the second, the roads and road-vehicles. From our standpoint, these changes influenced the foundation of a number of towns: Sir John Lowther began the great expansion of Whitehaven on his estate in the 1660's not only as a coaling port for his own mines, but as a shipbuilding port and a general carrier's port. By 1690, its population had grown from about 200, round the pier built by Sir John's father, to over 2,200; by 1730, to 6,000; and at its peak as a port, in the period around 1770, to about 9,000.

Commercially, the foundation (for it can be counted as such, since what went before was so minute) was a great success. From the very beginning it provoked the hostility of Newcastle, upon whose London coal-trade it encroached, and at its 18th century height, the Port of Whitehaven (which included Workington, Maryport, Harrington and Parton) ranked second only to London in tonnage cleared – handling well over twice as much as Liverpool, Newcastle or Bristol. Its prosperity rested largely on its own fleet, which was around 200 strong (excluding the neighbouring villages) at its peak.

Indeed, Whitehaven only began to slip back from its status as the third largest town in the North (after Newcastle and York) and the second largest port by volume in the country, in the 19th century as Liverpool's great

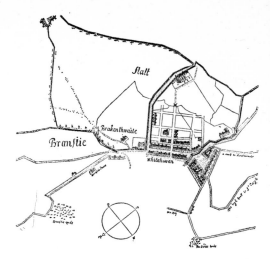

Whitehaven – c.1693. Sir John Lowther's grid stands out clearly, although it was not yet fully built up.

industrial hinterland was developed – and Cumberland remained a rural county of obstructive fells and poor roads.

The plan laid down by Sir John Lowther was a regular grid, with one oblong block left free for a Church, squeezed into the shallow valley leading down to the harbour. Sir John had obtained from Charles II at the Restoration a grant of the lands of the monastery (long-dissolved) of St Bees, which augmented the family holdings in the area substantially, not least in terms of coal, and had also secured the right of the town (before it existed as such) to a market and a fair. His zeal for the project was well-founded in personal advantage, but he nevertheless brought to it the progressive paternalism one might expect of a friend of Wren, member of the Royal Society, and tolerator of dissent. He specified the sort of houses to be built on his new, wide streets: 'to be of three storeys high, not less than 28 feet from the level of the street to the square of the side walls, the windows of the first and second storeys to be transomed, and the same, together with the doors, to be of hewn stone.' Sir John also made provision for gardens, and a later Lowther, Sir James, first Earl of Lonsdale, who re-united Lowthers of Lowther and Lowthers of Whitehaven, engaged in extensive redevelopment in the 1760's, again to splendid standards. Even so, the success of the foundation militated against its remaining gracious, airy and attractive: the gardens were built over, the spaces filled in, and the broad sweep of the grid was obscured under a rash of predestined slums, so that by the middle of the 19th century a visitor could

Whitehaven, 1738. The grid has obviously begun to fill up, but the Church still enjoys its island site, and there are good gardens. If anything, Matthias Read has under-represented the ship traffic of the Port by this time.

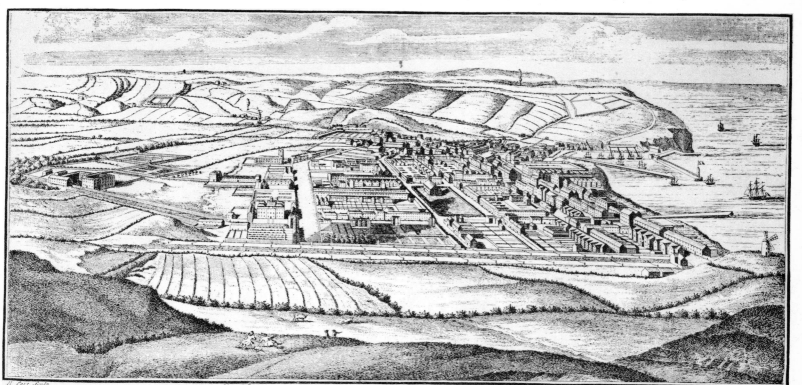

R. Parr Sculp.

To the Honble Sr JAMES LOWTHER BAR.^t F.R.S. & Knight of the Shire for the County of CUMBERLAND this East Prospect of the Town and Harbour of WHITEHAVEN is humbly Inscribed.

write: 'Houses, shops, jerry shops, courts, public houses, everything you come on speaks plainly of overcrowding. Sallow looking women, covered with rags, thrust their heads and half their bodies through the windows to look after you, and as they do this, they appear to gasp for fresh air.'

Whitehaven seems to have influenced its neighbours strongly. Its grid pattern was imitated in the middle of the 18th century when Humphrey Senhouse decided that his coal-mines could also do with their own port, and founded Maryport (his wife's name was Mary). The new section of Workington, laid out in 1775, centred on Portland Square, has a similar grid, and Dr Graham of Netherby Hall laid out both Longtown and the harbour at Sarkfoot on Whitehaven lines.

In the same group with Whitehaven we could class the very first post-mediæval foundation in England – since Queenborough in 1368 – Falmouth. Sir John Killigrew's new port of 1613, near the cottage called Penny-come-Quick, was understandably petitioned against by Penryn, Helston and Truro, whose trade and eminence it stole away. There had been an earlier, abortive, Elizabethan scheme for a 'new Dover' which was equally inspired by the expanding maritime trade, and, contemporaneously with Whitehaven, old Deal had New or Lower Deal added to it. At the end of the 18th century, for the same commercial reasons, Sir William Hamilton procured an Act of Parliament to enable him, 'his heirs and assigns to make and provide Quays, Docks and Piers and other erections' at what became Milford Haven. Hamilton, whose nautical interests were unusually catholic, delegated the project to Charles Francis Greville, and Greville hired Louis Barallier of Toulon – one of Europe's greatest naval bases – to design the town: this in 1790, after the Revolution but still, obviously, before the outbreak of the Revolutionary Wars.

Barallier planned the town as a simple grid with three main parallel streets, intersected by regular subsidiaries at right-angles. The main streets began life as Front, Middle, and Back Streets, became First, Second and Third, and were decently antiqued into Hamilton Terrace, Charles Street and Robert Street in the middle of the 19th century. Toulon itself was of course equally disciplined and gridded, the product of fortification by both Henri de Navarre and Vauban.

There are many other ports which began in this period of sustained commercial growth: Amlwch, the port for the great Anglesey copper mines, with its attendant housing for the miners; Helensburgh, named after the wife of Sir James Colquhoun, the owner of the land, was planted in 1776 at the mouth of the Gareloch to share the Clyde trade – and its first Provost, Henry Bell, used its jetty for the trials of his steamship, the Comet, which began the steam age on European waters in 1812; Ardrossan, Aberaeron, Portmadoc – town-founders' enthusiasm for the coast, always high, was most intense in the 18th and 19th centuries. The coast bears ample evidence of the commercial expansion of British merchants, and of the naval expansion which that so intimately affected. Milford, for example, became a Naval dockyard almost as soon as it was founded, with general trade, and the Waterford Packet, in view – it only lost the dockyard to Pembroke at the close of the wars. Straightforward road transport also expanded, but its architectural impact on the countryside is naturally much less pronounced. Roads, and vehicles to travel upon the roads, were vastly improved, but the object of the exercise was to improve connections between existing towns, rather than to create new ones, nor did it require new ones to be built for it to be carried out. Turnpikes leave tollhouses, not towns; new roads encourage the growth of existing settlements – as the Holyhead road revivified Bangor – or strangulate old ones. As it happens, the Holyhead Road did arguably produce one new town, the little settlement of Menai Bridge, on the Anglesey side of Telford's bridge of 1826, but it can hardly be called a conscious plantation or expansion.

In Scotland, there is no doubt that the immense road-building schemes of the 18th century made possible much urban development and in places was closely associated with new foundations – Fort George (Ardersier), Fort William, Fort Augustus – but there is equally no doubt that one should class much of that Vauban-esque plantation with the bastides of Wales rather than with the commercial building of the modern age. And in any case, it is all too easy to exaggerate the importance of those military roads. After Boswell and Johnson had travelled the Army road from Fort Augustus to Bernera, in 1773, it sank gradually back into the heather, used neither by conquerors nor the dwindling number of inhabitants, the Seaforths having sold their land to one Hugh Innes, who pursued a clearance policy undeterred by any inbred guilt or loyalty.

Canals, like roads, were built to link existing towns; but unlike roads, they need more than occasional bridges or toll-booths to support them. If they are to take anything like the shortest (or flattest) route, they need locks, basins at intersections, and provision for the feeding of both men and horses on towpaths that may not pass near existing inns, stores or stables. They also need barges, which must be fashioned by carpenters and smiths beside the water (one could hardly move a narrow-boat cross-country on the poor roads and worse carts of the 18th century) and maintained whilst in the water. And the use of canals naturally encourages new commercial and industrial development beside the waterway. Once one builds canals, one must also build terminals and docks. In fact, the great canal age inevitably·produced canal towns.

The age itself, and thus the towns, owed a great deal to Elizabeth, Duchess of Hamilton, Duchess of Argyll, almost Duchess of Bridgewater, and mother of four Dukes. One of the beautiful, if wilful, Gunning sisters, who invaded London society in 1751 (they were poor, Irish, in their teens, and so rapidly famed for their looks that on one occasion their presence at an Inn attracted a crowd of seven hundred admirers) Elizabeth was courted, after her first two Ducal husbands had died, by Francis Egerton, 3rd Duke of Bridgewater. He had graduated from being 'ignorant, awkward and unruly' at seventeen, via the Grand Tour, to being distinctly dissolute and pig-headed at twenty-three. Despite his own experience of debauchery, and lack of grace (or perhaps because of it), his proposal to Elizabeth stipulated that she break off with her sister, Lady Coventry, on the grounds that Lady Coventry's reputation, though based more on tactless idiocy than wickedness, was too scandalous for the Duke. Elizabeth refused to abandon her sister, and so the Duke stormed back from London to his estate at Worsley, near Manchester, to devote himself to its development, and to the cultivation of a life-long misogyny. All in all, the 3rd Duke of Bridgewater is a prize specimen of the bizarre peer: looking rather like the King, George III, he talked very little save of his passion for canals, never wrote a letter when he could avoid it, and when on his return from a visit to London he discovered that some flowers had been planted in his gardens, gave vent to his loathing of the merely decorative by whipping off their heads.

One of the prime resources of the Duke's estate was its coal-mines; and when he withdrew to it in 1758, he began immediately to consider a canal to carry his coal into Manchester. The normal method of transport at the time, as it had been for centuries, was on horse-back. The roads precluded heavy carts, and the householders of Manchester inevitably paid very dearly for their coal. Transport alone cost – for less than seven miles from Worsley – nine to ten shillings a ton. The Duke proposed to build a canal from the mine to Salford, but the engineer that he had engaged to build it, James Brindley, persuaded him instead to aim for Manchester itself – which meant carrying the canal by aqueduct across the River Irwell at Barton. The idea was sufficiently astonishing for the Duke to become instantly converted, not only to the scheme, but to its originator. The first canal in England to be entirely independent of a natural stream was also to be the first with such a flight of engineering brilliance.

Brindley was if anything more eccentric than his patron: the son of a Derbyshire crofter, he had been apprenticed to a millwright, struck off on his own in Leek, and experimented with a variety of water and steam powered mills. Bridgewater met him when he was working as a surveyor on the proposed canal to link the Trent and Mersey – the nearest Brindley had been to a canal, and a task for which he had been hired on the strength of his familiarity with mills – and the disgruntled Duke promptly employed the untrained engineer, largely on the grounds that both were fanatics for the idea of canals. Brindley, who was forty-two at the time, had had an even worse education than the Duke: according to the Dictionary of National Biography, 'he remained to the last illiterate, hardly able to write and quite unable to spell. He did most of his work in his head, without written calculations or drawings, and when he had a puzzling bit of work he would go to bed and think it out.' Samuel Smiles confirmed the peculiarity of Brindley's working methods in *Lives of the Engineers*: 'he has been known to be there (in bed) one, two or three days till he had attained the object in view. He would then get up and execute his design without any drawing or model. Indeed, it was never his custom to make either, unless he was obliged to do it to satisfy his employers.' Brindley's own note-books, masterpieces of taciturnity, occasionally interrupt the grudging outline of events with 'lay in bed'.

This exotic couple, neither of whom would of course now be permitted within a thousand miles of any engineering project, successfully built the Worsley-Manchester Canal, with its splendid aqueduct, in two years; it ran directly from the underground seams to Manchester, and promptly halved the price of coal in Manchester. Their enthusiasm vindicated in the market-place, Brindley and Bridgewater embarked on innumerable other canal projects: linking Manchester to the Mersey estuary, the Trent to the Mersey, and all the other feeders that went with that Grand Trunk – Stafford and Worcestershire, Coventry and Oxford, Birmingham and Wolverhampton. The frenzy was such, and Brindley's reputation so high, that Josiah Wedgwood wrote 'I think Mr Brindley, the great, the fortunate, money-getting Brindley, an object of pity and a real sufferer for the good of the public. He may get a few thousands, but what does he give in exchange? His health, and I fear, his life too.' Wedgwood's concern for any proven money-getter is no surprise, he wanted cheap Cornish clay to reach his potteries via the Mersey-Trent canal, but in fact Brindley did die, in 1772 at the age of fifty-six, worn out from over-work.

Before then, of course, the canals had begun to provoke the building boom which we have seen that both their own needs, and their novel routes, implied. Wedgwood's zeal for the canals went hand in hand with his plans to build a magnificent new works at Etruria, by the canal – indeed, with a canal feeder cut right into his factory yard – and every canal was naturally associated with similar projects. But the most significant piece of building was directly under the control of Brindley; as well as being the father of the canals, he is the father of the only town founded wholly to meet the needs of a canal, Stourport. Other towns, pre-eminently the small hamlet of Goole, transformed by the Aire and Calder Navigation Co., were immensely altered by the canals, but only Stourport can be called a completely new foundation.

'About 1766' wrote the local historian of Bewdley in Worcestershire, 'where the river Stour empties itself into the Severn below Milton, stood a little alehouse called Stourmouth. Near this Brindley has caused a town to be erected, made a port and dockyards, built a new and elegant bridge, established markets and made it the wonder not only of this county, but of the nation at large. In the year 1795 it consisted of 250 houses and about 1300 inhabitants. Thus was the sandy barren common at Stourport converted, in the space of thirty years, into a flourishing, healthy and very populous village'.

The people of Bewdley itself had contributed to this wonder of the nation: they declined to have Brindley's 'stinking ditch' at Wribbenhall, so the Staffordshire and Worcester Canal, on its way from the Trent to the Severn, was dug to join the latter close to where the Stour already emptied itself. Begun in 1765 and finished in 1771, the canal largely contributed to the decline in relative importance of Bewdley – now rather less than half the size of Stourport.

Although Bridgewater, who was involved in the project, had a reputation for mild philanthropy amongst his miners – building cottages, shops and markets for them, and encouraging sick clubs – there seems little or no evidence to suggest that the Canal company deliberated very long about the kind of town they were building. In the first instance, the land surrounding the basin became merely a camping and shanty site for the construction gangs, and as the work neared completion, houses for permanent employees, warehouses, barge sheds, seem to have gone up according to need rather than according to rigid master-plan. The result is that the street-plan of the centre does not suggest a new foundation at all, and follows existing roads, contours, and the canal itself.

Stourport: across this canal bridge, the Anglican inhabitants of the town had to walk to worship at Lower Mitton Church, now completely razed, before the building of a Stourport Parish Church in the 19th century.

Stourport: the last lock before the canal joins the Severn. On the right, the long, low shape of a barge-shed.

While the buildings, having been erected at a time when many existing country towns were indulging in rebuilding, merely suggest that Stourport was prosperous, and tasteful enough to indulge in lots of charming country-palladian, assembled by the local builders from the fashionable style-books of the 18th century. In fact, the only incontrovertible visual proof of the town's

Stourport: another lock to Stourport Basin, seen from the Severn side.

The Duke of Bridgewater's Navigable Canal. Made in 1766, this plan clearly shows the rapid expansion of the system after Brindley completed the initial stretch from Worsley (top right-hand by the title) to Manchester. The famous aqueduct over the Irwell is illustrated, top left.

plantation origins lie in the placing of canal and basin in relation to what are clearly the traditional main streets; no canal company would have paid the price for so much freehold in the centre of an existing town, and on that basis, it is evident which came first.

There are many pretty Georgian houses, and groups of houses, in the

[107]

AVERAGE RATES OF FREIGHTS, UPON THE CANALS.

		d.	
Goods perishable,	—	3	per Ton
Goods not perishable,	—	2½	per Mile.

UPON HIS GRACE THE DUKE OF BRIDGWATER'S CANAL.

	s.	d.	
From Preston to Stockton Quay, near Warrington,	2	6	per Ton.
From Preston to Manchester,	5	0	

UPON RIVER NAVIGATIONS.

	s.	d.	
From Shardlow to Gainsbro',	10	0	per Ton.
From Stourport to Bristol,	10	0	
From Preston to Liverpool,	3	4	

F I N I S.

Left

The Duke of Bridgewater at the age of 31 in 1767 – the bridge over the Irwell at his left hand.

Right

Average rates of freights upon the canals: although many canals were to abuse their monopoly position to exact massive profits (thus making life easier for their railway rivals at the beginning of the conflict), this shows how cheap the canals could be compared with the old pack-horse and wagon rates – which could easily reach ten shillings a ton-mile.

[106]

STAFFORDSHIRE AND WORCESTERSHIRE CANAL.

Nº								
	Haywood, the Junction with the Canal from the Trent to the [Mersey.							
29	5							Radford Bridge, near Stafford.
30	10	5						Penkridge.
31	12½	7½	2½					Gailey Bridge.
32	18	13	8	5½				Crofs Green.
33	21½	16½	11½	8½	3½			Junction with the Birmingham Canal.
34	23½	18½	13½	10½	5½	2		Compton Wharf.
35	28½	23½	18½	15½	10½	7	5	Gigetty Wharf.
36	31½	26½	21½	18½	13½	10	8	3	Green Forge.
37	34½	29½	24½	21½	16½	13	11	6	3	Stewpony Wharf.
38	42½	37½	32½	29½	24½	20½	18½	13½	10½	7½	Kidderminster.
39	46½	41½	36½	33½	28½	25	23	18	15	12	4½	Stourport, [the Junction with the River Severn.

BIRMINGHAM CANAL.

Nº							
	Autherly, the Junction with the Staffordshire and Worcestershire Canal.						
40	2						Price's Wharf, Wolverhampton.
41	8½	6½					Gofpel Oak.
42	11½	9½	3				Tipton Green.
43	12½	10½	4	1			Dudley Road.
44	14	12	5½	2½	1½		Brad's Wharf.
45	16	14	7½	4½	3½	2	Spon Lane.
46	22½	20½	14½	11½	10½	8½	6½	Birmingham [Wharf.

Left

A Plan of the Navigable Canals Intended to be made: reaching from Liverpool to Bristol, this was the spine of the Grand Trunk Canal – and, on this proposed plan of 1766, there is only Lower Mitton at the junction with the Severn, not Stourport.

Right

Tables of distance between quays enabled canal customers to work out in advance both the cost, and the likely duration, of any given delivery.

Stourport: the Basin, with, on the left, the rear of the Tontine Hotel, built by the Canal Company before 1776, and, on the right, the early 19th century warehouse. The Severn runs beyond the Inn.

Stourport: the Basin from the Tontine, looking towards the town.

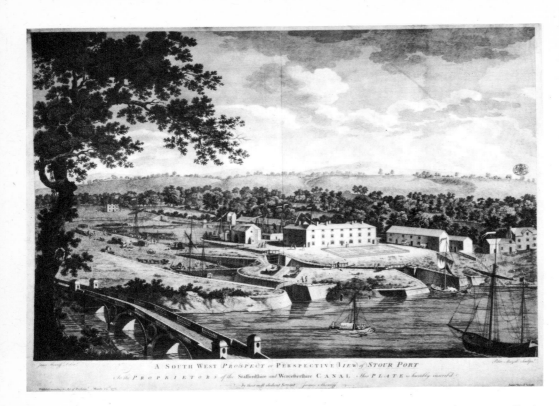

A SOUTH WEST PROSPECT or PERSPECTIVE VIEW of STOUR PORT
To the PROPRIETORS of the Staffordshire and Worcestershire CANAL, this PLATE is humbly inscribed

*Stourport: A South-West Prospect of 1776.
Apart from Basin and locks, there is only the
Tontine, the new Bridge, sundry warehouses,
and stables.*

winding and curving streets that slope down towards the water, but very little
sign of any organised estate-building. Even the town's essential civil facilities –
Churches, Town Hall, Inns – seem to have concerned the Company, let alone
the busy Brindley, very little. The Tontine Inn, beside the water, was put up
by the Company, as an essential; but the new bridge was not built until 1775,
after Brindley's death, and was in any case swept away by flood in 1794. For
religious purposes, new Stourport was happily left to the care of old Lower
Mitton. The Parish Church there now is by George Gilbert Scott, *circa* 1875,
long after the canal boom. Wesley went there twice on his endless peregrina-
tions. He noted in 1788 a 'small well-built village,' and in 1790 that it was 'twice
as large as two years ago.' The religious character of the Stourport people, who
were after all a classic example of the uprooted generation, upset Wesley: 'They
seemed to be serious and attentive while I was speaking, but the moment I
ceased, fourscore or a hundred of them began talking all at once. I do not
remember ever to have been present at such a scene before. This must be
amended, otherwise (if I should live) I will see Stourport no more.' He didn't,
dying in the following March, but there is some indication that they did,
embracing Methodism with all that distasteful enthusiasm which it seemed to
evoke so often amongst the labouring classes. Nonconformity in Stourport can
claim to be distinctly senior to the established Church.

   The curious lack of all the common signs of foundation – no grid, no vistas,
no unified style or placing of either houses or important buildings, no evidence
of social meddling – might be taken to represent the unconcern of busy men
(and a vindication of laissez-faire in architecture), or a masterpiece of self-

Opposite page
Stourport.

Upper left
Lichfield Street.

Upper right
Mart Lane.

Lower left
Mitton Street.

Lower right
9 Mitton Street, doors.

Opposite page
Stourport.

Upper left
Lichfield Street, courtyard and pump.

Upper right
Foundry Street.

Lower left
New Street.

Lower right
Mitton Street.

effacing pastiche of an organic town. By the time, fifty years later, that another Canal company found it necessary to create a town, round the diminutive township of Goole, the interfering hand of the planner had once more asserted itself. The Aire and Calder Navigation Company wanted a new port on the Yorkshire Ouse for just the same reason that the Stockton and Darlington Railway were to find they needed a new port on the Tees, and for the same reason ultimately that Bridgewater hired Brindley: to move coal more efficiently. The port at Selby was too far up-river for the increasing flow of South Yorkshire coal, and the 'want of docks suitable to the reception of Brigs had been much complained of', so the Canal company employed George Leather, in 1819, to survey a route for a new canal from Knottingley to Goole.

Stourport: off Mitton Street.

John Rennie was appointed to do the planning of the work, both canal and terminal, but when he died in 1821 Leather took over everything. The Company had recognised that they would need to build more than docks and warehouses, and bought an estate at the mouth of Vermuyden's Dutch River, opposite the handful of houses where the three hundred or so existing inhabitants of Goole lived. In August 1822 Leather was told to plan the streets for this estate, and in December, a five-man Building Committee was appointed. Their principal task was to get the great new port built, but they were expected in addition to provide homes for the influx of merchants and managers, navvies and dockers. For the middle-classes, the Committee ordered terraces of three-storey brick town-houses, like those surviving in Aire Street, and for the humbler orders, two-storey brick cottages, like those of Ouse Street. They had twenty-one houses built by 1826, when the brand new canal and harbour was opened with conviviality lasting until 'a late hour of the night' on July 20th, and the rate rose rapidly once labour and materials were liberated from the harbour works: 156 houses by 1828, and by 1829, proper housing for the thousand people who now lived in new Goole. There was no need for a Town Hall, since the Company administered its town through the same employees who ran the docks, and for entertainment and enlightenment, the Company presumably took the view that no man could want more than to be allowed to see the awesome sight of the whole of Goole basin being used as a lock – the water-level being lowered to meet that of the rising tide outside the gates. The works and town were built by Jolliffe & Banks, the civil engineers

Stourport: looking North along the canal, Lion Hill on the right.

Goole: entrance to Goole Basin, 1831.

who had built Waterloo, Southwark and London bridges, and Mr Banks gave his own name to the most imposing building in the town, the handsome hotel sited conveniently at the harbour end of Aire Street. Banks Hotel became, when Mr Banks died in 1835, the Lowther, after the former Chairman of the Company, Sir John Lowther. It is still there, fading, but markedly more proud

Goole: the Lowther Hotel, Aire Street, from the quay.

and grand than the younger buildings between it and the railway station.

Goole is far more the company town of the great industrialisation than was Stourport, and far more obviously planted (modern Goole can hardly be denied plantation status, despite the antiquity of its name; much of it rests on top of layers of alluvial warp deliberately deposited via controlled flooding at Leather's orders in 1823), but this sample of two precludes any generalisation about canal towns, save that they were originally focused on the basin, their houses faced the water, and their streets ran down to the water's edge. In other words, the canal is treated in precisely the same way as abbey, market square, great house or traditional harbour.

Canals themselves, of course, were not in the long run successful, and neither Stourport nor Goole has been able to survive without diversification. Both were also forced to permit the railway to penetrate close to their quays, bringing the illusion of extra traffic and the certainty of eventual slump. And, from our viewpoint, customarily wrecking the balance of each town it reached, planned or not, with its divisive lines, and commercially seductive station.

Every reason that one might adduce for building following the canals must be multiplied time and time again for the phenomenon of the railway boom. Apart from the fact that the mere arrival of the railway normally incited growth in any town (just as to be by-passed meant stagnation), the railways required vast new junctions and workshops, and the demands and incentives of the railways caused coal, iron, steel, engineering, docks and shipping, ship-building and food production, every kind of manufacture, service and distributive trade to grow. In 1846, for example, with about 2,000 miles of railway under construction (on top of the 2,500 or so already built), it was thought that there were over a quarter of a million men employed directly in construction or operation of railways – out of a population of only nineteen million – and that their wages came to two per cent of the entire national income. That consumer spending power, in common with dividends and the £150 million that the Companies raised in capital between 1846 and 1850, and used to equip their lines (with, for example, about two million tons of iron rails in 1847), helped transform the country and its people.

Very few towns of any size do not bear the marks of change induced by the railways, quite directly; and fewer still, if any, show no signs of their indirect influence. But we need not discuss even such as Doncaster and Darlington, ancient towns wholly swallowed by the railway companies, let alone the railway impact on York or Carlisle or Northampton. There is no need to discuss the railways' role in the history of our towns in terms of suburbs, changing use-zones and commercial foci. The railway companies built enough towns from scratch to be judged by their completed performance.

Middlesbrough and Crewe, Swindon and Wolverton, Eastleigh and Barrow-in-Furness were all the feudal plantations of a new aristocracy; the railways even created their own seaside, the better to run excursions – Skegness, Cleethorpes, Mablethorpe. They bought canals, as often to obliterate the competition as to rationalise their combined operations, bought and built docks and quays. The Manchester, Sheffield & Lincolnshire Railway deliber-ately revived the faltering port of Grimsby to such effect that the rival rail and canal companies of Goole had together to subsidise Goole's shipping to fight off the Grimsby competition. The towns the railways smiled upon seem quite arbitrary in some cases; Rhyl, Colwyn Bay and Llandudno, like Skegness, are resorts made by the railways, and Beaumaris and Freeston Shore, ones brought to their knees by railway disinterest.

The boom did not wait for the Liverpool & Manchester's Rainhill trials of 1829 to get under way: railways can, and did, exist without steam locomotives, and in any case, the first company to be authorised to use them, the Stockton & Darlington in 1825, had expressed itself unimpressed by their profit-making potential. Even on a line carrying nothing but Durham coal from the pit-head, they had found it impossible to reduce running costs by more than thirty per cent of the horse-drawn figure, and were understandably gloomy about the general application – on lines less favourably placed for fuel – of the principle. But, with heavier wagons running on the improved wrought-iron rail (edged rather than flanged, wrought rather than cast, Birkinshaw's rail of 1820 could cope with greater weight of traffic, and be made in longer sections, than its brittle predecessor) no matter if they were drawn by horse or stationary engine, the growing trade of the country could be tempted off the canals and roads and on to the railways. And so it is that the very first town founded by a railway company was begun before the Rainhill trials, and begun by a company which was still using horses when the first service to its new town was introduced. It is a very special example of the town-building of the 19th century, and one which changed its function within a generation of its birth, but it deserves close

Plan of the Collieries on the Rivers Tyne and Wear, 1788. From this sketch, it seems clear that an ordinary pit in the North-East was using horse-drawn railway wagons, steam power for draining the workings, flat barges at staithes equipped with chutes, and was obviously ready for any and every innovation.

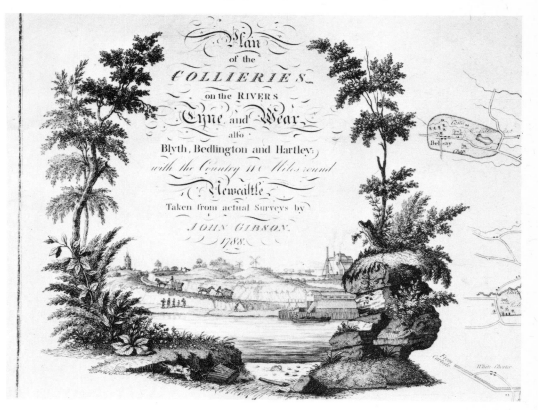

examination. It fascinated the Victorians, and has since then fascinated historians; it was appropriately described as 'a specimen of town manufacture of which neither Old World or New affords a parallel . . . the great type of the Iron Age'.

Gladstone called it an infant – 'an infant Hercules'. The Victorians in general, with their amazing capacity for self-congratulation, rhapsodized about this awesome offspring of their generation. Its neighbourhood 'rich as the mines of Golconda in subterranean wealth', the giant's growth, according to its own Official Guide, 'was unregulated, haphazard and aggressively utilitarian'. For visitors to England in the later 19th century, Middlesbrough was a more important sight than any cathedral: most nations had cathedrals, but only the English had this monstrous vision of the industrial future.

When Gladstone came to honour it, in 1862, Middlesbrough had a population of about twenty thousand. By 1891 it had reached 75,532, and in 1968 its expansion finally overwhelmed the older neighbours to its flanks and embraced them all in one great County Borough of Tees-side – in which, whatever Stockton may pretend, the dominating partner is the adult Hercules.

Dobbin's sketch of the opening of the Stockton-Darlington Railway, 1825. The great majority of the guests are plainly riding in coal-wagons, and despite the magnificent new Stephenson locomotive, there is apparently a horse ahead of it, against the eventuality of break-down.

But Gladstone's comments were not just remarkably perceptive of the future – they were occasioned by the events of the recent past. Writing in 1801, a local historian of the Cleveland district casually remarked that 'in the Northern extremity of the parish [Acklam] lies the township or Chapelry of Middlesbrough, which consists only of four farm houses'. In 1821, there appears to have been only one left. There is no reason to suppose that this site on the southern bank of the Tees, close enough to Stockton for the market, but too remote to be engrossed by any normal suburban growth, would to this day have had more than a family or two of farmers, had it not been for Joseph Pease.

Joseph Pease had, at the age of twenty-one, been involved with his father in the foundation of a tramway from Darlington to Stockton. It opened in 1821, exclusively for the hauling of coal from the Durham pits to the Tees, using horse-drawn wagons on its sunken lines. That same year, an engineer called George Stephenson introduced himself to the wealthy Quaker entrepreneur, Edward Pease, and persuaded him of the potential advantages of steam locomotion, and the obvious superiority of raised railway over recessed tramway. Pease put up the capital with which Stephenson repaired to Newcastle to begin constructing locomotives, and both Peases set about organising the Stockton & Darlington Railway. The Company was exclusively Quaker, and their line was commonly known as the Quakers' line.

The Stockton & Darlington began business, as we have seen, in 1825, with authority to try out steam locomotion – but with perfectly practical expectations of the Durham coal trade, steam or horse-drawn. In 1826, Joseph Pease forecast that the export of coal from Tees-side might be expected to run at ten thousand tons a year; but his partners readily agreed that the export would be infinitely aided if the Railway could find suitable deep-water staiths, instead of using the shallow water of Stockton, too far up-river for easy navigation by large boats.

Joseph Pease took upon himself the search for another site, further down the river, and in 1828 he settled upon one: Port Darlington, as it was proposed to christen the Railway's new dockside terminus, should be six miles down the Tees from Stockton (which as an ancient town did not take kindly to this perfidious scheme on the part of the Railway) in the Chapelry of Middlesbrough.

As Pease related in his diary, he 'sailed up to Middlesbrough' (then notable merely for its farmhouse and the vanished priory of Whitby Abbey which had flourished there six centuries before) 'to take a view of the proposed termination of the contemplated extension of the railway' and was 'much pleased'. 'Its adaptation to the purpose far exceeded any anticipations I had formed. Imagination here has very ample scope in fancying a coming day when the bare fields we then were traversing will be covered with a busy multitude, and numerous vessels crowding to these banks denote the busy Seaport.' For, of course, prescient as he was, Pease's plan for Middlesbrough was based on the existing coal trade, and could not anticipate the even greater transformation that was to be wrought by the ironmasters in the 'fifties.

Having seen and approved the site, Pease formed a company with his father, two Norwich bankers, Simon Martin and Henry Birkbeck, a Saffron

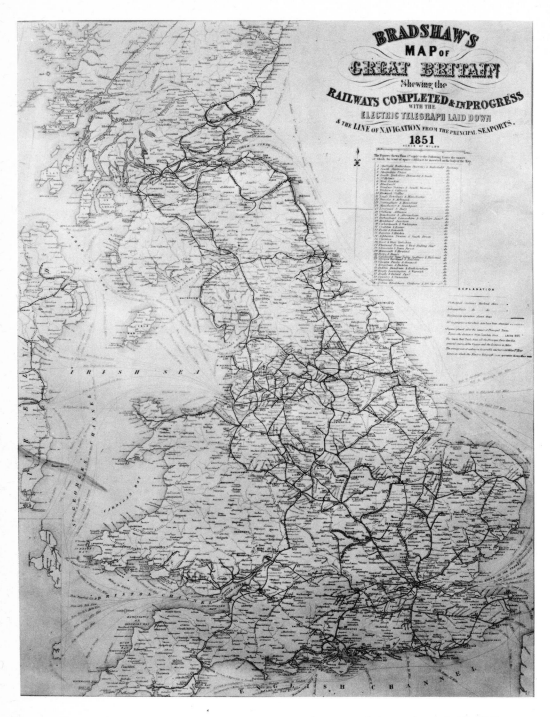

Bradshaw's Railway Map of Great Britain, 1851. Twenty-six years since the Stockton & Darlington opened, twenty-one since the Rainhill Trials, and there were already about 5,000 miles of railway in Britain (by 1886 there were 16,708) and it was having its effect: the coastal traffic of Boston, Wisbech and King's Lynn had gone for ever, and odd new names are on the map – Bishopstoke (Eastleigh), Great Ormes Head (Llandudno).

Walden brewer, Frank Gibson, and a gentleman of Stamford Hill, Thomas Richardson. All were Quakers. The company, informatively named the Owners of the Middlesbrough Estate, bought 500 acres in 1829 for £30,000, and drew up its plans for the new township on the small mound there which alone among the salt marshes offered any dry foundations.

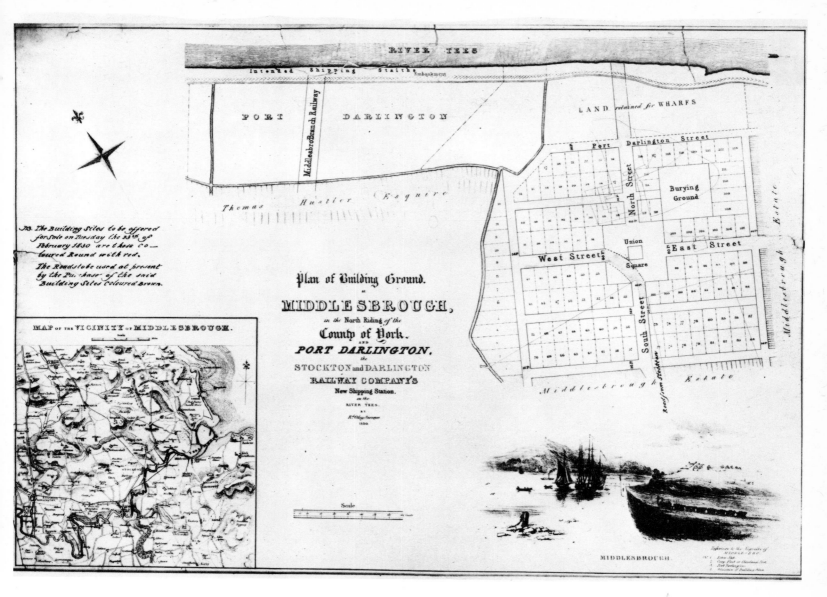

Plan of Building Ground at Middlesbrough – this, Pease's plan, drawn in 1829, can easily be recognised on all subsequent maps: the Burying Ground becomes St Hilda's, but otherwise there is little change for a hundred years.

For this eminence (imperceptible beneath the concrete, it ranges from twenty five to forty feet above OD sea-level) Pease planned in 1830 a grid-iron town of thirty-two acres. He divided his neatly-drawn square into 125 plots, each two hundred feet by sixty feet, centred on a core of Church and market, and with a spare section in the north-east for a burial ground. The wide central square, on the peak of the knoll, was the intersection for four main streets, each fifty-six foot wide; between each of these there ran subsidiary streets in parallel ranks, thirty-six foot wide. Five of these, Dacre, Feversham, Gosforth, Richmond and Suffield Streets, offered some form of grateful immortality to the five peers who had championed the Middlesbrough Railway Extension Act through the Lords.

The earliest buildings to appear met the new foundation's immediate

Middlesbrough: the Ship Inn, Stockton Road. One of the very first buildings to join the old farmhouse, and the only one of its generation to survive. It has been altered to face the road – originally, its front was towards the wharf, the modern rear.

needs. The railway station[1], a wooden hut, on Stockton Road near Watson's Wharf; the Ship Inn, handily nearby, first licensed in 1831 and still surviving, lost in a wilderness of council flats. Housing began, in April 1830, with West Street: for many years the first house 'erected by Mr George Chapman' in 'the new town of Middlesbrough upon Tees' bore a plaque to that effect. It has since been replaced by a block of flats, where, although there is provision for the tablet, it cannot be risked for fear of the inhabitants.

Although the town that eventually grew up had some of the most appalling slums in Britain, Pease's plan expected better: the Estate dictated not only the layout of their town, they required that purchasers of building plots should observe certain standards of construction. A Subscription to a Deed of Covenant of 1831 was asked, 'for the purpose of preserving some uniformity and respectability in the houses to be built', which laid down guides on building height, roofing material and door and window sizes.

Industry was originally confined – quite practically as well as philanthropically – to the river's side, and for the first fifteen years of the new town's life it was a credit to Pease's plan. The grid gradually filled up, shops, offices and houses almost evenly dispersed, although with a slight predominance of commerce in the north, around its handsome central square. In the northeast corner of the square was (and is, coal-black) St Hilda's Church, on a site designated by Pease, and with a striking spire. In its centre, completed six years after the church in 1846, a graceful town-hall with clock tower, the focus for all four main-street vistas. There had already begun in some sections

[1]The first service opened between Stockton and the new staiths was still horse-drawn, and the passenger service, thrice daily in a coach named 'Majestic' shared line, horse and coachman with the coal-wagons. 'The speed, never remarkable for its violence, slackened into something approaching a walking pace, much to the chagrin of the limited number of passengers and the intense relief of the horse.'

Middlesbrough: Trimmer House, a council block on West Street, has on its end wall, at the level of the first-floor balcony, space for a plaque recording that it stands on the site of Middlesbrough's first house. But experience has shown that if the plaque is put in position, modern Middlesbrough residents throw rocks at it.

the in-filling of the grid by extra, narrow streets, by courtyards and back-to-backing, but in the main it was fair to say in 1846, the year the original farm-house finally disappeared, that it was 'a handsome, well-built, commodious town', as well as that the 'proud array of ships, docks, warehouses, churches, foundries, wharves' seemed like 'some Arabian Nights' vision'.

Pease and his fellow-owners were not especially philanthropic. Although, as Quaker gentlemen, they were a great deal more humanitarian than some of their contemporaries – and successors – they were relatively unmarked by the great tide of utopian community-planning which was rising throughout England at the time, and which we discuss later. Pease's own instincts for improvement seem to have been given quite as much rein outside Middlesbrough as within it, for despite the magnitude of the task he had begun, his career was not confined to the railway and the town. In 1832 he was elected Member for South Durham, becoming the first Quaker M.P., and, consequently, the cause of some constitutional discomfort when he refused to take the oath upon the Bible. As a politician, he spoke frequently on questions of social and political reform, invariably evading the use of titles when addressing the House, and clinging to his distinctive Quaker style of dress. He was President of the Peace Society from 1860, and continued to publish and promote Quaker works after he went blind in 1865. He and his wife, Emma, also managed to have five sons and four daughters.

Although Pease and his partners were not, in the very practical context of their town, excessively concerned with social engineering, they did subscribe

135

Middlesbrough: South Street in 1855. Looking towards the first Town Hall and St Hilda's Church. Even if the artist has idealised the mud and squalor of the street, it would of course have been possible and natural to use the street for bargaining and strolling.

Middlesbrough: the old Town Hall in the Market Place (Pease's Union Square), now marooned in a wilderness of flat-blocks.

to certain common principles. It was, after all, their estate, whose property values had to be protected, and their bounden duty to provide an environment in which the bright new engineering civilisation could and should be seen to be superior to the old. Despite their own religious belief, the Owners readily gave the land on which St Hilda's Church was built, and Pease arranged as well for land, in Stockton Road, on which the first school was opened in 1838.

Nevertheless, although the growing town rapidly acquired both a reputation for drunkenness and a complement of Churches (Centenary Wesleyan Methodist Chapel 1840, Richmond Street Primitive Methodist Chapel 1841), the Owners' Plan provided for no library, no parks, no improving Institutes, nor indeed a hospital. The Covenant laid down broad lines for builders – about the visible elements of their work: built on a marsh, many Middlesbrough houses had no real foundations, nor proper damp courses. The town's character was inevitably unpolished; full of jobs for strong young men, it displayed for years the effects of a 'Klondyke' population – overwhelmingly of one sex, one age group, and one class.

It meant that Middlesbrough went in for drinking, fighting, and prostitution, as well as working, religious enthusiasm and the determined development of both friendly societies and trades unions. The society it bred was abrasively masculine and unrefined: 'not one gentleman in the place' they said in 1838, and those that counted themselves such later were self-made specimens. Harsh as was the intellectual and cultural atmosphere, it nevertheless remained more healthy than that of nature.

Damp was one of the two great curses of the town; the other was the unceasing smoke. 'When Mr Pease and his colleagues bought the Middlesbrough Estate' remarked their first historian, 'they purchased also the fresh air.' But while the smoke at least meant full employment and good profits – the town's Mayor in 1889 told the Prince of Wales 'If there is one thing more than another that Middlesbrough can be said to be proud of, it is the smoke' – the damp, combined with overcrowding and poor building, brought only disease.

The site itself demanded especial attention to drainage, and it did not get it. It is predominantly low-lying, in a meander of the Tees, founded on alluvium and clay. In the earliest days it was noted that one could not walk from house to house 'without sinking up to the calves' in mire, and in the 1850's a report on drains remarked that 'in almost all instances the drains are above the basements of the houses'. Things got worse throughout the century, with sewer gas driven up into the streets from tide-locked outfalls, sewage proper backing up whenever heavy rainfall met high tide, and several of the lowest streets subject to flooding since they were below the river's high water level. No-one would have chosen the site if their first consideration had been the people rather than the coal.

However, by the general standards of the time, first-generation Middlesbrough was quite civilised. After fifteen years it was overwhelmingly residential, with ownership widely dispersed, and with sufficient industry (pottery, shipbuilding, engineering) to deny the railway any monopolistic employment

power. The streets were muddy, but wide, the shops conveniently spread, the general character uniform as a result not only of the Owners' influence, but of the almost universal use of local brick and tile.

There had already taken place, however, an event that led to the explosive growth of smoky Ironopolis: in 1841, the year before they opened the Dock to which Pease had looked forward from the start, the Owners sold six acres of the river bank to H. W. Bolckow and John Vaughan. Bolckow, a German who had been in business in Newcastle, and Vaughan were apostles of the iron age, eager to begin the rebuilding of the world on iron rails. They chose to start their partnership in Middlesbrough because it offered ready access to coal – by train – and pig iron, by boat from Scotland. In 1846, in an effort to produce their own pigs for the rolling mill at Middlesbrough, the partners set up blast furnaces at Whitton. Insufficient ore was found there, and eventually the furnaces were fed by ore from Whitby which was transshipped through Middlesbrough on its way to Whitton on its way to Middlesbrough!

Their arrival in Middlesbrough was to prove the most significant event in the history of the town; and within ten years, it proved amongst the most

significant in the wider history of the country. It became enshrined in Yorkshire lore that John Vaughan's passion for the sporting life led to his casual discovery one day, whilst shooting on the Cleveland Hills, of fragments of ironstone, and thus re-founded at a stroke the mediæval Yorkshire iron trade. It is regrettably nearer the truth to say that Vaughan had been deliberately and conscientiously prospecting and assaying for some time before the 'discovery' became known, but an interesting survival of Victorian Public Relations that the romantic story is still told. At any rate, the first quarry for the stone was opened in 1850, and in 1851 a branch railway was completed from Eston to the rolling mill. The mill had employed 400 men; the new discovery, the direct line, and two new blast furnaces on the site brought that rapidly up to 1,600. Middlesbrough began making its own iron, and the old railway town, increasingly boxed in by the railway lines, began to sink beneath the spreading pall of unceasing fires.

The original plantation of the Owners, planned as a necessary adjunct to their business interests elsewhere, had been populated in the main by Yorkshiremen: the rise from forty in 1821 to 5,467 in 1841, although dramatic,

Middlesbrough: old cottages awaiting demolition, St Barnabas Road (outside Pease's town).

Middlesbrough: Princess Place, early 1900's. The photographer, the local Medical Officer of Health, may have posed the boy, who doesn't look like a spontaneous paddler.

Middlesbrough: Dover Street, early 1900's. No-one yet expected motor-traffic in this sort of neighbourhood – the sidewalk is paved, but the causeway appears to be mud.

Middlesbrough: St Hilda's Ward, early 1900's. The common water-tap in these closes only came on at certain times, and had to be queued for, with as big a bucket as could be managed.

hardly made the new town more than a singularly homogeneous village. The arrival of the ironmasters (and between 1851 and 1870 ten companies opened forty furnaces) demanded something more revolutionary. It coincided with the great depopulation of Ireland and the Scottish Highlands, and in 1871 the 39,563 citizens of the borough first incorporated in 1853 – with Bolckow as its first Mayor – included 50 per cent born outside Yorkshire, 18 per cent of the total being born outside England, and almost 10 per cent of the town being Irish. Over one-third of those arrested in 1869 were Irish; it was the time of the foundation of the Catholic cathedral, Catholic schools, and of innumerable beer-licences, primarily in the old square town, although by then the boundaries had extended well beyond Pease's grid. Although the growth – and æsthetic degeneration – of the town was temporarily halted in the 'seventies, it picked up once more when steel began to be produced, rather late, in the 'eighties.

The iron and steel Middlesbrough was not, however, the planned town of Pease: although the old centre continued to be its heart, with St Hilda's market and the Town Hall, the expansion had perforce to take place on the other side of the railway. Nevertheless, Pease's predilection for the grid crossed the railway with the people, since the Owners continued to be the source of building land. They bought it, laid out the street-lines and the sewers, then re-sold it to the speculators and the jerry-builders. Half-a-century after they arrived, the Owners still owned more than half the built-up land. There is a uniformity about Middlesbrough on both sides of the tracks which has only recently begun to pass with the erection of vast new estates. It is the uniformity of the grid, red bricks, and no grass.

The old Owners continued – personally as well as corporately – to play a major part in the town after the ironmasters came to power: Pease, who had in any case been instrumental in persuading Bolckow and Vaughan to come to his new town, remained a force throughout his life, involved in iron-works as he had been in railways and in docks. But the burden of civic pride naturally fell on the ironmasters' shoulders. Bolckow was not only first Mayor, but the donor of Albert Park in 1853, the town's first official lung.[2] And in 1889 a new, more grandiose, and far less graceful, Town Hall went up, at what has become the modern heart of the town, the Linthorpe Road intersection. This marks the final rape of the original town by its monstrous progeny, for although St Hilda's market still continued to be important until the First World War, St Hilda's Ward had become the cess-pit of the town. The older wards, St Hilda's, Cannon, Newport, contained a high proportion of worn-out housing, at a high density, overwhelmingly without baths (or even internal water) and had death rates well above the average. St Hilda's itself, in 1939, was 92 per cent pre-1875 in construction, 83 per cent bath-less, and had a death-rate per 1,000 of 27.31 – nearly three times that of the new residential suburbs. The town's motto, *Erimus*, full of Yorkshire pride and ambition, looks a little desperate cut into the filthy stone of the old town that still survives. The ironmasters and the strong may well look forward to what they will be and continue to be, but the weak went to St Hilda's, and to the wall, rotted by bronchitis, tuberculosis, cholera and rheumatism

[2]He put up two-thirds of the £8,500 for the Royal Infirmary, 1864, led the campaign for the Royal Exchange, 1868, gave £6,000 to build St Hilda's School, 1869, and spent £30,000 on the Park.

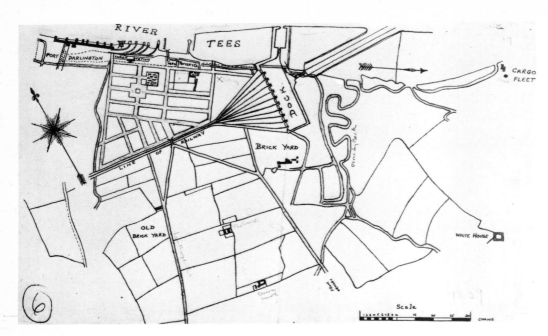

Middlesbrough: this map shows the plan of the town, the railway, and the Owners' Estate, in 1839. It demonstrates quite clearly why all subsequent expansion had to be across the tracks.

Middlesbrough: the Market Place, with St Hilda's and the old Town Hall, late in the 19th century – after the surrounding streets had decayed, but while the market itself maintained its importance.

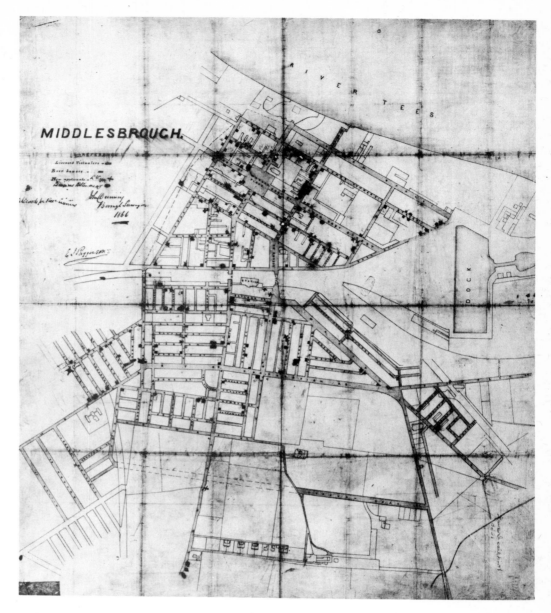

The nature of the town could hardly have been different: it was born of and thrived on the philosophy of aggressive industrialisation. Its industries – not railways, but docks, engineering, coal, iron and steel – are traditionally 'hard' industries, in which employers and employed both hold to extreme views of the nature of work and of the class struggle. Middlesbrough beer remains unusually strong, and Middlesbrough consumption remains high. Ladies are not served to this day in the Ship Inn, new flats are wrecked at record speed, and one whole model development has had to be abandoned because the industrial pollution in the air killed the plants, stripped the paint and put the people on the panel. As an exercise in urban planning, Middlesbrough demonstrated unexceptional taste for the regular and symmetric, without great concern for the spiritual environment, and despite Pease's optimistic – and accurate – forecasts for its growth, made no allowance for expansion, cutting off the plantation from its natural growth by the line of the railway.

Much of the old town has now been razed, together with large tracts across the lines in the area of the first expansion. St Hilda's and the old Town Hall (now a police station) still stand, but surrounded by council blocks. No effort has been made to restore the focal nature of the grid, the balance having irrevocably swung across the town to Linthorpe Road, or indeed to preserve the intimate nature of the district. Built in haste to serve industrial need, on an engineer's ideal of urban management, it has been destroyed with equal heartlessness. No-one presumably could feel nostalgic for what St Hilda's Ward had long become, and in any case, modern Tees-side has grown as a linear sprawl along the river, rather than in the concentric ranks originally planned. Throughout its history, the 'great type of the iron age' has been dedicated to the view that a town is the place where people live, as uniformly as they may, in the trivial hours between the shifts.

Wolverton: an aerial view of the pride of the L.N.W.R. Its monotonous regularity is apparent, even at height.

This uniformity is not atypical of railway towns, even if Middlesbrough itself is – being both the first railway town and eventually over-run by another industry. The Great Western.Railway's Swindon, the Midland's Wolverton, the London & South Western's Eastleigh, all lacked any real distinction in plan or detail. All three date from the period 1838-1845 in origin, heavily over-built later in the century.

New Swindon (Old Swindon remained distinct and separate until 1900) was the by-product of Brunel's London-Bristol line, completed in 1842. Swindon station, appropriately magnificent in appearance and appointments, was opened in 1842, the railway works in 1843, and the first houses of the new town followed. The Railway had distinctly grand ideas about its role. Having built a station at which all trains had to stop for ten minutes' admiration of the late Classical elegance of the buildings, and for refreshment at the superior hotel above the booking hall, and having then commissioned Sir Giles Gilbert Scott to build them a Church for their new town (Old Swindon procured itself a rival Scott Church six years later, in 1851), the Directors got around to letting it be known that 'the Company have made arrangements for the erection of 300 houses.' Old Swindon, at the time when the G.W.R. decided that its tracks should run north of it, and that it would be a good site for their repair and loco works, had a population of only 2,000. New Swindon was clearly to be as large again from the very beginning: by 1853, 243 cottages had been built to the probable design of Sir Matthew Digby Wyatt, and the building which is now the Railway Museum had passed from its first career – lodging-house for Irish navigators – to its second – overnight lodging for loco crews. Its third, in the 1860's, was as a Methodist Chapel.

The cottages, all terraced and of stone, were small, undistinguished and laid out on a banal plan. Squeezed between the loco works and Farringdon Road, bounded by East Street and Church Place, the estate streets all run East to West, with the only interruption across the line being Emlyn Square. The centre of the group was formed by the Mechanic's Institution, largely rebuilt in 1892, and the Market Hall, now gone. The Company provided a School, in Bristol Street, as well as Church and Institution, but the whole exercise was devoid of taste or passion – passion of any sort, conviction of any kind. The values of the property rapidly went down, and the Company's Hotel failed.

Eastleigh was an even more complete foundation. Bishopstoke Junction, a station only, was built in 1839 in open fields. In 1842 another line, to Gosport, was laid, and in 1847 a third, for Salisbury. The growing importance of the station led to the gradual growth of a permanent railway colony in its shadow, and this encampment took from a neighbouring farm the name of Eastleigh. It grew by a process of accretion, acquiring the standard Company Church in 1868, on a grid pattern for fifty years, and only began to expand at speed after the removal to it of the Nine Elms carriage works (1891), the Southampton engine repair sheds (1903) and the Nine Elms loco workshops (1910).

Wolverton, like Swindon, is now New Wolverton overpowering the Old. The year that the London – Birmingham line was opened, the Midland Railway carriage works were opened there (1838), between the main road and the canal. A township was planned and built to the south of the works, a grid mildly relieved by its long avenues of two-storeyed red-brick cottages with bay windows. Since this small and tidy plan proved inadequate, the Company also founded, slightly west of New Wolverton, New Bradwell, comprising, in 1858, just 150 brick cottages, a Church and a School, on a smaller version of the grid.

None of these foundations give evidence of real concern above and beyond the simple managerial level, nor have they any great character (that may be harsh on Swindon, marginally). There might indeed be an argument that one could not expect full-blooded industrial towns to thrive in Wiltshire, Hampshire or Buckinghamshire, and that a lack of either villainy or positive philanthropy by their founders is no more to blame than the surrounding disapproval of the countryside. In any case, not one of these three compared with early Middlesbrough in appearance, let alone with later Middlesbrough in growth or character; yet we might reasonably take them as representing railway ideals if we listen to the eulogy of *Stokers & Pokers*, a contemporary publication for, by and about railways and railwaymen. Wolverton moved someone, whether stoker or poker is now uncertain, to write 'It is a little red-brick town composed of 242 little red-brick houses – all running either this way or that way at right angles – three or four tall red-brick engine chimneys, a number of very large red-brick workshops, six red houses for officers, one red beer-shop, two red public houses and, we are glad to add, a substantial red school-room and a neat stone Church, the whole being lately built by order of a Railway Board, at a railway station, by a railway contractor, for railwaymen, railway women and railway children; in short, the round cast-iron plate over the door of every house, bearing the letters L.N.W.R., is the generic symbol of the town.' Given the source and the time, the note you hear is that of pride, not mockery.

However, the Railways did build better to the North, and it would not be fair to leave them without describing their successes. Of these, Crewe is almost certainly the finest, although much of the Crewe that the Grand Junction line planned and built has now been demolished – not merely house by house, but by the street, so that many of the old street-lines have disappeared. And Crewe dates from that same period, its first houses being occupied in 1842, and its Railway Church (Christ Church, still standing, bereft of all the little streets that used to lock it tightly in) was completed in 1845.

The early history, and geography, of Crewe is confusing, for the very good reason that, as a local riddle has it, 'The place which is Crewe is not Crewe: and the place which is not Crewe is Crewe'. Briefly, what it means is that the railway station built in 1837 was in the old township of Crewe, but that the new town called after the station was built, round the railway works which demanded it, to the west of the station in the township of Monks Coppenhall, half of the parish of Coppenhall. Crewe Station only became part of the municipal borough of Crewe in 1936.

The birth of Crewe followed the decision of the famous 'Liverpool Party' of entrepreneurs who dominated the Grand Junction Line – eventually part of

CREWE STATION
(L & N W. RAILWAY.)

Crewe: the Station in 1848. Clearly, railway lines held little more dread for pedestrians than did the quiet roads. A lithograph by A. F. Tait.

the giant London & North Western – to establish a railway engineering works at the place where their earlier efforts (financial and political) had secured the junction of the Birmingham-Liverpool and Birmingham-Manchester lines with the Birkenhead-Chester-Crewe. Thus, they made the tiny settlement (the total population of the parish of Coppenhall in 1831 was 498, spread over 2,871 acres) the focus for the whole North-Western traffic. Just as Stourport owes its existence to the distaste of Bewdley for a 'stinking ditch', so Crewe seems likely to be in the debt of Nantwich landowners who wanted too much for their land.

The Company took its responsibilities, if not demonstrably more heavily than other Railway Boards, with greater skill. Their Engineer, Joseph Locke, and architect, John Cunningham, were instructed to produce plans, and a Committee of the Grand Junction was appointed to superintend the settlement. The first houses were erected in 1842 (when the population of Monks Coppenhall rose from 203 in 1841 to 1,000) and the entire scheme for works and community, costing about £110,000, was celebrated with suitable festivities in November, 1843, on completion of the workshops. The *Illustrated London News* noticed the event: 'Certain factories having been recently completed, the directors determined to give the superintendents, clerks and workmen as well as their wives, families and acquaintances, a grand dinner, tea and ball; and having fixed the most convenient day, preparations were made on a most extensive and liberal scale. The workmen received each four tickets of admission, so that they might invite their friends and acquaintances (the females being admitted free to the tea and ball), the attendance was consequently very numerous – including not only the "beauty" of the village, but many of the farmers and their families for miles round the rapidly improving locality . . . All appeared to be delighted and the whole fete will be long remembered; and doubtless stand recorded as one of the first remarkable events in the annals of the "juvenile city of Crewe".' The farmers, whose enthusiasm for the original railway line had been distinctly bated, had good reason to attend: those who stayed had a large new market, and access to a greater still, on their doorsteps, and those who sold, as one did, might make £10,000 for a farm worth, a short few years before, £4,000.

The juvenile city laid out by Locke and Cunningham (with subsequent

Crewe: the Grand Junction Railway's Grand Dinner, Tea & Ball to mark the completion of their works at Crewe, in November 1843, was, naturally enough, held in a decorated engine shed.

assistance from R. S. Norris, the resident engineer) on the lands bought by the Company in 1840 was distinguished for the width and regularity of its streets, and the cleanliness and order imposed by decent standards of building and sanitation supported in the long term by Company policy: anyone whose behaviour seemed to be 'bringing discredit on the establishment and endangering the health of the town' was likely to be sacked and evicted.

The Directors' original feelings were expressed by John Moss, Chairman of the Board and himself one of the superintending Committee, when he recognised that 'the men around him had, no doubt, by coming there, dissevered many ties of kindred and affection . . . he and his brother directors were anxious to make them as comfortable as lay within their power'. In fact, nearly a thousand people had come to Crewe from Liverpool, where the Company's original workshops had been, and they came to houses carefully arranged in four classes. 'First, the villa-style lodges the superior officers; next a kind of ornamented Gothic constitutes the houses of the next in authority; the engineers domiciled in detached mansions, which accommodate four families, with gardens and separate entrances; and last, the labourer delights in neat cottages of four apartments, the entrances with ancient porches. The first, second and third have all gardens and yards; the fourth has also gardens.'

This system, regimented and hierarchic though it was, paid dividends for years to come: even in the 1870's, after much speculative building to standards well below the Railway's had begun to crowd in the centre, the people of

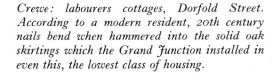

Crewe: labourers cottages, Dorfold Street. According to a modern resident, 20th century nails bend when hammered into the solid oak skirtings which the Grand Junction installed in even this, the lowest class of housing.

Crewe boasted proudly that they had no slums – unlike Chester and Nantwich. The railway had discovered at the very beginning that if they wanted anything, they would have to provide it, and so had laid on sewerage and water, gas and roads, education, refuse-collection, even policemen. All this meant that in the 1840's, Crewe represented the ideal against which men like Chadwick judged the squalor of the rest of industrial England.

The houses, 'rooms all capacious', 'ground-floors . . . tiled . . . the back and front are open, ventilation is perfect,' with gas and water[3] piped in, were designed to rent on the principle that the Company should earn $6\frac{1}{4}$ per cent on capital, but when the rents this produced (something over 3s. a week for a labourer's cottage) were found too high for the tenants, the Company gracefully reduced them, first to 2s. 9d. and then to 2s.

The Company did not confine itself – could not, as we have seen – to simple matters of building cottages; the Rector of Coppenhall told them that his Church was too small for the population they proposed to introduce, so they made immediate provision for Anglican services (with their own Chaplain) above an engine-shed until such time as Christ Church could be

[3]At first the lower classes were dependent on street-pipes: but it was intended, at least from 1846, to extend the service to every house.

Crewe: a Superior Villa, for executives of the Company. In Delamore Road, this was demolished in April 1968.

completed. They recognised that the people would need shops, schools, assembly rooms, a gasworks – and built them.

Part of this programme we can fairly attribute to human decency alone, and part to enlightened standards of industrial management in its own interest. The skilled men that the Company needed to staff its works – especially after they began the actual manufacture of locomotives there in 1845 – could always move their homes again if they or their families grew dissatisfied, so every effort was made to keep them happy. The Company's importation of an official surgeon, and a health insurance scheme (2d a week for a family) was clearly as much from business principles as philanthropy.

There is no doubt that Crewe is one of the successes of modern town-foundation. Its population grew from a few hundreds to four-and-a-half thousand in 1851, seventeen thousand in 1871, 42,074 in 1901. Its main industry, the loco works, built 4,000 locomotives between 1845 and 1900, and auxiliary industries, such as cheese (Crewe is after all in the middle of the Cheshire Cheese district), steel and fustian-cutting joined the Railways early on. It is of course a prime example of success based on nothing but geographic

position; Crewe has no minerals, if the salt that extends into the parish is excluded, and has absolutely nothing to recommend it for development unless one assumes a railway, and the previous existence of Birmingham, Manchester and Birkenhead in their actual positions. There is water, essential to a steam-based industry, but not in great abundance: the first M.O.H. of Crewe remarked in 1864, 'I am bound to mention that . . . it did sometimes happen that the tap got stopped up with something other than fish. Mere mud was hardly noticed, much less talked about.'

Furthermore, its success as a town from the very start was not just a matter of efficiency and profit – it was actually pleasing to the eye. The ground-plan was orthodox, and the architecture mundane, but the use of wide streets, gardens, the provision of every aid to cleanliness (even human: the Railway built a public baths in 1845, a great novelty) made Crewe civilised where Wolverton was mean. The Railway Company's concern for their tenant-employees' moral welfare may have been self-interested (no pubs on their land, and complaints to the magistrates about those springing up next door) but it may equally have been accepted. If the Company built Christ Church,

the employees were responsible for the rash of nonconformist Chapels – a dozen assorted kinds of Methodist chapel were opened before the end of the century, plus sundry Baptist and Presbyterian foundations. According to the *Directory of Cheshire* in 1850, 'the town now contains upwards of 800 good houses, commodious and well furnished shops, elegant hotels and taverns, a beautiful Church, Town Hall, several handsome dissenting chapels and schools etc. have sprung up, and formed a town of magnitude as if by magic.' The numerous dissenting chapels probably had much to do with the relatively slight evidence that Crewe was, like Middlesbrough, a frontier town – prone to drinking, fighting, and promiscuity.

The last of the Railway towns cannot help but be compared with Middlesbrough because Barrow-in-Furness, though the official offspring of the Furness Railway Company, only really took off into sustained growth with the discovery of the Park deposits of hæmatite – and the busy Barrow of the 'sixties and 'seventies, when house building was the town's second largest industry, was the Barrow of the steelmakers, jute spinners, shipbuilders, and docks, not that presaged by the erection of ten cottages at Salthouse in 1846.

In fact, Barrow could be attributed to iron before the railways. As early as 1711, ironmasters from Staffordshire and Cheshire had arrived there, and the local Backbarrow Company had provided accommodation for workers, like so many other industries of the late 18th and early 19th centuries, as a matter of course. The Furness region naturally attracted industry, since it had woods for charcoal (its ironmasters were still using charcoal long after most others had followed Darby into coke smelting), streams for power and transport, rich ore deposits, and of course, a splendid coastal position.

The railways only came in 1844, bringing with them a twenty-two-year-old assistant engineer called James Ramsden. There were many more important men associated with the Company at that stage, including the Earl of Burlington, but Ramsden is the one who matters most in the history of Barrow. At any rate, the line was opened in 1845, very largely to transport the ore from Barrow to more developed iron smelting districts, and the Company erected an engine shed and smith's shop at Salthouse, near the village of Barrow. The next year, in order to accommodate their employees, they put up ten cottages, forming a short terrace opposite the sheds, which still survive as Numbers 1 – 10, Salthouse Road. In 1848, although the growth of the district remained

Barrow-in-Furness: the first cottages, 1 – 10, Salthouse Road.

very slow, Ramsden was one of those who founded the Barrow Building Society, having by then been made Locomotive Superintendent.

The role of Vaughan in Barrow was played by the speculator, H. W. Schneider, and it was his investigations which led in 1850 to the discovery of the great new deposits of high-quality ore at Barrow. Thereafter, town and railway began to expand more rapidly, the railway extending to Carnforth, Whitehaven, Broughton, Ulverston and gradually forging a network linking all the ironfield, and linking West Cumberland with Lancashire. And the Railway, in 1854, recognising the growing pressure of development, bought the Hindpool Estate. Ramsden, who became general manager and Secretary of the line in 1857, also became chief promoter of the new town, and prepared a master plan for its construction. His own involvement, already deep, became deeper still in 1858 when he was appointed one of the directors of the Barrow Hæmatite Steel Company; and the building of new ironworks and greatly improved furnaces in the following year gave the town additional impetus.

Ramsden's plan laid great emphasis on space: main roads were to be fifty to sixty feet wide, side roads forty to fifty feet wide. There were no parks, since, like Crewe, the town sat in the middle of open country easily reached by walking in any direction (save seaward) for a few minutes. In addition, Ramsden hoped for grandeur, and for economic incentive, from proposed development of the water-front, and from a policy of imposing façades, dignified buildings, and noble vistas. Indeed, Ramsden is almost unique amongst industrialist-planners in that he gave little attention to housing, or to social services, but was concerned with such grandiose notions as avenues and squares. By and large, Barrow left the houses to private speculators, and the Railway Company concentrated on the provision of a suitably imposing framework. It would not be stretching very far to say that Ramsden approached the problem from the viewpoint of a business-minded Wren or Evelyn, rather than an Owen or a Moss.

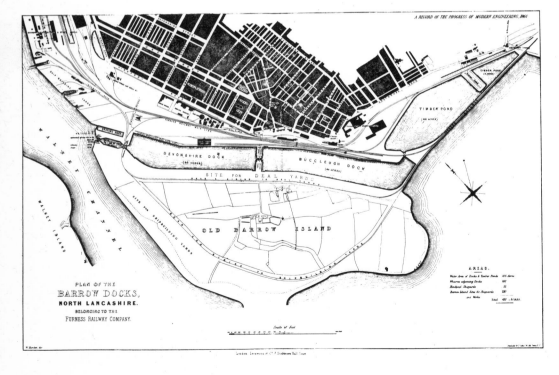

Barrow-in-Furness: Ramsden's original Plan, 1856, dwarfed the existing town.

Barrow-in-Furness: this Map, from 1866, shows that already the important central area has begun to be boxed-in by meaner streets and that the great theme of squares and avenues has begun to dissipate itself.

The Railway all this time – from its arrival, that is, until 1867 – had borne the responsibility for running nearly everything: Dalton-in-Furness manorial court was no more competent to deal with rapid urbanisation than was Monks Coppenhall Township. But by 1867, Barrow was big enough (it rose from 3,135 in 1861 to 18,911 in 1871) to seek its charter as a Corporation. Its first Mayor, inevitably, was James Ramsden, and he held the job for four successive years. In that same year, the first Barrow Dock was opened, beginning another great industry.

Ramsden and the Railway continued to dominate the town despite the constant expansion: nearly every other business venture in the town, dependent as it had to be on railway land, railway services, railway goodwill, involved railway participation; and houses, for which the demand was growing faster than supply could cope, were built on land either owned or sold by the Railway. In 1874, the Customs Inspectors' Report remarked 'houses are taken as soon as the foundations are laid . . . some of the beds in the lodging houses are never cool.'

The pressure was immense. The flooding immigration of the 'sixties was easily surpassed by that of the 'seventies, when the population rose yet again, this time to 47,259 in 1881. The flax and jute mills had opened in 1869, on top of the steel, the docks and shipbuilding, and Barrow became a magnet to working families all over the North-West – and, of course, from Ireland and Scotland, usually via Liverpool. Ramsden gave the town a public baths in 1872, and in return the town put up Noble's bronze statue of Ramsden on the 21st of May. In June, Ramsden was summoned to Windsor Castle and knighted for his efforts, and in 1873 he became Sheriff of Lancashire. Even the 10th Lancashire Rifle Volunteers had had time, in 1874, to make him their honorary Colonel before the Furness Railway Company got around to appointing him Managing Director in 1876.

The public baths were no longer quite such a mark of grace as they had been when Crewe had theirs, and the social conscience of Barrow, and of Ramsden, seem to have been well in control. In 1865 the Barrow Hæmatite Steel Company voted £4,000 for a new Church, and £500 for educational and medical services; and in 1878, when the long-delayed cottage hospital had just twenty-five beds for the town's forty thousand people, four new Churches were consecrated on one day. Naturally, Victorian principles would have endorsed the need for rapid provision of Churches with far greater alacrity than we can now, but even so there is a distinct impression left that Barrow may have been more sanctimonious than saintly.

The visual product of this explosive growth, so slow to start but then so frenzied, is distinctly odd. The wide streets and imposing arrangements of Ramsden often seem to have been lapped by a dirty tide, leaving behind, in the crevices, nondescript terrace houses, with small back-yards and narrow back-lanes, wholly out of scale with the visionary Barrow of the Plan. The Plan was all fine large blocks; the reality has many of them, but they have been nudged in by lesser groupings, and the folly of the Company, in permitting so much of its land to be developed by speculators, remains quite clear. It might also be argued that Ramsden's scale, appropriate as it was to his

THE NEW RAILWAY STEAM-BOAT DOCKS, BARROW-IN-FURNESS, NORTH LANCASHIRE.

Barrow-in-Furness: the immense Palace at the dockside illustrates in silhouette against puny Barrow, the artistic priorities of 1867.

Barrow-in-Furness: Lord Frederick Cavendish, Earl of Burlington, whose ancestor built Burlington House and Savile Row, gives the Town Hall a look of eternal aristocratic puzzlement.

Barrow-in-Furness: the Town Hall of 1878 is out of scale with the modern public lavatory, let alone with the contemporary cottage-shops.

Barrow-in-Furness: the impressive Gothic porch of the Town Hall.

ambitions for his town, inevitably suffers from Barrow's failure to grow to fit it. For, successful as it was in the booming days, Barrow in the longer run has fallen distinctly short of the wilder dreams of its sponsors, suffering acutely the effects of the depression of the iron and jute trades which set in just as Barrow was most over-stretched, at the end of the 'seventies.

Overall, the railway foundations have then in common not much more than the obvious: that all have suffered to some degree from the peculiar limitations on growth and regeneration imposed by the railway lines: that all were naturally sited with engineering rather than amenity in mind; that all went up in great haste at a time of erratic architectural taste. It may be simple prejudice that inclines one to think that Brindley's Stourport is infinitely preferable to Digby Wyatt's Swindon, but in any case the difference is hardly canals or railways (Goole is scarcely picturesque), but a difference of two generations. What seems always to be true of one-purpose towns, where the purpose requires important space and access, is that either failure of the central function or too great success can dislocate the balance of the town with equal vigour. Indeed, a limited failure, as with Stourport, or many Castle towns, may produce much the finest effects, where a dramatic success, like Middlesbrough, can wreck the scheme, consuming town in function and making, in one generation, slums of city centres.

Tied Towns

Any kind of classification of planted towns rapidly breaks down under close analysis, and no more so than when discussing the vast clutter of foundations, or profound and determined expansions, which follow the great revival of town-building in the 18th century. There will often be arguments of equal weight to suggest that a certain town be classed among those born of social, or political, or religious, conviction – or of blatant economic interest. Most lines of distinction are blurred when a foundation becomes successful – that is, proceeds to grow organically – and no amount of fine sub-division, onto-logical or teleological, can resolve problems like that of the embarrassing incident at Hull Garden Suburb. Apparently inspired by the humanitarian and æsthetic arguments of the Garden Cities movement, it was fortuitously close to the Reckitt factory, a large number of whose employees were among the first inhabitants, and at its formal opening in 1908, its greatest advocate, Sir James Reckitt, said 'I urge people of wealth and influence to make proper use of their property, to avert possibly a disastrous uprising.' Convinced cynics, and convinced marxists, may regard this as refreshing evidence of what they have always known to be true; for the rest of us, it is an uncomfortable flash of what lay behind many great improving schemes. The problem really is that by the 19th century, anyone who had any need to build a new community was the prisoner of the prevailing wind of improving theory, and of the practical truths revealed by the Parliamentary inquiries into the Sanitary Condition of the Working Classes and the Health of Towns. None but a fool would build all over again the kind of streets and houses which debilitated and slaughtered the workers, at no great saving in fixed capital over decent building, if the workers were going to be working at his own factory.[1] We may therefore remark upon the tolerably enlightened building of innumerable industrial villages and suburbs, not that every great industrialist was an Owen or Salt, but that few of them were either fools, or deliberately wicked – just as few were unnecessarily good and generous. The community-building of the 18th and 19th centuries, if classified by motive, includes many putative Reckitts, some Owens, quite a lot of eminently sensible, pragmatic men, and a few who must be classed as visionaries – or eccentrics.

The eccentrics, such was the distribution of wealth, were normally only able to carry out their schemes if of the peerage (however recent), and town-building history in the 18th century fills once again with noble names, reminiscent of the great periods of seigniorial plantation. And projects such as those of the Duke of Gordon at Portgordon, the Marquess of Stafford at Helmsdale, and the Earl of Elgin at Charlestown (two fishing ports and a limestone-quarry) could have as easily taken place in the Middle Ages – great landowners enriching their estates by plantation. But there were others which smacked more of self-indulgent despotism than of practical development. Lowther, Blanchland, Harewood, Milton Abbas, Fochabers, Inveraray, Archiestoun, are all where they are very largely because it suited their founders that it should be so – the last five, replacing older homes that did not suit the founder's taste or fancy.

Lowther, in Westmoreland, had best be cleared up first, if only because the name is one that dogs this book; various branches of the Lowther family

[1] In many cases, those who provided decent housing made a good profit anyway: the Herculaneum Pottery in 1807 discovered their cottages were yielding 10 per cent per annum.

(itself so complicated that it trapped Macaulay[2] into a wrong attribution) are associated with the foundation of Whitehaven, Goole and Lowther itself. Whitehaven and Goole are dealt with in the section on transport towns, but Lowther's *raison d'être*, apart from the fiat of James Lowther, Earl of Lonsdale, is unclear. One suggestion has it that it was meant to billet troops against the restive populace, and, since Lonsdale was capable of closing down all his pits (and thus effectively starving all his miners) in a fit of pique over losing an action over subsidence, and his managers forbade Inquests into deaths in the mines – 'such enquiry being ... calculated to frighten the ignorant and discourage them from going into the pits' – there may well be something in it. Few men were more likely to need the protection of the militia than 'the Bad Earl', of whom Alexander Carlyle remarked that he was 'more detested than any man alive ... an intolerable tyrant over his tenants and dependants ... truly a madman, though too rich to be confined.' Lonsdale owned seven parliamentary seats, and bought two more. His placemen were known as 'Jemmy's Ninepins' and of this peer's connexion and his tenants, it was recorded that:

> 'one sad servitude alike denotes
> the slave that labours, and the slave that votes.'

At any rate, whatever the reason, and one would naturally incline to the worst available, it was this Lowther who coincidentally united both the Whitehaven and the Westmoreland branches of the family in his person, succeeding to the baronetcy of Lowther in 1751 and the Viscountcy of Lonsdale, with the Whitehaven estate, in 1755, who founded the attractive but incomplete, village of Lowther. Built in the yellow local stone, it is a group of two closes and a crescent, with the implicit suggestion that the crescent was intended to be but one half of a circus. Built in the 1760's, there is no reason why a deranged Earl should not wish to emulate the style of the Woods' Bath in a tiny northern village. It is most agreeable, and must, together with his patronage of Pitt the Younger, whom he got in for his Appleby fief at the election of 1781, be put to Lonsdale's credit.

Blanchland, in Northumberland, was a Premonstratensian Abbey for nearly four hundred years, until the Dissolution in 1539; thereafter, the Abbey decayed and no new occupants arrived until, in 1752, the whole estate came to the Crewe trustees (John Crewe, later 1st Lord Crewe, being only ten at his father's death). In order to work the nearby lead mines, the trustees had to provide accommodation, and chose to build a model village in and around the ruined Abbey. From the bridge over the Derwent, entering the village from the south, it appears to be composed of a regular oblong of two-storeyed houses, but in fact the east side is stepped in, possibly to correspond with some vestige of the Abbey buildings, and the oblong is actually a thick L-shape. On the east side is the handsome hotel named for Lord Crewe[3] and the whole venture is a tribute to the taste of the advisers to a family whose next generation (John, 2nd Baron Crewe) rashly sold land from their ancestral estate in Cheshire to a railway company, and whose next (Hungerford, 3rd Baron) was forced to plant trees to hide the railway's new town from view. The 3rd Lord Crewe had no enthusiasm at all for the town which bears his

[2]And Ashton & Sykes in their *The Coal Industry of the Eighteenth Century*. We *think* we have them all right, but . . .

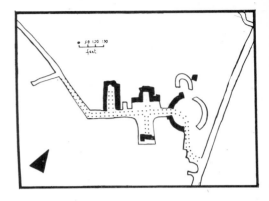

Lowther, Westmorland: the uncompleted nature of this scheme is as apparent as its ambitious model – with Circus and Closes.

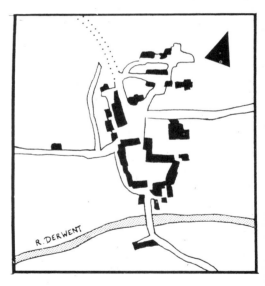

Blanchland, Northumberland.

[3]Although Lady Crewe deserved commemoration more: her beauty inspired the Prince Regent's famous toast, coupling Foxite politics with her in 'True Blue – and Mrs Crewe!'

name, and would instruct his coachman 'Anywhere but the New Town' at the outset of his daily drive.

The houses at Blanchland are of local stone, with stone slab roofs, and complement the successful whole: they are the finest in appearance of the lead-villages by far, though there is no evidence to suggest that the Crewe estate rivalled the social and managerial sophistication of their neighbours at Nenthead, the London (Quaker) Lead Company, who not only provided homes, but pioneered various welfare schemes – and evolved one of the earliest programmes for management training – in the 18th century. The Quakers provided schools, shops, supplying the latter from their own farms, sickness insurance, and a watchful eye on any 'tippling, fighting, night-rambling, mischief and other disreputable conduct', all of which were punishable by the sack, which was, as usual in these communities, tantamount to expulsion.

With Harewood, we come face to face with the whims of the rich at a time when the rich fortunately had sufficient taste not to abuse the total freedom from planning permissions and consents which prevailed. The Harewood estate, including the unusual 14th century Castle with its four great corner towers, was bought by Henry Lascelles, a man grown rich from the ribbon trade, his Directorship of the East India Company, and, far from least, his farming of the Barbados Customs, in the 18th century. His son, Edwin, 1st Lord Harewood, proposed to put the finishing touches to such novel aristocracy by having a suitably grand country mansion built, and hired John Carr to provide one in 1759. Carr, the son of a mason, graduated via the building of a grandstand for York Races, Harewood House, marriage to a Lascelles, and the Lord Mayoralty of York, to a contented death at the age of eighty-four, leaving £150,000 behind, an exemplary 18th century career. Anyway, Carr and Lascelles agreed that no decent house could be built whilst the surrounding park was cluttered up with the cottages of the village, and announced that the village would have to be moved. They were prepared to let the Church stay,

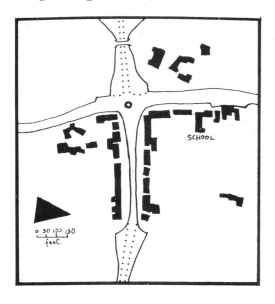

Harewood, Yorks: the triumphal avenue character of the plan, very much subordinating the Village to the great House, can be seen.

Harewood, Yorks: original houses and shops.

165

Churches being both politically and physically cumbersome, and in any case quite attractive and convenient appointments for one's garden, but the rest was shifted in its entirety to the gates of the magnificent new Harewood House. Carr's work on the House was subsequently altered by Robert Adam, but the village remains his.

The principal consideration being the grandeur and delight of the new nobility, the village lies on either side of a long avenue which begins several miles east of the site and runs straight for the gates of the Park, where it becomes the driveway. The houses of the new village, stone-built, are in terrace groups, some two-storeyed with punctuating two-and-a-half storey accents, others of two-and-a-half storeys punctuated by threes. The north side of the street is rather more formal than the south, but the village as a whole is undoubtedly a successful composition. High-handed as the inhabitants no doubt felt their landlord was, the fact that he regarded their homes as part of his view effectively guaranteed them well-built houses of good appearance.

Much the same can be said (and was no doubt thought) of Milton Abbas. Joseph Damer, M.P. for Weymouth 1741–47, for Bramber 1747–54, and for

Milton Abbas, Dorset: the self-sufficient, tree-sheltered nature of the village shows up from the air – at the centre, Church and Almshouses are opposite each other.

Dorchester, his birthplace, 1754–62, augmented his father's modest mercantile fortune in the course of his political career to the point where he was able, in 1752, to buy the estate and ruins of Milton Abbey. His problem was precisely that of Lascelles: wanting to build a mansion on his site, around which, most inconsiderately, there had grown up over the preceding centuries a small market town, he was forced to move the lot. What he built was just as appropriate to the Dorset countryside as Harewood's stone to Yorkshire. Milton Abbas consists of two gently curved rows (flanking the road) of paired, thatched, cottages, with, between each pair, a plot of land, and a splendid chestnut tree. The whole exercise, complete with new Church, was finished in 1787, five years before Damer finally converted his hard-won Barony into the Earldom of Dorchester.

Milton Abbas is a peculiarly well-finished project: sealed in with trees, this artificial example of a classical street-village is practically and æsthetically self-sufficient. Its north-eastern end is guarded by school and Inn, the south-west by brewery and smithy, and in the centre of the village, Church and almshouses face each other across the road.

Similarly autocratic gestures are, if anything, more common in Scotland, where the despotism of the native aristocracy has been reinforced not merely by trade and political corruption, but by infusions of English arrogance, made the more unfeeling by customary absenteeism out of season. For, well-built and attractive as so many transplanted villages and towns may be, one should not forget that modern experience has shown quite significant numbers who would rather accept poor housing than be moved away to new towns and estates. It is always a delicate task to justify the imposition of taste from above, and particularly so when one is discussing, not the television programmes, but the homes of the politically impotent.

The Dukes of Argyll have traditionally found it hard to credit that what they did was not irreproachable in this life, if indeed they could envisage argument from the Deity, and it doubtless came as no surprise to the people of Inveraray when they were moved. The 3rd Duke objected to their proximity to his Castle, and began both to pull down the existing town, and build another, between 1743 and 1761. But although a few existing buildings date from this period (for example, the Town House and the Argyll Arms Inn), the majority of modern Inveraray dates from later in the century, in the reign of the 5th Duke. The plan of the town is rather that of nave and transept, with the junction marked by the Church: a single street, broken by the place around the Church. Inveraray offers open views over Loch Fyne in both directions, since it is built parallel to the line of the water on a small, blunt, promontory. The houses are plain, two and three-storeyed, of local rubble-stone, some colour-washed, with pitched slate roofs and solid Scotch chimneys. Both John Adam and Robert Mylne worked on parts of it, and the town as a whole demonstrates that it is possible for a small harbour to be successful in a style other than tumbling snug.

There is another very similar foundation from this period on the Isle of Islay: Bowmore, founded as a jetty, a sweep of houses, and a circular Church, bears a sign in the Church that it was built by Daniel Campbell, 'Lord of this

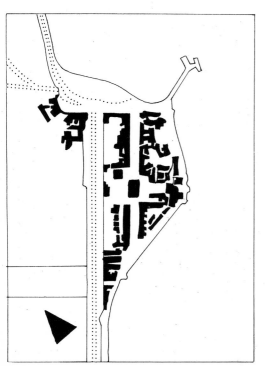

Inveraray, Argyll: this Plan, from the South, illustrates both the cruciform shape of the town, and its avoidance of the obvious focus, the pier.

Island' in 1767. However, the habit of moving and founding dates much further back than that in Scotland: old Yester became ornamental, landscaped new Gifford (it is near Haddington) in 1710, and the Marquess of Tweeddale's concern for his people extended to the provision of soup for the poor three times a week directly from his own kitchen. And Sir Alexander Fraser may deserve the credit for the first post-mediæval foundation of all, perhaps, with Fraserburgh in 1570.

The Dukes of Gordon had, in north-eastern Scotland, quite as much self-confidence as the Campbells in Argyll; and the same Duke of Gordon who planted Portgordon on the Banffshire shore of the Spey Bay as a herring port, took exception to the traditional site of Fochabers in Morayshire. Dating from the 1790's, planned Fochabers is a simple grid with a central square, in which are Church, small green, and shops. Although not all the buildings were completed in the century, they have all been built to the same pattern, and are of one or two storeys in plain harled stone, with slate roofs. There are a number of very similar grid-towns in grey stone and slate in this corner of the country, including the linen town of Tomintoul (Banff), the whisky centre of Grantown-on-Spey (Moray) and the Earl of Fife's Dufftown (Moray), all of which are very like Fochabers – or, since the first dates from 1775 and the second from 1765, perhaps one should say that Fochabers, Tomintoul and Dufftown (1817) are very like Grantown.

Linen was responsible for a number of Scots towns. Since it was the country's premier industry in the 18th century, with production rising from 4,720,105 yards in 1733 to 24,235,633 yards in 1800, one can hardly be surprised. And since the Returns of 1839 showed that all but twenty-one of the 183 flax-spinning mills in Scotland were in the north-east, where 15,000 out of a total 18,000 engaged in the trade worked in Angus, Fife and Aberdeen, it is equally to be expected that most of the foundations were in this area. The common origin can be illustrated at Stuartfield, Aberdeenshire: Lewis in

1846 explained its origin as 'built on the estate of Mr Burnett, of Denns, who, in 1783, established a bleachfield here for the encouragement of the linen and yarn manufactures'. Joseph Cumine's Cuminestown, dating from the middle of the century, Sir William Forbes's New Pitsligo (finished in 1828, and, according to Lewis 'houses neatly-built, and attached to each of them some acres of arable land'), Mr Ferguson of Pitfour's early 19th-century Fetterangus, Mr Graham of Ochil's Newtown of Pitcairn, and the ribbon-foundations of successive Earls of Fife at Keith, were all intended for the encouragement of the linen trade. Efforts were being made by landowners all over Scotland to grow flax and spin its fibres, and where the capital was lacking, there was always the British Linen Company, after 1746, with its nominal capital of £100,000 and actual funds of well over that figure, eager to develop, finance, and rationalise Scotland's staple.

Keith is perhaps the most curious of these foundations, the great majority of which remained small villages while the trade centred more and more on Dundee, Dunfermline and Paisley. Old Keith is a genuinely old, presumably organic town: Newmills, New Keith and Fife-Keith have all been subsequently

Fochabers, Moray. Despite minor ribboning along the Keith road, the classic grid remains unimpaired. This could be Winchelsea.

added to it, and all are regular, right-angled plans. Newmills, still outside the town, was built in the middle of the 18th century, by the great-grandfather of the Earl of Fife who built Fife-Keith in 1816, to the same plan of parallel streets and central square as New Keith, which pre-dates both.

There are two plantations in the north-east which are distinctly irregular, showing no signs of the ubiquitous grid. Gardenstown, in Banff, was built around 1720 by Alexander Garden of Troup, as a fishing village, and at the foot of the cliffs round Gamrie Bay, also founded by Mr Garden, lies the smaller fishing village of Crovie.

One could hardly leave the Highlands without mentioning one instance of the 'clearance towns' – for there were some landowners who were prepared to re-house their tenants in Scotland, rather than ship them off to Canada or Australia, and indeed many of the small-industry towns of the time, like the Marquess of Stafford's Helmsdale for fishing and Brora for coal-mining, were in a sense alternatives to emigration. Sir Archibald Grant of Monymusk, having cleared the crofters from much of his Moray estate, built for them in the 1760's the immodest Archiestown: another grid with central square, it was partly burned down in 1783, and subsequently reconstructed. Scottish land-owners were not all so uninventive, or so unromantic: Sir James Clark attempted to found a town at Penicuik, in Midlothian, which would retain a wholly rural atmosphere. He was altogether too successful, insofar as all that remains of it is his Parish Church, thickly surrounded by the unrural developments since 1770. The 5th Earl of Elgin's Charlestown, although prosaic in intent – the housing of workers for the local limestone quarry – was original in plan, being shaped like the letter E. At about the same time, in the 1760's, the 10th Earl of Renfrew founded a cotton-spinning town on his estates, Eaglesham, and adopted for his plan the letter A. Between the two legs of the triangle there was room for a fifteen-acre common. The shape is supposed to have been inspired by a Swiss or Austrian village which had captured the

Eaglesham: Polnoon Street.

Earl's fancy. In any case, having dictated the shape, the unfortunate Earl surprised a poacher on his lands, and, contrary to all the prevailing game laws, allowed the poacher to shoot him. Thus, from 1769 the building of the town was in the hands of the 12th Earl, Hugh Montgomerie, who had practical civil engineering experience as Inspector of Military Roads in the subjugated Highlands. He completed Eaglesham – 'it consists of two rows of elegantly built houses, all of freestone, with a large space laid out in fine green fields, interspersed with trees with a fine gurgling streamlet in the middle', according to Calder's *New Statistical Account of Scotland* – rebuilt Eglinton Castle, and commissioned Peter Nicholson to build him a port at Ardrossan which he optimistically thought might become a rival for Port Glasgow. Nicholson

Eaglesham: the A stands out, as does the common land that such a shape makes available.

Eaglesham: 19 Polnoon Street. This handsome door-case is one of the surprising details in what at first seems a typically dour Scots street-village.

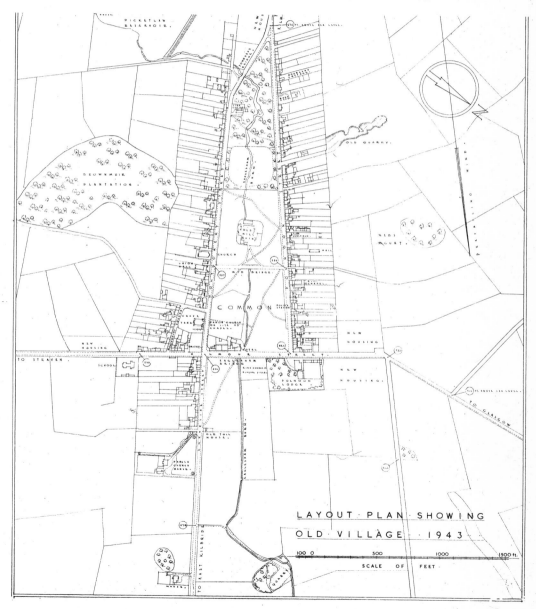

LAYOUT PLAN SHOWING
OLD VILLAGE · 1943

produced a grid plan, its streets lined with two-storey houses 'well-finished, neat and comfortable' but its completion, and its ambition, failed for lack of money. Eaglesham was finished sometime late in the 1790's, and Ardrossan begun in 1806.

There were plenty of Scottish plantations which failed to live up to their sponsor's hopes. George Dempster, of the Stanley Mills (and attendant village) planted in Perthshire in 1785 by local interests in partnership with Arkwright, attempted to repeat the process at Spinningdale in Sutherland, but it burned to the ground in 1808. The 3rd Duke of Buccleuch founded Newcastleton in Roxburgh in 1793 for the hand-loom weaving (not the greatest growth industry of the succeeding thirty years), on a sophisticated grid plan whose central street began and ended in a small square, having passed through a larger at the centre. The British Fisheries Society, having planted Ullapool and Tobermory in 1788 as ideal fishing villages, commissioned Thomas Telford himself to plan them a model fishing-town, Pultneytown, near Wick. Although Telford's Plan dates from 1808, building did not begin until 1830, and even though the one and two-storey houses had extra-large attics for the gear, the project has never caused serious concern to the fishers of Peterhead and Fraserburgh (its own 1815 redevelopment was on a grid-plan), or indeed of Ullapool.

Since there were something over 150 foundations in Scotland in the period 1745-1845, it was inevitable there would be failures, and failures by every sort of criterion; but the great building passion was not confined to Scotland, any more than to aristocrats, and there were many foundations, and failures, else-where. The handsome re-building of Blandford Forum, Dorset, in 1732, under the provision of a special Act of Parliament, with money raised from Church collections all over the country, followed a series of failures by fire: Blandford burned in 1579, was sacked in the Civil War, burned again in 1677 and 1713, and had a final conflagration in 1731. Its reconstruction was, in the circum-stances, a conspicuous act of faith, notably by the Bastard brothers, John and William, who designed and built the Church, the Town Hall, the Old Red Lion and the Crown Hotel: the overall effect of this new town after so many 'organic' failures was to suggest that Blandford, with its confident buildings, and large market place, was ready for greatness. In fact, although it has had, during its chequered history, periods of relative fame for pillow lace-making, glass painting and button making, nothing save the fires ever seems to have really taken there.

Purely on the ground of propinquity, one might mention at this juncture the curious plantation at Blaise, in Somerset: dating from 1811, it belongs among the whims of the rich, since its patron was J. S. Harford, of Blaise Castle, who wished, rather than move an existing village, to have supplied a picturesque hamlet as part of the sylvan scene. John Nash, who had earlier designed a conservatory at the Castle, planned Blaise Hamlet, which consists of ten cottages in a curious, and unique, style whose overtones of Hansel and Gretel reappeared later in the century at Port Sunlight and in much of the wilder garden suburbery. No two front doors in this small group, set on an oval village green, face the same way, the central pump incorporates a sundial, there are thatches, tiles, and rustic touches from half-a-dozen periods. Both

patron and architect were oblivious of economic function or social management; Blaise Hamlet is straightforward æsthetic indulgence.

Nash may have also been concerned with the port-foundation of Aberaeron; he certainly seems to have built Monachty, the Llanon home of the Reverend Alban Thomas Jones Gwynne, father of Aberaeron. And the town itself, although perfectly practically aimed at exploiting the conjunction of receptive coast-line with good inland access via the Aeron valley, has appropriately baroque overtones. Gwynne, having obtained an Act of Parliament in 1807 to build piers and provide shipping facilities, maintained strict control of the subsequent development, which falls into two principal sections: the harbour district, and Alban Square. The harbour front, Quay Parade, was designed for elegance, but the rectangular terrace-blocks behind it were more modest in size and ambition, although regularly laid out, and on streets of uniform width. Alban Square is a Piazza, straight out of the Italy of the Renaissance – or Wren's ideal London. Unfortunately, Aberaeron is even less suited to this scale of architecture (or level of sophisticated, sun-warmed life) than London, and Alban Square is tentatively bordered by buildings much too small for the context, and is in any case itself irredeemably Welshed, having become a grass football pitch rather than a paved piazza. As an experiment, it is quite credibly of Nash, but his direct influence can more readily be seen in the detail of many of the terraced houses. The aspirations for grandeur in this case seem to have been the Reverend Gwynne's. Grandiose ambitions were not uncommon at the time, and another contemporary Welshman, William Maddocks, founded two towns, conveniently named, since they are at the entrance to the Vale of Madoc, both after their founder and a great Welsh hero. Tremadoc and Portmadoc can both be explained in terms of misplaced economic analysis, but must even so suggest something of the rich eccentric's whim. Maddocks bought a large estate in the Vale and embarked, in 1800, on a massive project to reclaim nearly two thousand acres of tidal marshland at the seaward end of the Glaslyn Valley – Traeth Mawr. Having seized back the land from the sea, he decided to plant on its western side a new town, Madoc's Town, which would be the capital, the principal centre and market of the district. The market opened in 1805, embraced by an attractive square beneath a great slate cliff. In 1833, the town was described as 'situated on a portion of the tract first recovered from the sea, and is built on the sides of a spacious quadrangular area, having in the centre a lofty column. . . The Houses are of handsome appearance, and the town promises, when the plan is fully completed, to be a great ornament to this part of the coast.' The description is still perfectly accurate, but Tremadoc has yet to live up to its founder's aspirations, or Lewis's forecast. One fine square it began, and one fine square it remains. Oddly enough, what Maddocks saw as its subsidiary, the slate-port of Portmadoc, has grown since its foundation, although hardly to the stature that Maddocks foresaw (usurping Holyhead's role in the Irish trade). Portmadoc came after Tremadoc, being authorised by Act of Parliament (as a harbour) in 1821. It was the consequence of Maddocks's immense embankment-causeway-coffer, now known as Portmadoc Embankment, which took between three and four hundred men three years to build, largely by throwing stones into the water at great speed. No sooner was it complete, reclaiming another

Tremadoc: the Town Hall from the Square. The looming presence of the slate-cliff does not succeed in dwarfing this rather pretty building.

7,000 acres as a result, than a storm broached its central section. The whole of North Wales was canvassed for funds to repair the damage (one of the canvassers being Shelley, who spent 1812–13 at Tan-yr-allt, near Tremadoc) and Maddocks's gangs of stone-throwers returned: the total cost of the barrier was over £100,000. Today, Portmadoc is four times the size of Tremadoc,

Tremadoc: the road to Portmadoc from the Market Square. The regularity of the cottages, and the abrupt end of the tiny town, can be seen.

Tremadoc: Market Square, seen from entry of the Western road.

Tremadoc: looking East from the Square. Again, the abrupt end of the town can be appreciated.

but neither can really be considered a great success in economic terms, although Tremadoc as a whole, and the original section of Portmadoc at the Green, are satisfying in other ways.

Wales has had a remarkable record of foundations overall: from the first, Rhuddlan, early in the 10th century, to Portmeirion early in the 20th. Indeed, it has been argued that there are practically no modern Welsh towns which are not plantations, that is, none that have developed in a straight line from the *mærdrefi* of the chieftains, let alone grown from some point in time so remote that we cannot date it. The castle-towns associated with the English conquest, the ports, the holiday towns, the great markets and junctions, are all planted. And if Wales has a high proportion of the repressive foundations, she has nevertheless representatives of nearly every other sort. Industrial housing began in Wales (with Sir Humphrey Mackworth's estate for miners at Neath in 1700) as early as anywhere, and produced a number of the best-known towns of the mining districts. Merthyr Tydfil was the creation of the iron industry, and the unscrupulous land-exploitation of Crawshay, Plymouth, that of iron and Richard Hill, whose workers were housed as a very profitable speculation by an English financier, while the coal industry produced towns virtually everywhere it sank a shaft. Some of the industrial housing was out of the ordinary. Morriston, now part of Swansea, dates from the removal of Lockwood, Morris & Company's copper smelting works from Llangyfelach to the Forest Copper Works, in 1727; long-term labour shortages inspired Sir John Morris, the next generation of family management, to commission the civil engineer William Edwards to build a model village. Begun in 1790 and completed in 1796, Edwards's Morriston was on a grid-plan, and laid down firm lines for the houses, which were, however, to be built by the lessees of the standard-size plots. At a ground-rent of 7s 6d a year, on leases of either three lives or fifty years, the plots, and the house-building responsibility, would have been available only to the steadiest and most skilled men, for the average wage of a miner, without promotion and responsibility, was only about 15s a week – though there was a substantial infrastructure of foremen, overlookers, under-managers, mine captains, earning from a guinea a week up to as much as £4. To encourage these incomers (South Wales depended on the immigration of miners from Cornwall and Derby, metal workers from the Midlands at this period) Morris provided extra allotments 'sufficient to keep a cow'. He also provided a Church, subsidised a Chapel, and provided decent sewerage. It was a great improvement on the *ad hoc* slums which sprang up round many a similar enterprise, but neither unique, nor thought to be.

What we must recognise is that very large numbers of entrepreneurs found themselves willy-nilly in the position of developers. Many of the first and second generation industries of the revolution had no option but to go into empty country: mills seeking water, mines sunk where the lodes were to be found. If every master who housed his employees must be counted, then we shall lose all sight of the towns, lost amidst the factory villages – and worse: Matthew Boulton and James Watt had to house their workers at the Soho Works, and chose to put them on the top floor of one wing of the factory; Sir James Morris, at Neath, housed forty families of colliers in a 'castellated lofty mansion of a collegiate appearance'.

It is in fact rather difficult to draw the line, save by hunch or fancy. When Adam Bogle of Blantyre calculated that two-shift working would necessitate expenditure of some £15,000 or £20,000 on workers' houses, he was clearly moving into the founding class, rather than offering a few scanty lodgings. Furthermore, Blantyre was one of the developments where the masters used their power not only to impose discipline (the colliers of the north-east were habitually threatened with eviction from their tied hovels when they grew militant), but to improve men's souls – not least by forbidding pubs; the Findlays of Deanston, Catrine and Ballindalloch, Owen at New Lanark, Salt at Saltaire, the Liverpool Party at Crewe, Busby at Mearns, McGregor at New Kilpatrick, the Quaker Lead Company of Nenthead, all, and more, had firm rules about drink.

Whether one takes sheer size, absolute novelty of site, provision of more than rudimentary housing, concern for and interference in the moral and physical welfare of the people, or any other possible criterion, anomalies must remain. Gaskell, for example, remarked on the phenomenon in 1836: 'An inspection of Belper, Cromford, Hyde, Duckenfield, Stayley Bridge, the villages and hamlets around Oldham, Bolton, Manchester, Stockport, Preston, Glasgow, etc., etc., will show many magnificent factories surrounded by ranges of cottages, often exhibiting signs of comfort and cleanliness highly honourable to the proprietor and the occupants. These cottages are generally the property of the mill-owner and the occupants are universally his dependents.'

Well, one would incline to let the Strutts at Belper in as founders: they built the North and South Long Rows there in 1792, and thereafter continued a building policy which produced 300 company cottages by 1831, and undoubtedly stimulated the growth of the community as a whole so that it expanded nearly four times over in the period. Many Strutt houses had large gardens, and many of their tenants also rented, for 1d a week, additional 'potatoe lots'. The Company homes were of brick or gritstone, regularly repaired; their interiors were whitewashed at frequent intervals, a measure credited by Jedediah Strutt for the rarity of infectious diseases. The owners built a Unitarian Chapel at their other village of Milford, and made a sub-stantial contribution to the Anglican Church at Belper. They founded schools, in 1807, at both villages, on the principles of the educationalist Joseph Lancaster (thirty copies of his *Improvements in Education* went on the ledger that year at a cost of £3). They organised a forty-strong choir and orchestra, and paid full wages while members played, and gave community-wide banquets to celebrate great events – the Peace of Amiens, the Coronation of George IV, the passing of the Great Reform Act (4,800 lbs. of beef, 3,184 lbs. of plum pudding, 7,000 penny loaves and 2,550 quarts of ale were supplied for that festival of emancipation). Yes, the Strutts seem to qualify, from Gaskell's list; but their mills were among the largest in the country, employing 1,600 hands in 1818 (only New Lanark, with the same approximate strength, was in the same class – the Gregs at Styal only had 252, Deanston by then had slumped from 800 in the 1780's to 377) and one would expect them to be in the van of the 168 firms, out of 881 questioned by the Factories Commission of 1833, who declared that they provided some housing for their workers.

On the other hand, it would be stretching more than a minor point to grant Henry Houldsworth any status for his demesnes of Anderston and Woodside, near Glasgow, other than that of barrack-master. He certainly provided roofs for his hands, but not even that arch-apologist for the munificence of the factory-system and factory-owners, Andrew Ure, could find anything good to say about the roofs – save that they were well-ventilated.

What it boils down to is a continuity along a very broad spectrum, beginning with those the Sanitary Condition of the Labouring Population Report described: 'the proprietor . . . would see it advantageous to build a few cottages; these were often of the worst description; in such a case the prevailing consideration was not how to promote the health and comfort of the occupants, but how many cottages could be built upon the smallest space of ground and at the least possible cost.' And at the opposite extreme, just short of the Saltaire level, one found some like Samuel Greg the younger, at Bollington, with his gymnasium, drawing and singing classes, Order of the Silver Cross for young women of exemplary conduct, and meticulously-kept cottages and gardens; or like Thomas Ashton of Hyde, whose work was described by Leon Faucher in 1844. 'The little town of Hyde was, at the commencement of the present century, a little hamlet, of only 800 souls, on the summit of a barren hill, the soil of which did not yield sufficient for the inhabitants. The brothers Ashton have peopled and enriched this desert. Ten thousand persons are now established in their five factories, and in which their daily wages are £1,000, or £300,000 per annum. . . . The houses inhabited by the work-people form long and large streets. Mr Ashton has built three hundred of them, which he lets at 3s or 3s 6d per week. Each house contains upon the ground floor, a sitting-room, a kitchen, and a back-yard, and above, are two or three bed-rooms. The proprietor furnishes, at his own charge, water to the houses, keeps them in good repair, and pays the local rates.' For every Ashton, Greg, Ashworth of Turton, there was someone nearer a Gilchrist of Bervie ('a picture of filth and want of comfort') or a Sykes of Ashton-under-Lyne, who sacked a man for leaving his work in order to answer a summons from the House of Lords committee on the employment of children in cotton manufactories.

Having made the case that it was, and had to be, a commonplace for an industrialist to be a builder too, and that his standards of construction might vary just as widely as his standards of factory discipline or overall responsibility, one must then say that there may be seen throughout this period, beginning as early as the 17th century, the gradual coming together of two powerful themes in the establishment of new communities: utopianism, millenarianism, chiliasm, communism – the idealist theme – and straightforward economic advantage – the practical (and highly traditional) theme. What happens as they grow steadily towards each other is that, to some extent, utopians become rather harder-headed, and, much more important, the practical profit-makers perceive that their profits will be, if not necessarily greater, more secure if the whole lives of the people are improved. The climax of the process may be Howard (or Sir James Reckitt) but the beginnings lie a long way back, and, as we have seen, conflicting symptoms of the process can readily be found in the course of industrialisation.

Often enough, the projector of a new foundation has felt and expressed strong convictions about the sort of people he wished his citizens to be, or to become. But not until the 18th century did this magisterial whim become a significant aspect of practical town-building. Fantasists – they were hardly so close to realisation that they should be called theoreticians – from Plato to More, Andreae and Bacon, have always stressed the intimate relation of human character and human habitation; builders, from Roman generals to le Waleys or James Craig, have not often dabbled in such nebulous speculation.

The first real combination of the two, the real and the ideal, came, like so much else in British intellectual life, with the rise of nonconformity.

In this discussion of the philanthropic and paternalist foundations of the great industrialisation, we must encounter Owen, a religious libertarian in partnership with Quakers, Salt, a Congregationalist, the Cadburys, Quakers, Lever, Congregationalist, Greg, Unitarian, Strutt, Unitarian, and dozens of others, all convinced that the condition of their work-people was both their Christian (or Deist) responsibility and their managerial concern. Architecture, or environment, in their view played the role of literacy in the philanthropy of the more leisured class – it helped God.

In this context, to light upon New Lanark requires some stringent definition. There is nothing in the history of town-planning, or industrialisation, which makes any one of New Lanark's policies or artefacts stand out as unique, only their combination, and Owen's open advocacy, his belief in disseminating what he believed, and what he felt he had proved. Industry itself is not intrinsically opposed to improvement, once it knows that it is possible, and wise. It was, after all, the wealth of industry that made possible the great rebuilding of London, Newcastle, Edinburgh, that made desirable the resorts of Brighton and Bournemouth, as well as throwing up innumerable coal and iron and textile towns.

Nevertheless, New Lanark, more than any other town of remotely comparable size, demands some special care. Although its population never exceeded 2,500 (and is now sinking rapidly beneath 500) it has had greater impact on the ultimate nature of industrial society than a dozen Coketowns, since above all else it made the case that it was not necessary to counterbalance productivity and profits by misery and squalor. Every industrialist and politician, Ford and Lloyd George, Lever and Beveridge, who has argued for investment in a happy workforce has been in debt to David Dale and Robert Owen.

New Lanark was not founded by Owen, although his is the name we justly associate most strongly with it. David Dale, a Glasgow banker and industrialist, chose a site near the Falls of Clyde, Lanark, for a Cotton Spinning Manufactory in 1784. Associated with the venture (as with so many others) was the ubiquitous Richard Arkwright[4], inventor of the waterframe.

The site was chosen for its abundant free power, rushing down the adolescent Clyde. It did not have a ready source of labour, nor decent roads, nor any substantial inhabitation. In order to work his Mill, Dale had to

[4]Richard Arkwright began his career in partnership with the elder Strutt; together they ran mills at Belper, Milford, Cromford, Derby. We have seen that the Strutts were great builders – after the partnership dissolved, and Arkwright took Cromford – but so was he. He spent £1,000 on roads alone at Bakewell, and, if Father of the Factory System, he was no less the forerunner of the factory village-maker. Sir Edward Baines said of him, in the *History of the Cotton Manufacture in Great Britain 1835*, that 'his concerns in Derbyshire, Lancashire and Scotland, were so extensive and numerous, as to show at once his astonishing power of transacting business, and his all grasping spirit. In many of these he had partners, but he generally managed in such a way, that, whoever lost, he himself was a gainer . . .' Among his partners was Oldknow at Mellor, like Dale and Strutt a major builder; and Archibald Buchanan, partner and manager for the Findlays, responsible in part or whole for Catrine, Deanston and Ballindalloch, had been trained at Cromford before beginning his Scottish career as Arkwright's agent. In fact, practically everybody in the cotton industry had to lease Arkwright's patent, and Arkwright always dictated terms: by the 1790's, it was said that he could have bought out the National Debt.

180

Opposite page
Upper left
New Lanark: from the hill on the Lanark side. The Mill is on the left, and the smoke makes it obvious that Dale & Owen's housing was still in service in 1968.
Upper right
New Lanark: the Mill, across the roofs of Caithness Row (and Owen's Grocery Store) from one of the hillside walks laid out by Owen.
Lower left
New Lanark: Owen's school, long since converted for industrial use, and now empty.
Lower right
New Lanark: the Institute for the Formation of Character.

This page
Left
New Lanark: the Counting House. It is the natural focus for the arriving visitor to the town, filling the end of the small space at the Mill gates – out of picture to the right.
Right
New Lanark: Caithness Row. These houses have been renovated by the New Lanark Association.

scavenge for labour, and to keep them there, had to provide a town. In the first instance, and according to common practice in an era when every Parish had a burden on its rates of batteries of orphans, Dale took over from the Workhouses of Edinburgh 500 children, for whom he built a large house. Their labour was hardly adequate to run the mill alone, and in order to attract reluctant adults from the land into the confined factory, Dale also began erecting low-rent houses on the rising bank. Even so, the venture would have foundered from lack of hands if Dale had not one day appeared on board a ship at Greenock, laden with Skye families cleared from their homes and consigned away to North America. After a spirited harangue on the security of New Lanark and the dangers of the West, Dale led ashore a work-force, sullen, dispirited and unskilled, but the beginnings of a stable population for his town.

Owen was later to write that 'the population originally brought to the establishment was, with few exceptions, a collection of the most ignorant and destitute from all parts of Scotland, possessing the usual characteristics of poverty and ignorance.' Even allowing for his natural inclination, both as reformer and an Anglicised Welshman, to exaggerate the poverty of his raw material, there is no doubt that the rural Scots at the end of the 18th century were not ready for industrial civilisation, nor yet adjusted to the suicide of their own.

Dale's provision for the children was admirable: good food, clean, well-lit dormitories, attendant doctor and instructors. The only drawback for these infant paupers was that, in order to justify such Christian care (and Dale was a lay preacher as well as Chairman of the Board of the Royal Bank) they had to work in the Mill from six in the morning till seven at night. After work, their character and intelligence could be improved so long as they stayed awake, presumably not long for six, seven and eight-year-olds.

He could do less with the independent adults. As Owen observed of Manchester, the quickest way out was through drink, in any case the prevailing hobby of the Scottish poor. They had their homes and wages, but Dale could do little but regret the lives they chose to lead outside his Mill. By 1796 he had four mills in operation, employing 1,340 hands, 750 of them children, and half of those under nine years old. By the standards of the time, Dale was a model Master – but the standards were quite plainly appalling.

Owen met the Dales, among them David's daughter Rose, in 1799. He had already made a reputation, and a certain fortune, in Manchester. The Dales, father and daughter, were agreeably impressed, the one in any case eager to retire from business life, the other no doubt anxious as any girl to marry. Owen left them on the understanding he would try to find £60,000 to buy the mills and that he and Rose might marry. Within the year, he had persuaded the first of three consecutive consortia of Directors to put up the money, married Rose, and taken over New Lanark as General Manager. He was twenty-nine years old, and totally convinced that his duty lay in improving not merely manufacture, but men. Owen's distinction as an innovating manager lay not only in his proven practical success on his own, and for the mills of Drinkwater and the Chorlton Twist Company, but in his willingness to read outside the blueprints and the balance sheets. He was, for instance, almost certainly alone amongst his contemporary industrialists, in reading the Quaker John Bellars' 'Proposals for raising a College of Industry for all useful trades and husbandry with a profit for the Rich and plentiful living for the Poor, and a good education for Youth. Which will be an advantage to the Government by the Increase of the People and their Riches.'[5] Published in 1695, the title alone sums up Owen's life work. During his time at New Lanark, he built, out of the surplus profits voted by his Boards, a co-operative Grocery store, the Institute for the Formation of Character (where every morning improving calisthenics took place – the preachers chose to call it immoral dancing), a School, Bakery, Slaughter-house, Vegetable Market and Communal Wash-house. He also improved the houses that existed, and built new rows of solid homes to unheard-of standards: large rooms, good windows, and walls that still today stand straight and firm.

All this was done without impinging on the profits: the total profits made by the mills during Owen's twenty-five-year tenure amounted to £125,000. Each time he found it necessary to change his backers, having fallen out with one or more Directors over his remarkably forthright and inflexible conduct of affairs, the purchase price went up: £60,000 in 1799, £84,000 six years later, £101,400 nine years after that. The flocking visitors to New Lanark – about 15,000 during Owen's management – came not just to see an ideal community, but an efficient enterprise. The physical environment reflected Owen's purpose: his intention was not just to give better homes, a better town, to the workers, but to provide an environment which moulded their character.

[5]Francis Place took it to Owen, who reprinted it. It became a centrepiece of Socialism, if not of industrialism, being praised by Marx, Kautsky and Bernstein. The only influence that it had in Bellars' lifetime had been the foundation of Clerkenwell Workhouse on co-operative principles in 1701.

New Lanark: interior, first-floor living room, 12, Long Row. Taken immediately before modernisation in 1967, showing both Box bed and Hurley bed.

New Lanark: 12, Long Row again – the kitchen range, with iron pot-crane.

New Lanark: along the restricted Clyde, with tenements to the right, mill-buildings to the left.

Had he felt that windows harmed the character, he would certainly have tried to get the windows stopped. His insensitivity was remarkable; no doubt because he thought it was the product of his own devices, he disregarded his people's self-respect at work and in the town. At work, each hand had hung before him the 'silent monitor', a block of wood whose four sides ranged from black – bad work the previous day – through blue and yellow to white – excellent work. If Owen stumbled on a factory quarrel, he would carry off the quarrellers to some private place, and there explain to them his own solution to all human disputes until they quite forgot their argument in their frenzy to be free. Thieves, innumerable under Dale, became a rarity under Owen: 'by means so gradually introduced as to be almost imperceptible to them, they have been surrounded with those circumstances which were calculated first to check and then to remove their inducements to retain these inclinations' – by which Owen meant that he introduced a system of security so rigorous and determined that it was almost impossible to steal anything, and, once stolen, impossible to dispose of it. A thief when caught was subjected first to Owen's aweful lectures, and then to fining. The proceeds of these fines, like those levied on unfortunates detected by Owen in 'irregular intercourse of the sexes', went to the Support Fund, primarily financed from a one-sixth levy on all wages, and designed to yield a dole for the sick and aged. An excellent institution, but handed down from on high with suitable attendant homilies.

Once outside the mill, the people were not free from Owen's constant moral strictures. If he wrote some new work of reason and enlightenment – referring in some passing words to the savagery and ignorance of New Lanark's population – he would summon all the town's inhabitants from their homes and to the mill, there to listen while he read aloud, and at length. They could not even drink in peace: fines were imposed for drunkenness – or, more usually, for hangovers at the mill – and Owen propagandised ruthlessly against the pot-houses. On a more practical level, he offered some alternatives to drink – lectures, dances, handicrafts – and eventually put the whisky-shops out of business by stocking in his stores a decent brand which undercut the raw spirits of the competition.

Civic buildings, larger houses and an organised refuse collection were popular innovations; but, having provided them, Owen wanted to make sure they had their designed effect. It was hard, if not impossible, to evade the lectures and the gymnastics of the Institute, and to make sure that the homes were moulding character as they ought, Owen set up a Committee to inspect each household every week. The wives of New Lanark rebelled against the 'Committee of Bughunters', but even they could not prevail against Owen in the grip of some new obsession. Eventually, the weekly intrusion assumed the character of a status competition, the vanquished women vying to impress the Committee.[6]

The appearance of the community was plain. The large stone houses sit in parallel rows on the river bank, ranging upwards from the mills, and with their every view circumscribed by the steeper banks above them. The valley is both deep and narrow, and even such a small settlement has a strung-out quality, the wide roads trailing off to nowhere between the tall, flat house-fronts. The

[6] In 1833, the Factories Commission found fifteen other Scottish firms either providing, or inciting, regular cleaning and decorating in their cottages – including the Findlays.

social focus of the town, an irregular open space between the Mill gates, the counting house and the shop, is also the visual focus for most of the streets, but it has no especial distinction or grandeur. The mills themselves, although handsome, echo the shapes of the houses (although the reverse is presumably the actual truth) and contribute to an overall grey shabbiness. Owen provided walks along the hillside above the town, but no gardens in the town. The character he wished to mould – and he held that 'any general character, from the best to the worst, from the most ignorant to the most enlightened, may be given to any community' – was clean, honest, rational, sober and hard-working. Unfortunately, that kind of character, expressed in architecture, comes out as dour and tedious. One may imagine that Owen's conversation tended to be both as well.

Owen's experiment, and the others he took part in (New Harmony) or inspired (Orbiston and Ralahine), was in itself eventually a failure. Having run through three Boards, he finally sold out his share to the only director of the last Board he found at all acceptable, John Walker. A Quaker, Walker kept many of Owen's innovations going, without provoking quite the opposition

New Lanark: the absence of parked cars indicates the steady depopulation and impoverishment of the community since the Gourock Rope Company, who ran the Mill from 1903 to 1967, were forced to close it down.

that the increasingly anti-religious Owen had met. The physical appearance of the town has barely altered since then. The mills are now idle, probably for ever, and the population is ageing and diminishing. Since its fortunes have declined consistently throughout this century, New Lanark has never been worth developing, expanding, even metalling its roads. To walk now from the counting-house door past the Mill gates and up the long hill that leads to the Lanark road, leaving the gaunt grey stone beneath, must be much as it would have been – save that the mill would have been thriving, and the streets more lively.

However, the broader view reveals quite plainly that today's enlightened capitalism, and the welfare state, are strongly in Owen's debt, not perhaps because his ideas were wholly novel, but because of the consistent success with which he put them into practice in New Lanark, if nowhere else. He took the children out of his mills, and put them to school full-time from five till ten years old – little wonder that he found the Factories Acts of 1802 and 1819, with their derisory provisions for safeguarding infant workers, contemptible. His mill made money, his children grew up healthy and honest, and the infuriating thing was that 'no experiment could be more successful in proving the truth of the principle that the character is formed *for* and not *by* the individual – and that society now possesses the most ample means and power to well-form the character of every-one'. Yet society didn't do anything about it.

Important as he was, Owen was scarcely unique in his concern for the work-people. Samuel Oldknow had begun his philanthropic management at Mellor,

Mellor: Samuel Oldknow's Mill in 1803. The happy children in the foreground, despite Oldknow's care for the apprentices in his employ, suggest artistic licence.

in Cheshire, rather before Owen, in 1787. He bought a site on the river Goyt for a mill, and, needing to accommodate the necessary hands, raised a mortgage with the inevitable Richard Arkwright with which to buy the Mellor and Marple estates. To build his mill, he needed not only all the locally available labour, but had to induce extra men to come from miles around. Once the mill was finished, however, there arose a common social problem of the cotton age: in operation, a mill needs very few male workers (principally for supervision), and employs instead the wives and children of unemployed men. Oldknow, instead of accepting this as part of the immutable laws of economics, took it upon himself to employ the men about his estates, which in consequence enjoyed good roads and bridges, and in building and operating lime kilns. His interests in any case ranged far beyond mere muslin: he built the Peak Forest Canal, which descends through Marple by a flight of sixteen locks, the second steepest in the country, and crosses the Goyt on the Grand Aqueduct – 309 feet long, 93 feet high. He also mined for coal at Brickbridge, without much success; and was among the first to plant potatoes in the Midlands for human, rather than animal, consumption. Oldknow did more than create employment. Like Owen and the other 'interfering' masters, he regarded it as his concern that the wages he paid were wisely spent, and therefore instituted a Trucking system, paying in vouchers redeemable for cheap and wholesome goods at his own market place in Stone Row. This system was very common amongst philanthropic masters, despite the universally bad press it has subsequently received, and illustrates the strong paternalistic strain – where concern for the workers' well-being and productivity exceeds by far any rare glimmering of respect for their human dignity. No doubt, the motives might be often wholly altruistic, but the unscrupulous could use the system, like the tied cottage itself, to enslave the hands. Truck at New Lanark meant free support for 2,000 unemployed for four months: at Guest's Dowlais, the company store was the object of prolonged grievance culminating in riot.

Oldknow took great care of his apprentices, whose hours and food compared well with those customary in the Lancashire mills, and for whom he built Bottoms Hall as a boarding house (it survives as a farmhouse); and he exercised his influence for good by displaying improving posters in the mill, inveighing against drink and swearing. His town, like the mill itself, has unfortunately almost disappeared, and the district is one which shoves antiquities on display outside their context at some artificial site. However, the lime-kilns haven't yet been planted over with geraniums, and one can stand on the site of Oldknow's work. Even so, one could wish that far more of these early experiments (and Oldknow went bankrupt) had had the good fortune of nearby Styal, and been handed over to the National Trust, rather than being left to the erratic care of local authorities; there are few enough that have not, inevitably, been over-run by later spasms of industry.

Neither Owen nor Oldknow – let alone Bellars – appear to have exercised great influence on Titus Salt. By far the greatest commercial success of them all, Salt and Saltaire seem to have been inspired by Disraeli, who sketches in two pages of his *Sybil* the Model Factory and the Model Village: 'he felt that between them (the employer and employed) there should be other ties than the payment and receipt of wages' and 'recognized the baronial principle'.

New Lanark specialised in cotton tarpaulin, Mellor in muslin; Saltaire was founded on alpaca. Salt's own fortunes had been built over twenty-five years' successful mill-owning in Bradford, pioneering alpaca fibre in making worsted. Born poor in 1803, a devout Congregationalist, he owned half a dozen Bradford mills by 1848 when he became Mayor of the city. His concern for the welfare of the workers was neither the product of political ambition, nor of late-evening guilt. As Bradford's Mayor, he bought land for public recreation, just as, in all his mills, he had striven to mitigate the unhealthy nature of the trade; but in the context of Worstedopolis, everything was but feeble palliation of the desperate reality. After cataloguing its dungheaps, swill-tubs, open sewerage and gas-laden atmosphere, one witness of 1845 felt 'obliged to pronounce it to be the most filthy town I visited'.

At any rate, Salt resolved sometime in 1849, four years after *Sybil's* first appearance, to leave Bradford with all his businesses, and set up a single giant mill in more wholesome circumstances. His first biographer, and friend, quotes him as saying 'I will do all I can to avoid evils so great as those resulting from polluted air and water, and hope to draw around me a well-fed, contented and happy body of operatives. I have given instructions to my architect who is quite competent to carry them out that nothing should be spared to render the dwellings a pattern to the country.' For, of course, Salt was both compelled and anxious to surround his new mill with accommodation for the workers; his site, on the river Aire at Shipley Glen, was four miles north of Bradford,

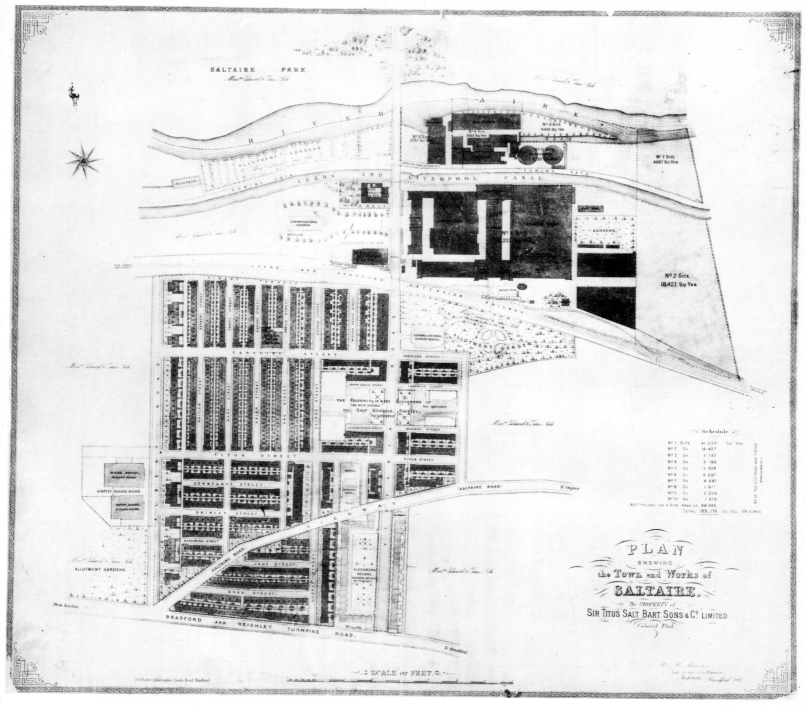

Saltaire: architect's Plan, 1881.

well placed both for the Leeds & Liverpool Canal and for the Midland Railway, but without existing houses.

His architect (or architects – Lockwood & Mawson of Bradford) had a full plate: laid out on a rigid grid system on the sloping southern bank of the river, Salt required a nine-and-a-half acre Mill, twenty-two streets, 805 houses,

forty-five almshouses, a Congregational church, a Wesleyan Chapel, a Primitive Methodist chapel, two Baptist chapels, a Sunday School, public baths, a public wash-house, a large assembly hall, a hospital and a school. All, from the 250-foot-high factory chimney in the style of an Italian campanile (a piece of confident audacity far beyond our own time, and remarkably impressive) to the smallest cottage, in that remarkable Victorian style, neo-Venetian Gothic. Salt himself proposed to live nearby his settlement, at Crow Nest: 'proximity to the employer brings cleanliness and order, because it brings observation and encouragement.' *Sybil* again.

The population of Saltaire – the mills opened in 1853 and virtually all the houses were complete by 1863 – got plenty of observation and encouragement. The baronial principle meant more than decent housing for the serfs,[7] and a high-minded contempt for the cash nexus. Salt did not care to see washing flapping in the streets, and although he provided a wash-house powered by three steam engines, so that the community could both wash and dry their clothes there, he flatly forbade any private-enterprise hanging out of clothes. He abhorred advertising, so that the shops along Victoria Road were con-

[7]Overlookers' houses cost £200 each to build, workmen's, £120. At the time, it was possible to erect a house, in brick, for £80.

Saltaire: backs, William Henry Street and George Street. The washing on the left would never have done for Sir Titus.

Saltaire: 43, George Street. One of the larger houses, used as architectural punctuation, and to offer a choice (most enlightened) to the potential tenants.

strained to announce their presence, and their stocks, with great discretion. And like so many other reformers who have seized upon the refuge from evil rather than its source, he steadfastly opposed drink: Saltaire, so magnificently appointed for the soul, did not have a single pub, for the spirit.

The operation was on a Yorkshire scale. The mill itself, 'exactly the length of St Paul's' at a proud 545 feet, and capped by the amazing chimney, was, when built for £100,000, among the largest in the world. It was opened, on Salt's fiftieth birthday, September 20th, 1853, with a certain ceremony and festivity: 3,750 guests, including hands, were summoned to a banquet, where they polished off '4 hind-quarters beef, 40 chines beef, 120 legs of mutton, 100 dishes of lamb, 40 hams, 40 tongues, 50 pigeon pies, 50 roast chickens, 20 roast ducks, 30 brace grouse, 30 brace partridges, 50 dishes potted meat, 320 plum puddings, 100 dishes of tartlets, 100 dishes of jellies, half-a-ton of potatoes, plus desserts.' Heaven knows what the desserts came to.

If Salt had himself a flair for the grand occasion – lacking only champagne, of course – loyal Balgarnie was its equal: 'At last, the great steam-engines begin to move, sending their motive power into every part of the vast system, which, as if touched by a mysterious hand, wakes up into life: the complicated wheels begin to revolve, the ponderous frames to quiver, the spindles to whirl, and the shuttles to glide. Now the silence of the place is broken by the din of machinery . . . and then comes forth the product of it all, the beautiful texture known as alpaca. How animated the scene!'

The mills employed between three and four thousand people (today it is about 2,000) and in 1870, when the residential village was complete, about

2,450 inhabitants of Saltaire worked there. This union of mill and town broke down gradually over the years and in 1933 had reached the point where the Company felt it proper to sell the village to the Bradford Property Trust Ltd., and since then the great majority of the houses have become owner-occupied, the Trust retaining only thirty. The present proportion of the mill hands living in the village is only about 10 per cent – substantially less, according to the official guide, than the 25 per cent made up of 'Poles, Ukrainians, Pakistanis, Indians and Italians'.

The quality of the housing was, and indeed remains, high. Perhaps the most remarkable piece of philanthropy on Salt's part – certainly the most enlightened – was to conduct a survey of the workers' actual housing needs. Saltaire had the great distinction, over not only most Victorian working-class housing but over many modern Council estates, of offering different units of accommodation. The number of desired rooms was seen by Salt to be a function of family size as well as of social station. There are therefore a mixture of two, three and four-bedroom houses of the sort intended for hands, as well as the more usual choice of size open to the managers and overlookers. The differing sizes, coupled with minor variations of style and decoration, enabled the architects to lay out the inexorably regular streets without too much monotony: at least the houses do not look identical, row by row.

Internally, the houses were of good standard. Each had a living room – a parlour – a kitchen, pantry and cellar in addition to the bedrooms, and most had a small yard, with coal and ash pits and outside lavatory. Few of them had gardens, although the 'managerial' houses in Albert Road had quite reasonable front-gardens. Bathing, like washing clothes, was expected to take place communally, and Salt provided twenty-four baths and a Turkish bath in Amelia Street.[8] They have now gone, of course, many of the houses having installed their own baths, and made way for garages. The allotments along Caroline Street have also gone, covered by a Working Men's Club, where drink is served. Disraeli's vision has slipped from view.

Disraeli's Mr Trafford did not forget his work-people when they left the factory: 'deeply had he pondered on the influence of the employer on the health and content of his work-people'; and Salt, having provided 'a village where every family might be well lodged', public baths, opportunities for horticulture, ample religious accommodation and an Institute with library, reading room, laboratory, billiards, bagatelle, smoking room, assembly hall, gymnasium, art-school, chess room and lecture theatre for adult education – all for a subscription of less than 2d a week – provided also a park with cricket, bowling, croquet, walks and floral displays. Furthermore, although his new foundation might have been expected from the start to attract young families, the very first plans called for forty-five almshouses, completed in 1868. With a garden and their own tiny chapel, the almshouses were for those 'of good moral character and incapacity for labour by reason of age, disease or infirmity'. They were rent-free, maintained by the Company, and carried pensions – ten shillings a week for a couple, 7s 6d for a single almsman or woman.

Although in so many respects akin to New Lanark – the Institute itself, with its education and gymnastics, was flanked by four stone lions symbolising

Saltaire: Vigilance, Determination, War and Peace stand guard over Salt's Institute and the School opposite on Victoria Road. Tradition, not noticeably supported by documentation, has it that they were originally sculptured by Thomas Milnes for the foot of Nelson's Column, London, but were rejected for being too small, and inadequately martial.

[8]He also distributed disinfectant during a cholera epidemic.

Vigilance, Determination, War and Peace – Saltaire was also well on the road, with its horticulture and parkland, towards Bournville,[9] Port Sunlight and Letchworth. It represented a realisation that environment was not only intimately connected with character, and directly related to industrial efficiency, but of itself important: Salt's houses showed concern not merely for the health of the inhabitants, and the imposition of habits of good order and cleanliness, but for their aesthetic surroundings. And, although the grid system shows little concern for the natural contours of the site, the townscaping is of a far superior order to that of New Lanark. Victoria Street, the central thoroughfare, sweeps down the long incline towards the river, wide and straight, flanked by houses of the larger sort, then by the Victoria Hall and the Old School (and the four lions), then by shops, the railway station and a Company office, the impressive Congregational Church, set back along an avenue, and completes its quite successful vista with the mill, slightly offset on the river so that there is a glimpse as well of the Park beyond.

The lesser streets, those parallel to the rail and river line, and connecting the three north-south roads, Albert, Exhibition and Victoria, are inevitably less striking. They lack the purpose given by a view of the mill or Park, and

[9]And Salt's canteen, like Akroyd's, anticipated Cadbury in providing free cooking for the workers' own food, or supplying cheap hot meals.

Saltaire: The Institute, Victoria Road.

Saltaire: the Congregationalist Church. A credit to the taste of Salt, his architects, Lockwood & Mawson, and to the continuing care of successive generations of Saltaire people.

Saltaire: George Street, looking towards the Congregationalist Church. The excellent preservation of the buildings, physically and socially, is apparent.

their narrowness is now accentuated by the endless lines of parked cars. Although the district is now a smokeless zone, the legacy of the years when it was not is irremovable. The earnest efforts at stylistic variety, the well-intentioned decency of streets and houses, cannot prevent the ultimate effect of dullness. Saltaire to look at today, and it has been preserved in respectability not by antiquarians or the smart, but by ordinary work-people wanting to live there, is a quiet grey-stone limbo. The Cumbernauld of the 1860's, it suffers from the seemingly admirable desire of its planners to create an environment to uniform standards and a uniform style. Walking its streets, one cannot help feeling like a sober, industrious working man of the better sort, tempted to steal furtively into dirty Bradford for a lubricious pint before hurrying back to the sand-table town where 'the men were well-clad; the women had a blooming cheek; drunkenness was unknown; while the moral condition of the softer sex was proportionately elevated'.

The philanthropic industrialist – by the standards of the day, vaguely humanitarian impulses qualified as philanthropy – was not confined to the textile trades, with their peculiar necessity to colonise river-banks and valley bottoms. Contemporaneously with Salt, for example, Prices Patent Candle Company moved part of its works from Battersea to Wilsontown (Bromborough) there to found a cholera-free industrial village. The Company was founded, in the 1830's, by William Wilson, a Scot from Carnwath, Lanarkshire. As a family, the Wilsons bridge the intellectual journey from Owen to Lever, since William knew New Lanark, and his sons, James and George, founded their village a few miles from where Port Sunlight was to be.

The site of Bromborough – which is its most familiar name, although both Wilsontown and Prices Village have been used – was bought by James and George in 1853. The Candle works had neither room for expansion in Battersea, nor were its employees fit for work in the prevailing miasma of the Thames-side slums.

The choice of Bromborough (near Bebington in the Wirral) was made for perfectly sound commercial reasons: an increasing proportion of the business lay in sales of 'cloth oil' for textile lubrication – and therefore was in Lancashire – and the raw material for it was West African palm oil, which came through Liverpool. Bromborough undoubtedly offered a much healthier setting for the works and workers, but it also substantially reduced transport costs. The Wilsons employed to design their village Julian Hill. His instructions, frequently augmented by the keenly interested brothers, were to provide high standards of sanitation and of horticulture. The regenerative effect of gardening was clearly rated very high by Disraeli's generation. By 1858 he had put up seventy-six houses, accommodating 460 citizens, with front and rear gardens, and water-borne sanitation. There was also a school, a cricket field and a bowling green: not quite so educational as Salt and Owen, but equally less extensively gymnastic. The idea of suburbanisation – for that is what it came to despite its industrial motive – was increasingly debated at this time. Already, the idea of the great city, of the purely urban virtues, had been shied away from in favour of the pseudo-rural dream that has dominated British planning for so long. In 1845, for instance, a Mr Moffatt, a London architect,

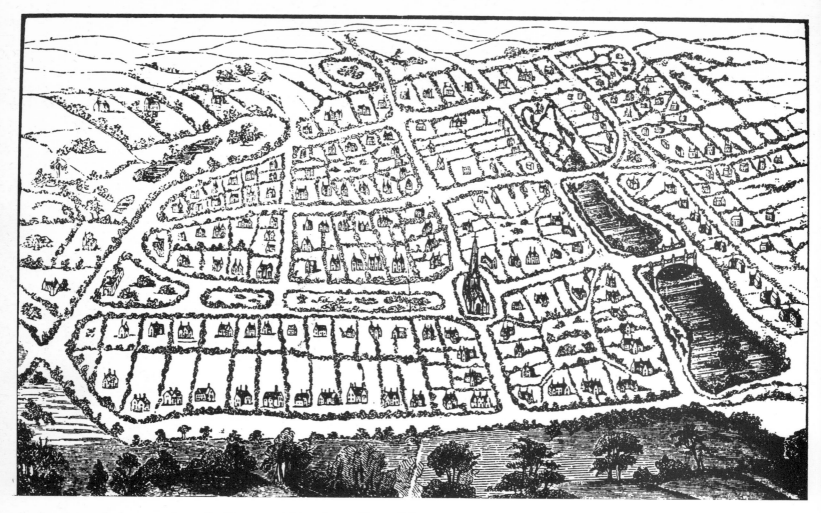

had proposed the erection of villages within the radius of four to ten miles of London; his scheme called for the housing of 350,000 people at a cost of £10 million. In 1848, the Edinburgh Magazine revealed a scheme to build a village of 5,000 people near Ilford Station; a capital of £250,000 in £5 shares was apparently called for, and the plan proposed 'air and space, wood and water, schools and churches, shrubberies and gardens, around pretty self-contained cottages, in a group neither too large to deprive it of a country character, nor too small to diminish the probabilities of social intercourse'. The commuting nature of the project was explicit: those taking houses at £40 per annum would automatically get a first-class season ticket to London, those in £30 houses second-class seasons, and the peasant-artisans paying between £12.10s and £18 per annum qualified for third-class seasons.

In 1849, James Silk Buckingham published *National Evils and Practical Remedies*. It combined authentic Owenism, in its plan for a Model-Town Association, with early Howard. Industry on the eight-hour day, free medical services, crêches, schools, baths, communal kitchens and laundries, no alcohol, tobacco or weapons, all on a radial plan with factories on the peri-

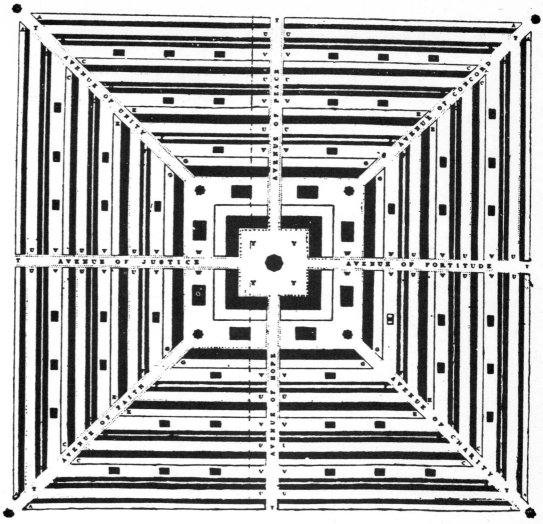

meter, houses and public buildings to the centre.

At the same time, Minter Morgan, like Buckingham solidly in the millenarian tradition, published his *The Christian Commonwealth*, advocating a self-supporting Trust for housing 300 families – without, of course, any beer-shops or 'other pernicious excitements'. The period was one when at least the threads of Christian communism (and fragments of the Diggers' thought turn up in the 19th century just as often as those of the Shakers) were beginning to become irrevocably entangled with other utopian schools – St Simon, Fourier, the Phalanx, Owenism – and the most obvious offspring of this long, and muddled, tradition of separatism, exclusivity, socialism and religious mania was the rise of practical Co-operation. No longer optimistic bands of the elect, taking off for great houses or dubious Mid-Western farms, but ordinary working men, running shops in their mutual interests. Out of the centuries of longing for a better life, for the rewards on earth traditionally retained for the hereafter, out of the bankruptcies of Orbiston and Ralahine, the persecutions of St George's Hill and Fulneck, there came at least the C.W.S.[10]

[10]There had also been the great enthusiasm of the Chartists: Feargus O'Connor's giant imagination founded O'Connorville, Lowbands, Charterville, Snig's End and Mathon, between 1846 and 1848, but the beginnings of the collapse could be seen before he bought the land for a sixth, Dodford, and their history strictly belongs either amongst that of naive utopias or that of semi-fraudulent lunacies rather than here.

There were still plenty of new developments in benevolent capitalism as well. Colonel Edward Akroyd built first Copley, then Akroydon, for his workers near Halifax. The mill at Copley dates from 1847, and an accompanying estate of terraced back-to-backs from 1847–53. Akroyd provided a school (1849), library (1850) and Church – St Stephens – designed by W. H. Crossland in 1863. The Copley canteen was capable of serving 600 meat-and-potato dinners at a sitting, costing 1½d or 2d. Akroydon came rather later, to accommodate the workers at the Haley Mills, and terraces of cottages were commissioned from Gilbert Scott, but designed eventually by Crossland once more. Straight rows of 'domestic Gothic', like Copley they had gardens (and both also had allotments and recreation ground), but Akroyd hoped to encourage owner-occupation there, and arranged for the assistance of the Halifax Permanent Benefit Building Society.

Copley and Akroydon were both suburbs (of Halifax), and development from this time on is increasingly suburban; there was no longer any industrial necessity to go out into the country (except on rare occasions, as when the City of Birmingham founded a village to go with its waterworks in the Elan Valley) and in any case the towns were relentlessly growing towards one another. Sir Edward Watkin's programme of house-building for fishermen in Grimsby, in 1860, followed the efforts of the Manchester, Sheffield & Lincolnshire Railway to resuscitate the port. We are approaching the time of the Peabody Trust, and the colonising of the decaying cities with the honest poor, rather than the empty countryside.

Nevertheless, late in the day as they were, a number of distinguished Victorians (Lords Shaftesbury and Aberdeen, Samuel Morley, Benjamin Jones of the C.W.S., Walter Hazell of the printers, Hazell, Watson & Co., among them) attempted to launch a crusade under the banner of the Society for Promoting Industrial Villages. Founded in 1883, it was of course long after the great era of the factory village, and already within the age of Norman Shaw and Ebenezer Howard. They rallied round the proposition that 'the true answer to the bitter cry of outcast London and other great towns is to be heard in the dreary half-depopulated rural districts of the Kingdom. The one evil must redress the other and the formation of Industrial Villages, on the plans recommended by the Society, will, we believe, best secure the object.' Their recommendations included gardens, libraries, schools, baths, co-operative stores (Jones was not involved for nothing), and, inevitably, no pubs at all. By 1887, the Society's accounts showed a subscription income of less than £50, and receipts from sale of literature amounting to exactly 7s in the year. Their only success seems to have been the foundation of a co-operative smallholding, thrillingly entitled the Total Abstainers' Industrial Farm.

In the same year, another group, with closely overlapping membership, announced the founding of the Improved Villa and Cottage Homes General Land and Building Company Ltd., with an authorized capital of £100,000. By early 1888, however, it was quite clear that it would never raise the capital, let alone 'acquire Freehold, Copyhold or Leasehold Agricultural and other land suitable for the promotion and formation of Industrial Villages'.

Overall, it is plain that the early Victorians saw the environment problem as an essential part of the Condition of England Question. And although it is undoubtedly true that most of their proposed solutions smacked of social and physical geometry, regular, consistent and ultimately arid, we have seen that that is almost inseparable from the founding instinct. It is greatly to be regretted that the variety and stimulus of much unplanned growth so seldom observes the minimum standards of the planners; but arguably one should regret rather more that so much of the planners' work (to which objective intelligence has in theory been applied) falls short of the emotional achievements of the happiest organic growth.

So much planned development is mysteriously sterile when complete because the original inspiration, the model for emulation, was inappropriate. It can fail because of simple anachronism, slavishly following an æsthetic wholly out of keeping with the practical, rather like the modern lunacy of flat-roofed Californian bungalows in extremely wet Welsh and Scottish hillside settings. Or it can fail from misplaced scale: there is nothing wrong with the square at Tremadoc that a few dozen surrounding streets would not put right, nor with the Alban Square 'Piazza' of Aberaeron, sunless and dour, that the arrival of a baroque metropolis would not redeem.

The next major development of paternal capitalist housing, Bournville and Port Sunlight, illustrates, if it does not entirely prove, this point. Both took as architectural models a pantomime vision of bucolic England, in Port Sunlight laid out on a European skein of avenues and boulevards. Individual houses in both tend to look like Anne Hathaway's Cottage with the electricity laid on, and the social aspirations of the foundations veer from Owenite improvement to straightforward Merrie: it doesn't matter desperately about the workers taking the occasional drink, so long as they take it after bell-ringing practice, in a half-timbered snug.

As a site, Bournville came first. The Cadbury's, a Devon Quaker family, had migrated to Birmingham in the person of Richard Tapper Cadbury in 1794. His son, John, opened a shop specialising in tea and coffee in Birmingham's Bull Street in 1824. One of his sidelines, cocoa, ground by hand from the beans in his cellar, became so popular that, in 1831, he took a small factory in Crooked Lane to concentrate on its manufacture. The factory prospered, and when, in 1847, the Oxford & Birmingham Railway line threatened it with demolition, Cadbury was able to move to larger premises in Bridge Street.

Allied to commercial success there was already the customary Quaker streak of philanthropy: Cadbury was an Overseer of the Poor, a pioneer in smoke abatement, among the first employers to allow a weekly half-day, and to let off younger employees an hour early twice a week in order to attend night-school.

In 1861, after a long down-turn in the factory's fortunes (the retail shop had been taken over by a nephew, Richard Cadbury Barrow, in 1849), John passed over the business to his sons, Richard and George: they were respectively twenty-five and twenty-two, and took over a business with diminishing profits, staff and reputation.

Although their first efforts were directed to stabilising the precarious conduct of the company, and to restoring its prosperity, the real turning point came in

George (left) and Richard Cadbury.

1866 when the brothers introduced the first pure Cocoa – one so refined that it did not need adulteration with starches to cut the fatty cocoa butter content. Much of the subsequent growth of the firm derived from this line, allied to the chocolate confectionery with which Cadbury's eventually took over the market in French sweetmeats.

By the end of the 1870's, the factory in Bridge Street was unequal to the rapidly-increasing turnover, and the brothers began to seek a new site. They rejected the various possibilities in Birmingham's vast industrial sector, not only because they felt that foodstuffs – particularly those selling on the slogan of purity – ought to be made in clean and healthy surroundings, but because George's work for Adult Schools had convinced them that the slums must be first escaped from, and then destroyed.

In 1878, the Bournbrook estate, four miles south-west of the city in still untouched countryside, came on the market. It adjoined a railway and a canal, lay between two main roads, and had ample water. The Cadburys bought $14\frac{1}{2}$ acres of the estate, including a good stretch of the Bourn, and built on it

Bournville: the factory in 1879. In fact, there are certain minor differences between the factory as built and this artist's impression, but the trees are not exaggerated.

Bournville: cottages and gardens, 1879. These are George Gadd's original homes, of which only one now survives, for essential workers.

Bournville: some Gadd cottages of 1879. All those shown here were demolished to make way for the works Dining Block.

a factory so much bigger than Bridge Street that the awed workers thought it impossible ever to sell enough cocoa to pay for it. They not only built a factory, they built, for some essential workers, twenty-four semi-detached houses, designed by George Gadd. They reflected, in their construction and of course their setting, George Cadbury's philosophy: 'The best way to improve a man's circumstances is to raise his ideals; but it is not enough to *talk* to him about ideals. How can he cultivate ideals when his home is a slum and his only place of recreation the public house?' Those first arrivals at Bournville (the name chosen in deference to the prestige of France in the chocolate trade) found a great deal of alternative recreation. Next to the factory was a field for cricket and football, and a garden with swings and benches; it was also possible to catch trout in the Bourn, for a time.

The factory itself was equipped from the beginning with a kitchen where the workers could heat their dinners, and heated changing rooms where wet clothes could be left on arrival. Apart from its size – and its gross floor-space has expanded fifty-fold since 1879, on a site swollen to eighty-one acres – the factory was striking: the sickly smell aside, the cocoa and chocolate industry is inoffensive, and without the dirt of other factories nearby, the vaguely classical lines of bright red-brick stand out sharply against the green surroundings.

George Cadbury's lifelong interest in social amelioration led in the 'nineties, when the Company's success was sufficiently assured for him to spare the time, to the foundation of Bournville Village proper. In 1893 he bought 120 acres near the Works and put into operation his desire, expressed in the later Trust Deed, 'of alleviating the evils which arise from the insanitary and insufficient accommodation supplied to large numbers of the working classes, and of securing to the workers in factories some of the advantages of outdoor village life.'

From its inception, Bournville Village has been both an industrial foundation – in that it took place around a great manufactory – and a suburb, since it has always been open to residents apart from Cadbury employees. The population in 1902, 405 households, included only 40 per cent whose head was employed at the Bournville works, and that proportion has remained fairly constant.

The earliest houses, those of 1879, were well spaced with large gardens, and adapted from the common 'tunnel-backs' of the industrial towns evolved in response to the Public Health Act of 1875, which required air-space on two sides of a house and thus ended the worst period of back-to-back building.

The 1894 homes included tunnel-back variations and cottage-styles. In blocks of twos, threes and fours, they were spaced twenty feet apart on the road-frontage, with large back gardens, and normally contained parlour, living room and kitchen on the ground floor with three bedrooms above. Few had separate bathrooms, largely because the chargeable rents were too low to allow such luxuries: philanthropy is all very well, as David Dale found out, but capital must be serviced. In 1901, some of the leaseholders objected to the erection of cheap cottages for the workers near their hard-won property – Cadbury having originally envisaged a community of small owner-occupiers –

Bournville: happy faces at the chocolate mill. Early 1900s.

Bournville. The Cadburys believed in keeping their girls fit: compulsory P.T. in the gymnasium, early 1900s.

Bournville: having decided to put baths in all new houses, the Trust resorted to some novel expedients in the cheaper cottages. This version, sunk into the kitchen floor with a strong lid supplied, dates from c. 1900.

and were told quite firmly that the project was in the interests of the working class. In fact, when built, the cottages let for rents rather above what genuine slum-dwellers could afford. In the early years there were frequent attacks on the project's high rents as 'more business than philanthropy'.

Bournville, unlike New Lanark or Saltaire, has grown continuously from 1879 to the present. The Cadbury Brothers original 14½ acres housed factory and workers' homes; George Cadbury's first purchase of purely housing land, in 1893, came to 120 acres; by 1900 there were 313 houses on 330 acres; by 1960, the Estate covered rather more than 1,000 acres, of which 750 acres were developed, had 4,000 dwellings, a population of 13,000; and the Trust, with its own architects, direct labour force and housing managers, was also

responsible for 2,169 acres of agricultural estate near the Lickey Hills; 456 acres of National Trust land; and a village in Warwickshire, Butlers Marston.

Most of the growth has come under the Trust administration. George Cadbury, having founded the Village, and imposed on it, seemingly permanently, his own vision of garden suburbanism, handed it over in 1900 to a non-profit Bournville Village Trust, with twelve trustees answerable only to the Charity Commissioners. The first trustees were all Cadburys, and George was Chairman, but since then it has become, if not less oligarchic, a more widely based oligarchy, with space for the placemen of the Corporation of Birmingham, the Society of Friends and the University of Birmingham.

Inevitably, with development so widely spread in time and space, there is rather more variety in housing style and setting than in single-period foundations. Paradoxically, the density of building, set by Cadbury at six houses to the acre, has worsened in response to the interference of municipal planners: the City of Birmingham has forced the rate up to twelve to fourteen houses per acre. However, it remains true that Bournville houses have gardens, many of them quite large gardens. It is strictly in the *Sybil* tradition, with horticulture on the reverse of the coin from shiftless, slum-dwelling drunkenness. Early Bournville tenants were greeted with a ready-dug garden and newly-planted fruit trees. The major component in the style is the cottage: that is, the compact, regular one or two-storey unit that most people would draw if asked to draw a house. In its time, and Bournville helped pioneer this return to simplicity, it was a vast improvement on the urban styles – terraced, back-to-back, tunnel-backed, basement and garreted. It is unfortunately prone to two visual failings: in the hands of a journeyman, it ends up as a brick box, and, should the architect strive to introduce some novelty, it usually results in glued-on half timbering, unhappy tiles following a thatch scalloping, hopelessly arch gables and oriels. The actual houses of Bournville, of all periods, are neither genuinely rural nor, of course, handsomely urban. They are archetypally suburban, the sort of well-built, undistinguished, family houses that delight building societies and estate agents.

The experiment has been much more fruitful in terms of overall planning, for although it has been bought and developed piecemeal, it has been carried out on common principles. At the very beginning, although houses were built in groups on large sites, rather than terraced, they tended to be set out along a common building line parallel with a straight road. This soon changed, and one of the Village's best points is its landscaping of roads along existing features, and the varying settings of the housing groups in relation to the road. Even quite mundane houses can be improved by being set in large gardens and in irregular patterns. Part of this technique, and a vital part, is the preservation of existing trees and the constant planting of new ones: nothing redeems Birmingham brick quite so much as a decent screen of branches.

Given Cadbury's rural vision, and his comparative flexibility of plan in every respect, Bournville was spared the grid. It has instead developed the close, the cul-de-sac, the crescent, all the minor tricks of building arrangement that make up the garden suburb. The principal thoroughfares are all curved, and unpredictably curved, and there are a number of open spaces as such in addition to the generous gardens and pavement borders. The Village as a whole was intended to have a natural social focus, the Green at the junction of Sycamore and Linden Roads (the street names are conscientiously bucolic – Haygreen Lane, Woodlands Park, Raddlebarn Lane, Hazel, Thorn, Acacia, Laburnum and so on) and despite the cellular growth imposed by the irregular acquisition of new land, the shopping centre at the Green (if not so much the conscious provision there of Primary Schools, Day Continuation College, College of Arts & Crafts, Parish Church and Friends' Meeting House) has kept it a real centre, while the weight of the housing has shifted from the skirts of the factory over to the south and west.

There can be no doubt that Bournville is a success: even more than Saltaire,

it has maintained its status as a desirable area whilst its contemporaries – the inner Birmingham suburbs – have gone downhill. It has a sense of community, and is free from the feudal aspects of many other tycoon foundations. In terms of real betterment of the people, it was noted very early in its history that the average death-rate for Bournville was 5.5 per 1,000 while that for Birmingham was 14.5 (of course, by its very nature, it was then and probably still is, demographically atypical, with a bias towards young families headed by active wage-earners). At the same time, infant mortality per 1,000 live births stood at thirty-seven, while in Birmingham as a whole it was 125. Gardens cannot supply the deficiencies of architecture, but they plainly contribute to physical health.

Bournville's great contemporary, Port Sunlight, was substantially more baronial in concept; W. H. Lever actually lived there for a time, the plan is suggestive of Versailles, and to this day the real authority there is that of Unilever (Merseyside) Limited. Like Bournville, it came into being as a by-product of business success. Lever's soap-works at Warrington had run out of room for expansion by 1887, and he settled upon a new site on the West bank of the Mersey, three miles south of Birkenhead. There is no doubt that he had in mind something more than a factory, but the relative importance of business and philanthropy can be gauged from the fact that the site was 'mostly but a few feet above high-water level and liable at any time to be flooded by high tides . . . Moreover an arm of Bromborough Pool spread in various directions filling ravines with slime and ooze'. On the other hand, it was far enough up-river to be outside the Liverpool Dock and Harbour dues, had an anchorage where incoming ships could transship cargo to lighters and thence into the works, materially strengthening Lever's bargaining position with the contiguous Birkenhead-Chester Railway line, had ample room for expansion, and

Port Sunlight: Queen Mary's Drive. The beams are real, as are the barge-boards, which may explain the superiority of these forerunners of suburban Tudor.

Port Sunlight: The Lady Lever Memorial Art Gallery, at the North-western end of The Diamond.

Port Sunlight: The Diamond, looking up the triumphal avenue from Art Gallery to Factory.

Port Sunlight: Lower Road group – one of the most cheerful compositions on the estate.

Port Sunlight. This Plan of 1917 already shows the village expanding to fill the natural site, and across the New Chester Road. It certainly demonstrates the multitude of interesting shapes on the ground-plan.

PORT SUNLIGHT
CHESHIRE
——— 1917 ———

could draw on the large labour pool of Birkenhead. As a later Minister to the Port Sunlight congregation was to observe, 'I sometimes feel that I am intended to be an advertisement for Sunlight Soap more than for the Kingdom of God.' Port Sunlight as a foundation, despite its undoubted architectural and social fascination, rests on a similar premise. 'The whole village', remarked Angus Watson 'was dominated by the spirit of Soap.'

Lever's social impulse was primarily an extension of his faith in profit-sharing. Although he acknowledged that part of his success derived from the surplus value produced by his employees (he was in no other conceivable sense Marxist) and that it was both morally appropriate and managerially intelligent to return some part of this, he had no confidence in the capacity of the lucky workers to use their dividends wisely. He chose instead to convert the workers' share of profits into improved housing, explaining that 'If I were to follow the usual mode of profit-sharing I would send my workmen and work-girls to the cash office at the end of the year and say to them "You are going to receive £8 each; you have earned this money: it belongs to you. Take it and make whatever use you like of your money." Instead of that I told them "£8 is an amount which is soon spent, and it will not do you much good if you send it down your throats in the form of bottles of whisky, bags of sweets or fat geese for Christmas. On the other hand, if you leave this money with me, I shall use it to provide for you everything which makes life pleasant – viz., nice houses, comfortable homes and healthy recreation".' He might have added, 'all of which will be in the shadow of the works, supervised by the officials of the Company, so lateness and absenteeism will cease forthwith.'

The working conditions were comparatively good: men worked a forty-eight hour week, girls forty-five hours; there was a guaranteed minimum wage of twenty-two shillings (which puts that £8 in perspective for both Lever and his workers: they might have thought it less trivial than he); there were medical inspections, exemplary safety precautions, and ample works canteens. The most irritating aspect of cold-blooded philanthropy is that it is in the long run of greater benefit than the wholly altruistic sort, if only because the Levers stay in business and the phalangistes go bankrupt at great speed.

Port Sunlight: in this gothic house, near The Dell, Lever himself lived for several years.

The development took place not only on a marsh, but amongst a series of ravines. Natural obstacles, which some might regard as a challenge to be circumvented or exploited by technique, Lever regarded as impertinence. When the Ministry of Housing listed Port Sunlight as a place of architectural and historic interest in 1965, their citation remarked drily enough 'the planned layout is of a kind quite unusual in this country and was dictated not by conditions of terrain'. Port Sunlight has vistas, perspectives, formal gardens and public buildings on the consciously grand scale: ravines have been filled in, contours scraped down, and what the Unilever publicity office call an 'informal feature', The Dell, is an erstwhile stream bed converted into a luxuriant garden and spanned by an unnecessary bridge in Gothic-Renaissance style, like a background to Beardsley.

Lever's view was that 'the convenience and life of the people can be achieved without any sacrifice to beauty or inspiring vistas'; what he meant becomes more clear if one replaces the 'to' by 'of'. His son, the second Lord

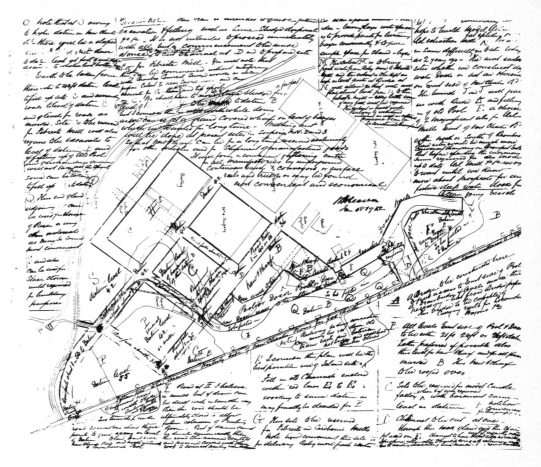

Port Sunlight: Lever's own detailed interest in planning is illustrated by this sketch-plan of his for industrial development in 1912.

Leverhulme, in a hagiographic work – filial piety or common gratitude – observes that 'the architects he employed all looked upon him as unique amongst their clients. He did not employ them, he collaborated with them.' One may infer therefore that any common factor in Port Sunlight's architecture is the Lever contribution: and it is only just to admit that the common factor in the parts, like the conception of the whole, is remarkable. Port Sunlight is a great deal too good to be dismissed lightly, although it is quite often very bad indeed.

To revert to the Ministry of Housing's encomium, 'whether one likes or does not like the buildings, the fact remains that it is a large and complete museum piece indicative of the thoughts and ideals of those *fin-de-siècle* architects working under the influence of the pre-Raphaelites.' Nearly every traditional European house-style has been plundered for inspiration, and put through the Gothic mill of *art nouveau*. There are Cheshire black-and-white groups next to Dutch Colonial, set on sweeping French loops; gables, crenellations, barge-boards, shutters, shingles, brick, stucco, nail-studded oak and traceries of stone, stained glass and wrought iron. In architectural style, no other planned foundation can compare with Port Sunlight's variety. Alternate generations have found it modern, vulgar and camp: a cycle that may well be repeated endlessly until it sinks back into the Bebington marshes.

The very first plan for the site was Lever's own, and the first development of it by William Owen, in 1888. He designed twenty-eight cottages and an entrance lodge to this private paradise. Although it began as a site of fifty-six acres (thirty-two residential, twenty-four for the factory) and grew to fill up the complete area between the factory, the railway and the Chester road – a mile long and a third of a mile wide – from the beginning Lever wanted the streets to reproduce the boulevards of France, rather than the mechanical grid or the cosy village. The houses, in blocks of three to seven mainly, were to be restricted to a density of seven or very slightly more to the acre. No block was to, or does, exactly match another in detail.

The continental model for the layout went further than the boulevard (Bolton Road, Greendale Road) and included Versailles – The Diamond and The Causeway. The Diamond, flanked by houses and two parallel avenues, is a long formal garden between, at one end, a raised, terraced garden with stone arch, and at the other, the deliberate, heavy bulk of the Lady Lever Art Gallery, decked out in symbolic figures. Running NNE–SSW across it, completing the crucifix, is a minor-key repetition, The Causeway. It too has a completed vista, pointing directly at Christ Church, which combines, in red stone, English perpendicular and French flamboyant. It also combines the grandeur of an Anglican building with the latitudinarian convenience of the Congregational Union.

The houses had between two and four bedrooms, and fall broadly into two main types – kitchen and parlour. They originally rented for 5s to 6s 3d a week for a kitchen house, and between 7s 6d and 10s for the grander parlour house. Bathrooms were, as elsewhere, a luxury, and many of the nearly 900 homes have had to be extensively rebuilt internally since the last War to accommodate baths, airing cupboards and modern sink units. Lever shared the prevailing obsession with gardening, and provided ample allotment land, placed so as to provide a green core to each enclosed building plot. He also allowed for a front garden throughout, but those were strictly tended by the company, to ensure uniformity throughout the village, and maintain the trim, formal appearance of his boulevards. The allotments are being swallowed now by simple gardens and more useful garages.

Despite the splendours of the Diamond, and despite the pub Lever was eventually constrained to allow[11] (in Coaching Inn style) a site on Bolton Road with the Church behind and a large garden opposite, the focus of the community is the main entrance of the factory. Public buildings, like public gardens, are scattered throughout the development: the Art Gallery nearly half a mile from the works, the Technical Institute as far from it as possible – the extreme northern corner of the village – the Cottage Hospital and the Schools, like Bridge Inn and Church, are in the centre, gymnasium and open-air bath on the south-western corner of Diamond and Causeway, Collegium, Hulme Hall, Auditorium and Lyceum (Port Sunlight has a vigorous amateur dramatic tradition, and needs it to keep its building busy) in the Bolton Road/Bath Street blocks. Even so, the short stretch of Greendale Road which bends from the Port Sunlight railway halt to the imposing front door of the factory, bordered as it is by shops and library to the left, bowling

Port Sunlight: The Bridge Inn. Vaguely modelled on a coaching Inn, with galleried courtyard, this was meant to be a teetotal house, but Lever reluctantly bowed to democracy in the shape of an eighty-per-cent vote to go wet.

[11]The inhabitants voted 80% to 20% in favour of a license.

green and Gladstone Hall to the right, is the communal centre. The shops cluster, with the Bank and Post Office, at the mouth of the cornucopia to snatch what they can; no-one in Port Sunlight can forget, as they spend their money, from whence it came. No doubt, just as the first Lord Leverhulme would wish, for his view of man's improveability was not, of course, the messianic radicalism of Owen, or the Tory democracy of Salt, or even the vaguely William Morris indulgence of Cadbury. Lever is capitalism enlightened strictly in its own interest, the higher management come to stay. Part Henry Ford, part Northcliffe, and, one has to allow, part Maecenas.

By the time of Port Sunlight, not only has the bestial hand been replaced by the respectable worker, immediate ancestor of consuming man, but the governing and owning classes as a whole have been converted to environmental reform. A series of Public Health Acts, and reforms of local government – coupled with the extension of the franchise to many of those condemned to live in the worst slums – had laid the administrative basis for improvement, re-development, and planning. The distance between Owen's vision of villages self-sufficient in agriculture, living in kibbutz-like communality, exchanging their surpluses with neighbouring villages – what Cobbett, seizing on the chinese-box zoning, called 'parallelograms of paupers' – and John Burns's Town Planning Act of 1909, like that between New Lanark and Letchworth, is not very far in hindsight. It had taken all the first full century of industrialisation. It might be argued that until industrialisation had reached the level of sophistication – the production of much that is not essential – where it requires a growing middle-class to operate it and to absorb its output, no-one needed middle-class housing.

There is no doubt that most of the improving environments offered the workers, in design and often in operation, imposed middle-class standards and aspirations. The middle class were busy conspiring to improve their own environments at the same time. The schemes of Moffatt, Buckingham, Dr Benjamin Richardson (his Hygeia's main novelty was to propose attic-kitchens, so that fumes did not pass through other rooms on their way out) had all remained schemes; but in 1876, the year of Hygeia, Norman Shaw laid out the first self-avowed garden suburb, Bedford Park, and the publication of Ebenezer Howard's *Tomorrow* (re-titled *Garden Cities of Tomorrow* subsequently) in 1898 led directly to the foundation of the Garden City Association and to the building from 1903 onwards, of Letchworth. Since them, private enterprise has built a number of other, similar bourgeois Bournvilles: Hampstead Garden suburb, Gidea Park, Ruislip, Ealing, Welwyn and so on. And the concept has been adopted by government and by local authorities. However, the garden city movement, and all planning after the first Town Planning Act, is beyond the scope of this book, and has been well recorded and discussed elsewhere.

Select Bibliography

This list is intended as a guide to further reading on major topics, and excludes obvious primary works (e.g. More's *Utopia*), periodicals, pamphlets (guide books, brief histories, etc.), and sources of contemporary comment (Fiennes, Lewis, Aubrey, Camden, etc.).

Abercrombie, Sir P.: *Town and Country Planning*; Oxford University Press, 1943.

Armytage, W. H. G.: *Heavens Below*; Routledge and Kegan Paul, 1961.

Ashworth, W.: *The Genesis of Modern British Town Planning*; Routledge and Kegan Paul, 1954.

Balgarnie, R.: *Sir Titus Salt, Baronet, His Life and its Lessons*; Hodder and Stoughton, 1877.

Barton, M.: *Tunbridge Wells*; Faber and Faber, 1937.

Benevolo, L.: *The Origins of Modern Town Planning*; Routledge and Kegan Paul, 1967.

Beresford, M.: *New Towns of the Middle Ages*; Lutterworth Press, 1967.

Boon, G. C.: *Roman Silchester*; Parrish, 1957.

Boucher, C. T. G.: *James Brindley, Engineer*.

Briggs, A.: *Victorian Cities*; Odhams, 1963.

Carter, H.: *The Towns of Wales*.

Chaloner, W.: *The Social and Economic Development of Crewe*; Economic History Series, Manchester University Press, 1951.

Checkland, S. G.: *The Rise of Industrial Society in England, 1815–1855*; Longmans, 1964.

Clark, G. Kitson: *The Making of Victorian England*; Methuen, 1962.

Cole, G. D. H.: *The Life of Robert Owen*; Macmillan, 1930.

Davis, T.: *John Nash, the Prince Regent's Architect*; Country Life, 1966.

Duckham, Baron F.: *The Yorkshire Ouse, the History of a River Navigation*; David and Charles, 1967.

Dunbar, J. G.: *Historic Architecture of Scotland*; Batsford, 1966.

Dyos, H. J., (ed.): *The Study of Urban History*; the Proceedings of an international round-table conference of the Urban History Group at Leicester University on 23–26 September 1966. Reproduced from typescript, 1968.

Fitton, R. S. and Wadsworth, A. P.: *The Strutts and the Arkwrights, 1785–1830*; Manchester University Press, 1958.

Gilbert, E. W.: *Brighton*; Methuen, 1954.

Hadfield, C.: *British Canals*; Phoenix House, 1950.

Hadfield, C.: *The Canals of the West Midlands*; David and Charles, 1966.

Hamilton, H.: *The Industrial Revolution in Scotland*; Oxford University Press, 1932.

Haverfield, F. J.: *Ancient Town Planning*; Oxford University Press, 1913.

Hay, D.: *Short History of Whitehaven*.

Holroyd, A.: *A Life of Sir Titus Salt*.

Hoskins, W. G.: *The Making of the English Landscape*; Hodder and Stoughton, 1955.

Howard, E.: *Garden Cities of Tomorrow*; Faber and Faber, 1946.

Hughes, T. H., and Lamborn, E. A. G.: *Towns and Town Planning, Ancient and Modern*; Oxford University Press, 1923.

Johns, E.: *British Townscapes*; Arnold, 1965.

Malet, H.: *The Canal Duke*; Phoenix House, 1961.

Mantoux, P.: *The Industrial Revolution* (new edition with preface by J. S. Ashton); Jonathan Cape, 1961; paperback edition, Methuen, 1964.

Marshall, J. D.: *An Economic History of Furness, 1711–1900 and the Town of Barrow, 1757–1897 with an Epilogue*; Barrow-in-Furness Library and Museum Committee, 1958.

Martin, G.: *The Town*; Vista Books, 1961.

Mate, C. H., and Riddle, C.: *Bournemouth, 1810–1910, the History of a Modern Health and Pleasure Resort*; W. Mate and Sons, Bournemouth, 1910.

Meakin, J. E. B.: *Model Factories and Villages: Ideal Conditions of Labour and Housing*; T. Fisher Unwin, 1905.

Moody, T. W.: *The Londonderry Plantation: 1609–41*; W. Mullan and Son, 1939.

Mumford, L.: *The City in History*; Secker and Warburg, 1961.

Pevsner, N.: *The Buildings of England* (series), passim; Penguin Books.

Pike, E.: *Royston: Human Documents of the Industrial Revolution in Britain*; Allen and Unwin, 1966.

Pimlott, J. A. R.: *The Englishman's Holiday*; Faber and Faber, 1947.

Pollard, S.: *The Genesis of Modern Management*; Arnold, 1965.

Purdom, C. B.: *The Garden City: a Study in the Development of a Modern Town*; J. M. Dent and Sons, 1913.

Richmond, I. A.: *Roman Britain*; Jonathan Cape, 1963.

Rosenau, H.: *The Ideal City*; Routledge and Kegan Paul, 1959.

Saalman, H.: *Mediæval Cities*; Studio Vista, 1968.

Salzman, L. F.: *Edward I*; Constable, 1968.

Savage, W.: *The Making of Our Towns*; Eyre and Spottiswoode, 1952.

Sennett, A. R.: *Garden Cities in Theory and Practice*; Bemrose, 1905.

Sharp, T.: *The Anatomy of the Village*; Penguin Books, 1946.

Simmons, J.: *Transport*; Vista Books, 1962.

Smiles, S.: *James Brindley and the Early Engineers*; 1864.

Summerson, Sir J.: *Georgian London*; Pleiades Books, 1945.

Summerson, Sir J.: *Sir Christopher Wren*; Collins, 1953.

Summerson, Sir J.: *John Nash*; Allen and Unwin, 1935, 1950.

Summerson, Sir J.: *Inigo Jones*; Penguin Books, 1966.

Tout, T. F.: *Mediæval Town Planning*; reprinted from *The Bulletin of the John Rylands Library*, University Press, Manchester, and Longmans, London, 1920.

Unwin, G.: *Samuel Oldknow and the Arkwrights, the Industrial Revolution at Stockport and Marple*; University of Manchester Press, Economic History Series, Vol. 1, 1924.

West, T. W.: *History of Architecture in Scotland*; University of London Press, 1967.

Williams, I. A.: *The Firm of Cadbury, 1831–1931*; Constable, 1931.

Wilson, C. L.: *History of Unilever*; Cassell, 1954.

Woods, E. C., and Brown, P. C.: *The Rise and Progress of Wallasey*; (2nd edition) 1960.

Youngson, A. J.: *The Making of Classical Edinburgh*.

Index

Page numbers in italic refer to illustrations